4942

LUTON SIXTH FORM COLLEGE

NAME	TUTOR GROUP	DATE ISSUED
G. Crawley		10/95
T. SHAH	FGSPH	9/97
T. CLARKE	J5JAR.	9/98
CASSANDER FINN	J5EMD	13/9/99
S. BI HUSSAIN		

HEINEMANN
INTRODUCTORY
POLITICS

UK
Government
& Politics

ANDY WILLIAMS

Heinemann Educational Publishers
Halley Court, Jordan Hill, Oxford OX2 8EJ

MADRID ATHENS PARIS
FLORENCE PRAGUE WARSAW
PORTSMOUTH NH CHICAGO SAO PAULO
SINGAPORE TOKYO MELBOURNE AUCKLAND
IBADAN GABORONE JOHANNESBURG

British Library Cataloguing in Publication Data
A catalogue record for this book is available from the British Library

ISBN 0 435 33154 X

Designed by Roger Denning
Typeset by CentraCet Limited, Cambridge
Cover illustration by Debbie Hinks
Cover design by Aricot Vert Design
Printed and bound in Great Britain by The Bath Press, Avon

Acknowledgements

The publishers would like to thank the following for the use of copyright material reproduced in this book.
The Associated Examining Board for the questions on pp. 30, 56, 77, 78, 152, 175, 183; BBC Education for the extract from *The Judiciary in the Nineties* by Lord Taylor, 1992, on p. 139; Blackwell Publishing for the extract from *The Commons in Perspective* by Philip Norton, 1985, on p. 61, and for the extract by Paul Addison, taken from *Ruling Performance: British Governments from Attlee to Thatcher*, edited by Peter Hennessy and Anthony Seldon, 1989, on p. 176; © *The Economist* for the extracts on pp. 14–15, 34, 75, 119–20, 161–2, 168, 170, 192; Faber & Faber Ltd for the extract from *Modern British Politics* by Samuel Beer, 1969, on p. 71; Fourth Estate for the extract from *Citizens' Britain: A Radical Agenda for the 1990s* by Paddy Ashdown, 1989, on p. 56; Lord Hailsham for the extract from his 1976 Guildhall lecture, on p. 12, and the extract from his lecture to the Holdsworth Club, on p. 124; Hamish Hamilton Ltd for the extract from *Whitehall: Tragedy and Farce* by Clive Ponting, 1986, on p. 104; HarperCollins Publishers Ltd for the extract from Richard Crossman's 'Introduction' to *The English Constitution* by Walter Bagehot, published by Fontana in 1963, on p. 96; Harvester Wheatsheaf for the extract from *Politics UK* by Bill Jones, Andrew Gray, Dennis Kavanagh, Michael Moran, Philip Norton and Anthony Seldon, 1994, on p. 28; Her Majesty's Stationery Office for the extract from 'The Civil Service: Continuity and Change', 1994, on p. 98, and for the extract from John Major's statement to the House of Commons on the Downing Street declaration, 1993, on pp. 200–1; Hodder & Stoughton for the extract from *The Essential Anatomy of Britain* by Anthony Sampson, published by Coronet, 1993, on p. 77, and for the extract from *Heseltine: The Unauthorised Biography* by Julian Critchley, published by Coronet, 1988, on p. 106; Neil Kinnock for the quotation on p. 108; Manchester University Press for the extract from *British Politics Today* by Bill Jones and Dennis Kavanagh, on p. 30; Oxford and Cambridge Schools Examination Board for the questions on pp. 14, 30, 77, 113, 139, 151, 175, 183; Penguin Books Ltd for the extracts from *Arguments for Democracy* by Tony Benn, 1979, on pp. 102, 110, and for the extract from *Post-war Britain: A Political History*, by Alan Sked and Chris Cook, 1984, on p. 183; Philip Allan Publishers Ltd for the extract from 'The Fall of a Prime Minister' by John Benyon, *Social Studies Review*, Vol. 6, No. 3, January 1991, on p. 50, and for the extract from *Contemporary Record* by Peter Hennessy, 1988, on p. 113; Prentice Hall Press for the extract from *Applied Economics*, by Alan Griffiths and John Wall, 1986, on p. 179; the Joseph Rowntree Foundation for the extract from *Local Government Since Widdicombe*, 1990, on p. 152; Secker & Warburg for the extract from *Whitehall* by Peter Hennessy, 1989, on pp. 103, 107; Chris Smith MP for the quotation on p. 73; University of Cambridge Local Examinations Syndicate for the questions on pp. 30, 49, 77, 78, 119, 151, 175; University of London Examinations and Assessment Council for the questions on pp. 14, 30, 49–50, 56, 77, 78, 95, 96, 113–14, 139, 151, 161, 174, 183, 192, 200; University of Oxford Delegacy of Local Examinations for the questions on pp. 30, 95, 113, 119, 151, 161, 175, 200; Hugo Young for the extract from *The Judges*, broadcast on BBC Radio 4, 13 April 1988, on p. 126.

The publishers have made every effort to trace copyright holders. However, if any material has been incorrectly acknowledged, we would be pleased to correct this at the earliest opportunity.

Contents

Introduction

In the past, many politics textbooks have been written in an attempt to help both A level students and undergraduates. As a result, A level students have been forced to wade through a mass of material, some of which is relevant to their course and some of which is not. While teachers provide a valuable guide inside the classroom, outside it, students have had little help in deciding whether material is fundamental, useful or merely interesting.

UK Government and Politics has been written with you, the A level student, in mind. It offers a complete grounding in the processes, institutions and policy areas of the British political system, as well as an introduction to the European dimension of British politics.

The book combines description, explanation and analysis – the three levels of understanding required of A level students. The basic workings of the institutions and processes are described to ensure that you understand how, for example, the British electoral system works and how a bill passes through Parliament, but simple description has been kept to a minimum.

The quality of written work at A level will depend on your ability to explain and to analyse the British political system, so this book looks closely at the political institutions and processes and analyses their effectiveness.

While it is designed to introduce you to the analysis of British politics, rather than its historical development, the elements of the system are to some extent the products of historical events and so each chapter puts its subject into historical context. For example, important political developments from medieval England are covered when considering the role of the monarchy and the background to the recent ceasefire in Northern Ireland is discussed. If you choose to read this book from beginning to end, rather than dipping into selected chapters, you will find that certain historical events are referred to many times, for example, electoral reform in the nineteenth century. This is deliberate as the events explain turning points in British political history and it is important that you understand their relevance to the development of today's politics.

As essential as the historical context are up-to-date examples. Every effort has been made to include as many of these as possible, but since political textbooks easily date, it is recommended that you keep in touch with the day-to-day developments in British politics through newspapers, television and radio.

Where the book describes the institutions of British politics, these are set in their historical context and then their position in the constitutional framework is considered. Therefore, many chapters include an outline of the traditional position of an institution in the British Constitution. Parliamentary sovereignty, cabinet government, civil service permanence, neutrality and anonymity are all covered at some length in order to establish the traditional foundations of British political institutions. However, the analysis then examines how far it can be argued that the reality conforms to the constitutional pattern.

In line with the recommendations for the new A level Government and Politics syllabuses, the performance of British political institutions and the effectivness of political processes are compared not only to constitutional theory but also to their counterparts overseas. Therefore, throughout the book you will find references to the American political system and, in some cases, to the political systems of Europe. The use of comparative politics is not intended to give an in-depth knowledge of other political systems but rather to enhance understanding of the British system through comparison.

The aim has been to make the material easily accessible, leaving you with a clear understanding of the British political system. However, politics, like chemistry, physics or economics, has its own technical terminology. Concepts like sovereignty, authority and legitimacy, as well as descriptive terms such as bicameral, access points and 'backwoodsmen' are not merely jargon designed to make the subject more complicated! The terminology forms the language of politics which you will need to understand and to use in your written work. To emphasize the importance of these terms and to help you become familiar with them, key words are listed at the beginning of each chapter and then highlighted in the text.

1 Concepts and constitutions

Questions to be answered in this chapter

- What is politics?
- What is power and where does it lie?
- What are states and governments?
- What are constitutions and why do states have them?
- How is the British Constitution made up and should it be changed?

Terms to know

Amendments	Influence
Adversarial politics	Judiciary
Authority	Legislature
bicameral	Legitimate
Bill of rights	Limited government
Civil rights	Parliamentary government
Codified	Parliamentary sovereignty
Consensus politics	Politics
Consent	Power
Constitution	Prescriptive constitution
Conventions	Presidential government
Descriptive constitution	Rule of law
Devolution	Separation of powers
Executive	Sovereignty
Federal	Unitary
Flexible	

Politics

When most people think about what is meant by **politics**, they usually define it as political parties, parliament and the prime minister, but all of these terms confine politics to the British system of government. Politics appears in a variety of forms in every country throughout the world and is not simply confined to the institutions of government. The trade union member is participating in politics just like the government minister and, in some countries, the priest is as involved as the army general.

Politics is about conflict. It is the disagreement between groups or individuals about the way in which their lives should be governed. In Britain the Conservative and Labour Parties embody the disagreements between conservatives and socialists. In the USA political divisions are between the Republican and Democratic Parties. But even in undemocratic countries politics is present. Military leaders who stage a coup in order to wrest a country from the control of politicians might ban political parties, but they are not abolishing politics. They are merely changing the context of

Conflict

politics and the divisions will now occur between the army and the navy or within the army.

In the former Soviet Union many observers saw the Communist Party of the Soviet Union as a monolithic party in which there was no disagreement. No other parties were allowed to exist, so they concluded that there was no political competition. Of course there was, but it took place behind closed doors, within the party.

So, politics will be with us so long as people continue to disagree. Many dictators have tried to remove disagreement by banning the symptoms of politics, such as freedom of speech, a free press and the freedom of association, but none have succeeded in extinguishing the human spirit to such an extent that all resistance, debate and feeling were destroyed.

Political power

In any conflict the winner is the player with the most **power**. That power could be derived from, among other things, supporters, money or skill. Politics is no exception, and the political players compete for power as energetically as a business executive, a footballer or a general. In politics the individual or party with the greatest power will be able to make decisions, according to their ideas and principles, about how the country is governed – the conflict will have been won.

Definition

It is relatively easy to see why politicians desire power. It is a much more difficult matter to define power or to observe it. The political scientist, Robert Dahl ('The Concept of Power', *Behavioural Science*, 1957) described his intuitive idea of power: 'A has power over B to the extent that he can get B to do something that B would otherwise not do.' This definition contains two important elements of any definition of power – a relationship and the removal of coincidence.

Relationship

Power is a relationship. A person sitting alone on a desert island has no power because there is no one over whom to wield that power – there is no 'B'. The ancient Greeks were no more powerful than the Chinese because they did not know of each other's existence and so the issue of which country was more powerful was irrelevant.

The issue of 'coincidence' raises the problem of observation. The effort to remove any coincidences is to ensure that if A does get B to do something B would not have done it anyway. If the power of the prime minister is assessed by observing how many of their proposals are approved by Cabinet, it is possible to be misled because the cabinet might be expected to agree with the prime minister anyway. Therefore, observations say little about the power of the prime minister.

Observation

Even in seemingly innocuous situations, power can be difficult to observe. For example, if the population of a country is given the opportunity to depose a dictator via the ballot box, it might be observed that power lies with the electorate. Given the situation, it might be expected that the voters would elect to oust the dictator. However, if they vote to retain the dictator, it is possible to imagine that power really lies with the dictator and the voters made their decision with the dictator's possible reprisals in mind. Therefore, despite the power to vote, the real power lies with the ruler.

Types of power

Robert Dahl's definition of power is extremely broad. It is helpful to divide power into three different types: coercion, **influence** and **authority**.

2

Coercion

Coercion is based on force. A is able to get B to do something that B would otherwise not do because of some explicit or implicit threat. Some commentators argue that the South African government was encouraged to release Nelson Mandela and to relinquish power to the African National Congress as a result of the sanctions imposed on South Africa by the rest of the world. This illustrates the negative aspects of coercive power. However, there are positive aspects to coercion. 'If you do not . . . we will impose sanctions' can become 'If you do . . . we will lift the sanctions'. In the latter, the end of coercion becomes a reward.

Sanction

Influence

Influence is based on persuasion. A has influence over B if A can persuade B to do something B otherwise would not do. Influence is most commonly associated with pressure groups such as trade unions, the Confederation of British Industry (CBI) and the British Medical Association (BMA). Pressure groups seek to persuade government to adopt policies that suit the needs of the pressure group, its members or society as a whole.

Persuasion

Authority

Authority is based on the right to wield power. A can get B to do something B otherwise would not have done because B believes A has the right to tell them what to do. A parent, a teacher, a priest or a government are all believed to have the right to tell their children, students, etc. what to do.

Right

The German sociologist Max Weber believed that authority could be divided into three types: traditional, legal and charismatic. Traditional authority includes the monarch, the Pope and a parent. Their authority is customary, well established and comes from experience as much as their position. Legal authority encompasses those who gain their authority from their office, for example, the prime minister and the US president. The final category is perhaps the most problematic, charisma. An individual is considered charismatic when the strength of his or her personality is so great that people will follow their lead. Charismatic leaders have included Winston Churchill, Adolf Hitler and Margaret Thatcher.

Weber

Weber's typology should be handled with care because it is difficult to separate clearly different types of authority as there is considerable overlap. Similarly, there is a degree of blurring between the different types of power. Most governments, for example, rely on people to obey the law due to the government's authority, however, they must also be able to turn to coercion to threaten those who do not respect the laws or the government's authority.

Consent and legitimacy

In democratic countries a government's authority is based on elections. Provided those elections are free and competitive (freedom of speech, a number of parties from which to choose, a secret ballot, etc.) they allow the people to give their **consent** to government. This means that the people are governed in a manner and by a government of which they approve. However, consent need not be achieved solely through elections. Many regimes that would not be considered democratic have tried to show that they have the consent of the people through demonstrations,

Elections and consent

3

marches and public shows of support. The Nazis in Germany in the 1930s tried to show their public support through mass rallies, and public support in Cuba for Fidel Castro has been shown by 'spontaneous' public demonstrations.

Legitimacy

However, in western states, elections are the usual means of gaining consent. An elected government is considered to be **legitimate**, in that it is the rightful government. From its legitimacy comes its authority.

Public order

Governments lay down laws in order to create predictable patterns of behaviour. These laws reflect the ideology and morals of the society. The fact that people abide by these laws is known as public order.

It is achieved by the legitimacy of the government making the laws. In Britain the House of Commons is elected and so makes law on behalf of the people. As a result the people obey the law made in their name.

Public order is necessary to create a stable society in which art, science and commerce can flourish. However, some degree of disorder is also necessary to allow progress. Absolute order implies no disagreement. Without disagreement ideas are not challenged and there is no progress.

The link between legitimacy and authority is extremely important in representative democracies. The fact that the people elect representatives makes the government legitimate. Those representatives then make the laws that will govern people's lives. People obey those laws because they believe that their elected representatives have the *right* or the *authority* to make law. Therefore, most people obey the laws not because they fear the sanctions that would follow from a breach of the law but because they believe the law was made in their name and that it should be obeyed. The result is public order.

International legitimacy

Legitimacy can also be bestowed by the international community, usually represented by the United Nations. If a government is considered to be the rightful government of a country, it will achieve recognition from other governments and will take up its seat at the United Nations. For many years the communist government of the Peoples' Republic of China was not recognized by western states, first, because it came to power via a revolution rather than democratic elections and second, because it joined the communist bloc during the Cold War.

Constitutions

Rules

Given that politicians compete fiercely for political power, rules are needed to regulate this competition. These rules are included in a constitution. They are intended to ensure that competition takes place within limits. In Britain the conflict between the Conservative and Labour Parties is fervent, but takes place through parliamentary debate, elections and in the media. It does not spill over into armed conflict or civil war. This is because Britain has a constitution by which all, or most, politicians are prepared to abide.

Formally, a constitution is a broad set of rules and principles by which a state is governed. It is important that the rules should be broad because a constitution must allow a political system to develop over time. If rules are very precise, they will date

Unconstitutional and anti-constitutional

Unconstitutional behaviour breaches the principles of the **constitution**. For example, if the government acts beyond the power given to it by Parliament it is said to have acted *ultra vires* (beyond its powers) – this is unconstitutional behaviour.

Anti-constitutional behaviour involves opposition to the constitution with a view to its overthrow. In the UK the Anarchist movement and the IRA might be considered anti-constitutional.

quickly and the constitution will break rather than bend with changes in circumstances.

A constitution should contain rules regarding the three main elements of a political system: the relationship between central and local government; the relationship between the institutions of central government; and the relationship between the government and the governed.

The central–local relationship

All states have a central government that takes responsibility for national policy making, but they also have smaller units of government that are responsible for policy at a regional or local level. The relationship between the centre and the local units varies considerably from state to state.

In Britain the state is **unitary**. This means that constitutionally power lies with central government, and units of local government are given a degree of power by the central government. In Britain local government is responsible for education, housing, police, fire services, etc. Depending on the government in power at Westminster, local government power has varied from freedom of action in these areas to acting merely as an agency for central government policies. It can be argued that the latter was particularly true under Margaret Thatcher's Conservative governments.

Unitary state

Britain has also experimented with regional government. In 1921 it set up a parliament in Northern Ireland at Stormont Castle. This had the power to make

State and government

A state is a legal, political and geographical entity.

Legal because states have an identity under international law and so can act illegally in the eyes of the international community.

Political because within a state all citizens are subject to a system of laws and are under the authority of a government.

Geographical because all of this takes place within a recognized geographical boundary. The boundary of a state does not necessarily coincide with the boundaries of a nation. Nation refers to an historical, linguistic and cultural identity.

Government can mean the system of government by which a state is governed, for example, parliamentary or presidential. More usually, it refers to the **executive** branch that governs the state on a day-to-day basis. The personnel of government may change while the state remains constant.

policy for the province. However as the 'troubles' in Northern Ireland escalated, Parliament decided that the province should be ruled directly from Westminster and in 1972 it revoked Stormont's powers and returned them to Westminster (see page 197). At no time did Westminster give up its **sovereignty** over the regional government.

Federalism

Such a system is in stark contrast to a **federal** system such as that which exists in the USA. It began life in 1776 as a loose grouping of independent states, the former British colonies. However, in 1787 each state decided to give up some of its independence in order to create a central government that could make policy for the USA as a whole. In this case, the power flowed from the peripheral states into the central government, not the other way round as is the case in the UK. As a result, individual states in the USA have the power to make their own laws on some areas of policy; hence the differences between states on the use of the death penalty, the availability of abortions and laws relating to alcohol.

The institutions of central government

Separation of powers

All systems of government need to be able to perform three functions: to make law, to implement law and to apply law. In modern states these functions are carried out by the **legislature**, **executive** and **judiciary** respectively and according to the doctrine of the **separation of powers**, as outlined by Baron Montesquieu in the eighteenth century, each unit of government should be independent of the others. Splitting up the powers of government between different institutions is intended to prevent the concentration of power in the hands of one individual, or institution, who would then have the power to remove the liberties of the citizens.

In Britain the legislative function is carried out by Parliament (see Chapter 5); the executive by the prime minister and the cabinet (see Chapter 6), supported by junior ministers and the civil service (see Chapter 7); and the judicial function by the courts (see Chapter 9). In the USA Congress is responsible for the legislative function; the president heads the executive branch and the Supreme Court sits at the head of the judiciary.

Parliamentary government

Having established the institutions of central government, we now look at the way in which they are arranged, i.e. the relationships between them. Britain has a *parliamentary* system. Any parliamentary system has three key components:
- an elected assembly
- an executive branch that is drawn from the assembly
- an executive branch that is accountable to the assembly.

Britain's Parliament is **bicameral** (made up of two houses): the House of Commons and the House of Lords. Only the former is elected; the latter is based on an hereditary system and more recently, a system of appointment.

Parliamentary executive

The composition of the House of Commons determines the party of government, or the executive branch. In the 1992 general election the Conservative Party won more seats in the House of Commons than all of the other political parties put together and is, therefore, said to have an *overall majority* in the House. Assuming that the party's MPs work together, the party will have the support of the House to form a government. The leader of the party becomes prime minister and has the power to appoint colleagues to sit with them in the cabinet. So, the executive branch of government is drawn from Parliament, giving Britain a *parliamentary executive*. Therefore, in Britain the executive is not elected directly.

Governmental functions

If we look at the example of a new education policy as it goes through the governmental process, we can see the role that each branch of government plays.

The executive usually initiates policy. It is formulated by ministers and their civil servants.

The policy is presented to the legislature in the form of a Bill. It is then debated and a vote follows.

If approved by the legislature, the responsibility for implementing the policy returns to the executive. The civil service informs schools of the policy change.

The judiciary may be called upon if a school fails to implement the policy correctly. The judges will apply the law to the specific case.

Finally, the executive is held accountable to Parliament by the concepts of *collective cabinet responsibility* and *individual ministerial responsibility*. The former means that the whole cabinet should take part in decision making, should publicly support decisions once made and should collectively stand or fall by those decisions. Individually, ministers are also responsible for the work of their civil service departments and might have to resign if a major error occurs.

Ministerial responsibility

The parliamentary structure of British government infringes upon Montesquieu's concept of the separation of powers between the three institutions of central government. Far from being separate, the executive branch is actually a part of the legislature with all members of the executive branch also holding seats in either the House of Lords or the House of Commons.

An added element to the relationship between the legislature and the other branches of government in Britain is the idea of *parliamentary sovereignty*. In other words, Parliament is the most powerful institution in the UK. According to A V Dicey, writing in the nineteenth century, this meant that 'Parliament . . . has, under the English Constitution, the right to make or unmake any law whatever; and, further, that no person or body is recognized by the law of England as having the right to override or set aside the legislation of Parliament'.

Parliamentary sovereignty

In terms of the relationships between the institutions of government, parliamentary sovereignty is probably the most important principle of the British Constitution. Parliament can make, amend or repeal any law. It can create or bring down a government and no Parliament can bind a future Parliament, meaning that the Parliament of today is always supreme and cannot be tied down by anything a Parliament has done in the past. Thus the executive, the judiciary and local government are all subordinate to Parliament.

The USA's political institutions are arranged not in a parliamentary structure but as a presidential system in which the head of the executive branch, the president, and the legislature, Congress, are elected separately. Therefore, the people choose the legislature and the head of the executive branch and so whoever becomes president has nothing whatsoever to do with the majorities in either house of Congress. The separation of powers is more strictly adhered to with members of the executive prohibited from holding seats in the legislature.

Presidential government

In addition, no single institution in the USA is sovereign. The president needs the

Limited government

support of Congress and vice versa. Therefore, a system of checks and balances is in place which is intended to create a **limited government**, no institution of which has unlimited power. Britain also has checks and balances, but they are much weaker because only the judiciary and the executive can be checked – not Parliament because it is sovereign.

However, Britain and the USA have one principle of central government organization in common – an independent judiciary. A fundamental tenet of western democracies is that judges should be free to apply the law without political interference (see page 121). This is intended to ensure that laws are applied equally to all citizens regardless of their standing in society, their wealth or their political beliefs. Law should be implemented according to a predictable and equitable pattern rather than on the whim of politicians. Thus is created a government of laws not of people.

Rule of law

This is the basis for A V Dicey's **rule of law**. According to this theory everyone is equally subject to the law, citizen and government; everyone is equal before the law and is entitled to a fair trial presided over by a non-partisan judge (see page 123). In order to achieve this, judges should be free from political interference and so the political branches of government should be separate from the judicial. Even so, in both Britain and the USA there are infringements of this separation, for example, judges are appointed by the executive branch (see pages 124–5).

The government and the governed

Bill of rights

A constitution should outline the relationship between the government of the state and the citizens of the state. Essentially, this concerns the rights and liberties that citizens can expect within a state. This is most clearly illustrated in those states that have a **bill of rights** incorporated into their constitutions. The first ten **amendments** to the American Constitution are collectively known as the *Bill of Rights* – here are enshrined freedom of speech, religion and assembly (1st Amendment); the right to bear arms (2nd Amendment); and the right not to incriminate oneself (5th Amendment).

The British Constitution contains a Bill of Rights which established the rights of Parliament over the monarchy in 1689. There is no bill establishing the rights of citizens in relation to the government. The main responsibility for upholding the rights of citizens lies with Parliament and the judiciary. Parliament should pass laws that uphold rights and liberties while the judiciary should apply these laws in fair and just manner to preserve rights and liberties.

Written and unwritten constitutions

Codified and uncodified

As well as in their contents, constitutions may also vary in the manner in which they are compiled. The American Constitution is a *written* constitution. More precisely, it is **codified**, written in a systematic way in a single document. At the end of most American politics textbooks, you will find the American Constitution and its amendments. This is not the case in Britain because the British Constitution is *unwritten* or *uncodified*. There is no single document in which the British Constitution can be found; instead it is made up of a variety of different elements, some of which are written down, some of which are not.

The British Constitution is one of the last remaining unwritten constitutions in the world. This is largely because most states have undergone significant upheavals during their recent political history and this has given an opportunity to formulate a written constitution. The American Revolution, the French Revolution, independence from colonial rule for India, Kenya, etc., defeat in war for Germany and Japan and a civil war in Spain have all given opportunities to write or rewrite constitutions.

Britain has not been free of major upheavals. The Civil War and the subsequent restoration of the monarchy (1642–60) and the Glorious Revolution (1688) were both significant turning points in British political history, but they came at the very beginning of talk of written contracts between government and citizens and so did not present an opportunity to codify the constitution.

Therefore, the British Constitution has evolved as political, economic and social circumstances have changed. In medieval England the king was absolute ruler until the barons began to resent his power, hence King John was forced to sign the Magna Carta in 1215. The power of the monarch and particularly King Charles I's relationship with Parliament, became a further source of conflict in the mid-seventeenth century, resulting in first the Civil War and then the Glorious Revolution. As a result, the power of the monarch was curbed and Parliament began to take the upper hand.

In the nineteenth century the electoral franchise was gradually extended in 1832, 1867 and 1884. This process continued into the twentieth century, until 1969 when the voting age was reduced from 21 to 18. The extension of the franchise made the House of Commons more democratic, so the power of the unelected House of Lords seemed hard to justify. Therefore, in 1911 and 1949 the power of the Lords was reduced.

Since then it is the power of the executive branch of government that has been on the increase. The prime minister and cabinet, backed by departments of civil servants, have come to dominate the policy-making process. The size and influence of the civil service has been particularly noticeable in the second half of the twentieth century (see page 101). Its responsibility has grown to such an extent that ministers are increasingly willing to ignore the doctrine of individual ministerial responsibility and refuse to resign in the wake of major departmental errors.

This outline of some important political developments in British history shows how the British Constitution has been added to, reinterpreted and modified to suit the changing environment. The ways in which it may be adjusted can be examined by looking at the sources of the British Constitution.

Sources

Historical documents

We have already seen that the Magna Carta and the Bill of Rights laid down important rules regarding the power of the monarch. They are stages in the development of the British Constitution and so are part of it.

Statute law

Parliament

Statute law is law made by Parliament. Any law that involves constitutional relationships becomes part of the constitution. The 1911 Parliament Act, for example, removed the House of Lords' power of veto and replaced it with the power to delay legislation for two years. It also prevented the Lords from examining financial legislation. Therefore, it is part of the constitution.

9

Common law

Judges

Common law is sometimes referred to as judge-made law. It concerns judicial interpretations of statute law. No law is so precise that it needs no interpretation, and as judges interpret the law they are deciding what it should mean and so are contributing to making that law work in practice (see page 126).

International treaties and agreements

Treaties

In recent years the signing of treaties and agreements has been one of the most significant sources of the British Constitution, largely due to Britain's membership of the European Community (EC), now known as the European Union (EU) (see Chapter 11).

Europe

In 1972 Britain signed the Treaty of Rome and Parliament passed the European Communities Act to allow Britain to become a member of the EC in 1973. In doing so, the British Constitution was fundamentally changed. Britain accepted the superiority of European law and for the first time Parliament was subject to an authority greater than its own. In other words, Parliament was no longer sovereign. Today British courts have the power to review acts of Parliament in the light of EU legislation and can suspend statute law if necessary. British courts did this in 1991 when the 1988 Merchant Shipping Act was suspended as part of the so-called Factortame case (see page 132).

Britain is also a signatory of other international agreements and treaties, all of which reduce its ability to act totally independently. For example, Britain is a member of the United Nations and the North Atlantic Treaty Organization (NATO) and is a signatory of the European Convention on Human Rights.

Conventions

Patterns of behaviour

As their name suggests, **conventions** are habitual or normal patterns of behaviour. They are an important part of the British Constitution, but are also perhaps the most difficult to understand. They are considered binding on those who should abide by the constitution, but they are not legally enforceable.

Examples of constitutional conventions include the relationship between the prime minister and the cabinet, royal prerogative (see page 116) and the conventions of individual and collective ministerial responsibility (see pages 80 and 99). Theoretically, the monarch retains the power to dissolve Parliament, appoint the prime minister and to grant the Royal Assent to bills. However, in reality the monarch dissolves Parliament on the advice of the prime minister – no monarch has declined to give the Royal Assent since 1708.

Legally, there is no punishment for the breach of a constitutional convention. Therefore, if a minister decides not to resign in the light of mistakes made by their civil service department, there is no recourse to any legal action. However, there might be political repercussions to such decisions, including a weakening of the minister's position, parliamentary and media criticism and perhaps the undermining of prime ministerial authority.

Academic opinion

Some famous commentators on the British Constitution have been so influential with regard to its interpretation that their work has become part of the constitution itself. Perhaps most famous are Walter Bagehot (1826–77) and A V Dicey (1835–1922). Again, such work is only interpretation and is not legally binding.

Bagehot and Dicey

Flexible and rigid constitutions

As the British Constitution is unwritten, or uncodified, it is often considered a **flexible** constitution. All that is needed to change it is a new law through a majority in Parliament, a change in an habitual pattern of behaviour or even a change in interpretation. It is this flexibility that has allowed the constitution to evolve with political circumstances.

Some observers have suggested that flexibility seriously weakens a constitution because it should be a set of broad rules which lay down the structure of the system, against which the branches of government should be judged. It should not be a set of rules that bend and contort to suit any political circumstance. In fact, Alexis de Tocqueville, the French eighteenth-century statesman and historian, even claimed that Britain had no constitution at all. It certainly does have a constitution, but perhaps it is best described as **descriptive**, outlining relationships as they *are*, rather more than as they *should be*.

Descriptive

The American Constitution is codified and **prescriptive** with a rigorous amendment procedure. In order to amend the constitution a two thirds majority in both the House of Representatives and the Senate is required, followed by the approval of three-quarters of the legislatures in the individual states. Since 1787 this has only been achieved 27 times – the first ten of which were all passed together in 1791. However, even the seemingly most rigid of constitutions can be kept up to date by the courts. In the USA the Supreme Court's interpretations of the document have changed dramatically as circumstances and attitudes have changed. The issue of **civil rights** illustrates this very clearly. In 1896 (*Plessy v. Ferguson*) the Supreme Court declared racial segregation constitutional, so long as the provision for both races was equal. In 1954 (*Brown v. Board of Education, Topeka, Kansas*) the court used the same document to declare racial segregation *unconstitutional*.

Prescriptive

Constitutional reform

Britain is faced with two possible routes to constitutional reform. The first is, in fact, a continuation of the evolutionary track followed to date. Reforms could be adopted on a piecemeal basis as and when it is seen fit. Examples of possible reforms might include the introduction of an electoral system based on proportional representation, fixed terms for Parliament and reform of the House of Lords and the monarchy. The Conservative Party tends to support such an approach because it favours the gradual evolution of institutions rather than radical reform or revolution.

Evolution or revolution

An alternative, and perhaps more radical, approach is that suggested by Charter 88, a pressure group which seeks a written constitution for Britain. Many of the proposals for piecemeal reform and for inclusion in a written constitution might well be similar; the radical element is in the demand for a codified document. The Liberal Democrat Party and to a lesser extent the Labour Party are supporters of such reforms.

Charter 88

Arguments for a written constitution

Limit Parliament

A major concern about Britain's unwritten constitution is the fact that Parliament is unrestrained. Its sovereignty, as we have seen, means that it can make or unmake any laws without restriction. The danger of this is that one branch of government has ultimate power and cannot be checked by any other branch. With the workload of Parliament being very heavy, there is the threat that Parliament will pass bad or ill-considered law.

Devolution

This is particularly worrying when parliamentary sovereignty is combined with the federal system. Parliament can make law which affects all areas of the state and might not be particularly sensitive to local conditions. Therefore, many groups including the Liberal Democrat and Labour Parties seek greater **devolution** of power to national and regional parliaments.

**Limit government
Elective dictatorship**

Under the present constitutional arrangement the executive branch of government can be checked by Parliament and by the courts. If it acts beyond the powers given to it by Parliament, it is acting *ultra vires*. However, parliamentary majorities, backed by strong party discipline, mean that the executive is able to dominate the legislature. This has led former Lord Chancellor Lord Hailsham to argue that Britain is an 'elective dictatorship'. In 1976 Lord Hailsham stated:

'The sovereignty of Parliament has increasingly become, in practice, the sovereignty of the Commons, and the sovereignty of the Commons has increasingly become the sovereignty of the Government which, in addition to its influence in Parliament, controls the party whips, the party machine, and the Civil Service. This means that what has always been an elective dictatorship in theory, but one in which the component parts operated in practice to control one another, has become a machine in which one of those parts has come to exercise a predominant influence over the rest.' Guildhall Lecture

Since 1976 the House of Commons has been less subservient than Lord Hailsham might have expected. The select committee system was reformed in 1979 and backbench revolts have become more common, but a written constitution would limit the power of Parliament and in turn that of the executive.

Electoral mandate

Many observers are keen to restrict the power of the government because they question the mandate to govern. Every government since 1945 has been elected with less than 50 per cent of the vote and so cannot claim to be representative of the majority of voters. This has been of particular concern since the mid-1970s, when Britain moved away from **consensus politics** towards **adversarial politics** with the two main parties becoming more polarized in the policies they sought to implement when in government. Supporters of the centre of British politics, such as Roy Jenkins and Shirley Williams, have been keen to remove the exaggerated mandate by reforming the electoral system.

Bill of rights

A further concern is that Britain does not have a bill of rights which outlines the rights of citizens. Therefore, nowhere are the rights and liberties of citizens clearly laid down. It is Parliament's duty to preserve those liberties, but it can remove them at any time. The Prevention of Terrorism Act was first imposed in 1974 in the wake of the Birmingham pub bombings and has been reimposed annually by every government since then. The act allows a suspected terrorist to be held for two days without access to any adviser and for a further five days, with access to a solicitor, upon the issue of a warrant by the home secretary. This is an infringement of the traditional right to be released after 24 hours unless charged.

The fear that civil liberties might be removed is of particular concern to minority groups. Parliament is elected and so is likely to be in tune with the majority of voters because the well-being of the majority is likely to determine the future of a political party. Minority groups are far less influential in the outcome of general election results. Therefore, the minority groups in society are in danger of having their rights removed by the 'tyranny of the majority'. Geoffrey Robertson QC has said:

'Majority rule resulting from free and fair elections does make most of us safe most of the time, and there is little likelihood that any Government would risk electoral reprisals by passing laws which deprive the majority of any right which they value. But it is minorities who are at risk – immigrants, homosexuals, persons suspected of crime, demonstrators, parents of children taken into care, mental patients and other classes of persons insufficiently numerous to wield electoral power but large enough to attract obloquy or resentment.' – Freedom, the Individual and the Law, Penguin, 1993

Arguments against a written constitution

Many of the arguments against a written constitution rest on the desirability of tradition. The Conservative Party, in particular, is keen to avoid radical change to the constitutional arrangement unless absolutely necessary. Britain's unwritten constitution has served us well to date, the argument goes, so why change it now? Furthermore, if it does need to be changed it could be done on a piecemeal basis to suit the circumstances – in other words, the constitution should continue to evolve.

Evolution

However, other arguments against a written constitution concentrate on the role that judges would play in the interpretation of a written constitution. If it is to survive, a written constitution must be relatively vague, in order to allow it to develop over time. Responsibility for interpreting and reinterpreting the constitution to suit the time would be the responsibility of the judiciary. This raises a number of difficulties.

Judicial interpretation

Judges are not elected, whereas the House of Commons is. Nevertheless, they would have the power to overrule the elected representatives of the people. If Parliament passed a law that was considered unconstitutional, the judges on a 'supreme court' would be able to veto it.

Unelected judges

Judges are also unaccountable. They do not have to answer to the electorate or even to Parliament for the decisions they make. This is to protect them from political influence, but if they were given the power to interpret a constitution, such freedom from accountability might be a cause for concern.

Unaccountable judges

In addition, they are unrepresentative of the people at large. John Griffith of the London School of Economics has argued that judges are biased in their attitudes against racial minorities, demonstrators and trade unionists. If this were true, the value of a bill of rights would be undermined if it were interpreted in a biased way and the groups most in need of protection might not receive it. (The role of judges in the preservation of civil liberties is discussed more fully on pages 133–9.)

Unrepresentative judges

There is also controversy about what should be included in a written constitution and a bill of rights. Socialists and conservatives, for example, emphasize different rights. A socialist might wish to emphasize a positive role for the state, giving people the right to work, to welfare and to some degree of economic equality. A conservative is more likely to highlight a limited role for the state with individuals being free to develop without governmental interference. These divisions have led critics of the idea of a bill of rights to argue that it might confuse, rather than clarify people's rights and liberties.

Content

Finally, a written constitution and a bill of rights are only as good as the willingness of politicians to abide by both documents. The courts, with their limited powers, would be unable to force a government to conform to constitutional requirements. Therefore, ultimately, rights and liberties rest on the constitutionalism of politicians.

Exercises

Short questions

1 a Why is British government described as constitutional?
   b Outline a case against such a description. (ULEAC, June 1993)
2 a Define public order.
   b To what extent is it an issue in British politics? (ULEAC, June 1994)
3 Distinguish between unconstitutional and anti-constitutional behaviour. Give an example of each.
4 Distinguish between a written and an unwritten constitution.
5 Distinguish between a flexible and a rigid constitution.

Essay questions

1 The British Constitution is what happens. Discuss. (ULEAC, January 1993)
2 Has the time come to draw up a written constitution for Britain? (ULEAC, January 1991)
3 What aspects of constitutional reform are most needed in Britain and why? (Oxford and Cambridge, June 1994)
4 Would a bill of rights make the British political system more democratic? (ULEAC, January 1994)

Data response question

'Outside Westminster the constitution has precious little authority. The public sees a government that does not hear its grievances, a House of Commons discredited by sleaze, an unaccountable quangocracy and a philandering monarchy. Only isolated ministers, advised by obsequious civil servants, could believe otherwise.

... The "efficient secret" of the British constitution, according to Walter Bagehot ... was the omnipotence of Parliament. Yet this is changing before our very eyes. Power flows up from Westminster to European institutions. As judges lose faith in the state, it flows out, to the courts ...

Meanwhile ministers are quite happy to change the constitution, sacred though it may be, whenever it suits them. Power flows from Westminster to Whitehall as the government waters down parliamentary accountability by establishing quangos and semi-autonomous agencies. It flows to the centre, in the form of a determined assault on the powers of local government. It flows out again as some of the powers local government has lost are handed to local schools. If and when peace is established in Northern Ireland, power will flow from Westminster back to Stormont – yet another in the myriad constitutional changes that have transformed the province's government over the century.

The "efficient secret" of the British constitution is not the one that Bagehot thought he had discovered. Its real secret lies in its adaptability to circumstances. And that, in turn, has been sustained by the ability of Britain's rulers, with good or ill grace, themselves to change the constitution in good time before its anachronisms destroy what remains sound and relevant.'

Source: *The Economist,* 17 December 1994

1 What factors have diminished the power of Parliament over recent years?
2 Explain the phrase, 'Its real secret lies in its adaptability to circumstances'.
3 Outline the case in favour of drawing up a written constitution in Britain.

2 British elections

Questions to be answered in this chapter
- What is democracy?
- Why are elections so important?
- How does the British electoral system work?
- Should the British electoral system be reformed?
- What would be the effects of reform?
- How can the way people vote be explained?

Terms to know

Additional Member System (AMS)	Minority government
Alternative Vote	Opinion polls
Class	Proportional representation (PR)
Coalition government	Representation
Democracy	Representative democracy
Expressive voting	Responsibility
First past the post (FPTP)	Single Transferable Vote (STV)
Hung parliament	Wasted votes
Instrumental voting	Winner-take-all system

Democracy

Origins

The word **democracy** comes from the Greek word *demokratia* meaning *demos* (people) and *kratos* (rule). From understanding the derivation of 'democracy', it is a short step to the words of American president Abraham Lincoln at Gettysburg in 1863 in which he described democracy as 'Government of the people, by the people, for the people'. However, this does not explain exactly how democracy can be put into practice in a political system.

Representative democracy

The city states of Ancient Greece had a 'pure' democracy which allowed citizens to participate directly in political decision making (women and slaves were not considered to be citizens and so could not take part). However, in modern societies direct participation is not practical. Britain's 58 million citizens cannot be regularly involved in political decision making. Therefore, liberal democrats in the eighteenth century introduced the idea of **representative democracy** to political theory.

In a representative democracy the citizens recognize that they cannot all participate directly and so they choose a smaller group of representatives to act on their behalf. The mechanisms by which representatives are chosen are elections. The adequacy of the system of elections is fundamental to the functioning of a country's democracy. An inadequate electoral system can undermine representative democracy.

Elections and democracy

In Western democracies the term *election* tends to conjure up images of political parties, campaigns, speeches, media interviews, the secret ballot and late-night declarations of results. We might believe, therefore, that all elections are automatically characterized by these things. This is not true.

Who votes?

In 1832, 5 per cent of the adult population were allowed to vote. In 1867 this increased to 13 per cent and reached 25 per cent in 1884. Women were not given the vote until 1918 and 1928 when the percentage reached 99 per cent of adults. In 1969 the 'adult' age was lowered from 21 to 18.

In order to vote an individual must be registered in a constituency and must be a British subject.

Peers, those certified insane and certain categories of criminal are not allowed to vote.

In many countries elections take place in difficult circumstances in which one party rules the country and will not tolerate opposition; the press is controlled by the government; voters are subject to intimidation and corruption; and the election result is always in danger of being overturned if it does not suit the ruling bodies. Therefore, elections alone do not make a democracy. Political toleration, multi-party competition, a free press, a constitutional commitment to abide by the results and, of course, the ability to vote for representatives to fill offices that actually have some power are all basic requirements of a true representative democracy.

Democracy

Broadly speaking, British democracy satisfies these requirements. Nevertheless, a great deal of controversy surrounds British general elections. This is not related to freedom of speech or political toleration but to the very system of election itself. The Liberal Democrats, in particular, argue that the British electoral system is biased against them and exaggerates the support for the two larger parties. For this reason, they argue, it is fundamentally unfair.

Before examining these claims, we need to understand how the British system of election works.

The British electoral system

Since the Parliament Act of 1911 the lifetime of a British Parliament has been limited to a maximum of five years. Within this period the prime minister must ask the monarch for a dissolution of Parliament; in other words, a general election must be called. British elections are not held on a fixed-term basis, so at which point during the five-year term the election should be called, is at the discretion of the prime minister. Usually, prime ministers call an election when they believe that their party has the best chance of victory, although occasionally they may be forced into one by the loss of a vote of no confidence in the House of Commons as happened in 1979 when the minority Labour government lost such a vote and went on to lose the election.

Life of Parliament

In a general election all adults over the age of 18 are, with very few exceptions, allowed to vote. This was not always the case. The male franchise was gradually

Electorate

widened throughout the nineteenth century by the Reform Acts of 1832, 1867 and 1884. Women did not receive the vote until 1918 and 1928. The voting age was lowered from 21 to 18 in 1969.

Secret ballot

The secret ballot was introduced in Britain in 1872. This was an important advance because for the first time voters could complete their ballot without the knowledge of their landlord, employer or any officials. As a result, they could cast their vote freely, without any interference from outsiders.

Electoral boundaries

There is a Boundary Commission responsible for England, Scotland, Wales and Northern Ireland. It reviews the distribution of parliamentary seats every 10–15 years and redraws boundaries in an effort to keep pace with movements in the population.

The ideal of constituencies of equal size is an important aspect of a representative democracy. It ensures that every person's vote is of equal worth. Nevertheless, there are significant divergences between constituencies.

The Boundary Commission revisions implemented in 1983 have benefited the Conservative Party as they have taken into account the growth of the population in suburbs and in the south, i.e. Conservative strongholds. It is expected that the changes due for implementation at the time of the next general election will also favour the Conservatives.

Constituencies

The UK is divided into 651 electoral constituencies, each sending one Member of Parliament (MP) to the House of Commons. To ensure that each citizen is equally represented by their MP the constituencies should all be of approximately the same size, around 65,000 people.

By-elections

By-elections are held whenever a seat falls vacant in the House of Commons.

They tend to attract a great deal of media and political attention, which in itself makes them unrepresentative of a normal constituency contest in a general election.

Governments often perform badly in by-elections as the electorate passes judgement on its performance in office. Generally, governments take by-election results as a jab in the ribs from the electorate.

The Liberal Democrats have often performed well in by-elections as the electorate uses the opportunity to protest against the two main parties.

The reliability of by-election results as a means of predicting a general election result is further undermined by the low turnout, which is often less than 50 per cent – compared to 70 per cent in general elections.

First past the post

The method of election is known as **first past the post (FPTP)**. This means that voters choose their MP by placing an 'X' on the ballot paper next to their preferred candidate. The candidate in each constituency with the most votes wins the election. The winning candidate need only poll more votes than their nearest rival – they do not require more than all of the other candidates put together nor do they need over 50 per cent of the vote.

The British electoral system does not, however, merely elect individual MPs to represent their constituents in Parliament. As Britain is a parliamentary system, by voting for individual MPs the electorate is indirectly determining the nature of the government. The British government is drawn from the House of Commons and relies on the support of the Commons. Therefore, the party with the majority of seats in the lower house is usually asked by the monarch to form the government after a general election.

Election of government

Assessing an electoral system

An electoral system should give the electorate the opportunity to select the people whom they would like to act on their behalf in the country's assembly and then it should give them the opportunity to remove those individuals at the next election if they are unhappy with their performance. These twin ideas are formalized in the concepts of **representation** and **responsibility**.

Representation

In Britain, the parliamentary system means that voters are seeking not only an MP who represents them but, indirectly, a representative government. Similarly, they need the ability to unelect a government by unelecting their MP. So the electoral system is operating at two levels: assembly (made up of MPs) and government (drawn from the assembly). It needs to be assessed using the criteria of representation and responsibility at both of these levels. This task is made difficult by the fact that the supporters and critics of first past the post are often using different definitions of these criteria.

The first-past-the-post system

Support for first past the post

According to supporters of the British electoral system, first past the post gives fair representation. They point to the fact that the majority of adults over the age of 18 have the right to vote for an MP to act on their behalf and that they do so in constituencies that the Boundary Commission makes every effort to ensure are of equal size.

Once elected, MPs should adhere to the view of philosopher Edmund Burke who believed that MPs are representatives and they should act on behalf of all of

Edmund Burke

Representatives and delegates

The nineteenth-century philosopher and MP Edmund Burke distinguished between delegates and representatives.

Delegates make decisions according to the instructions of others. They refer to those whom they represent whenever a decision is to be made. Representatives make decisions on the basis of their own judgement. Although they might consider their constituents' views when making decisions, they do not have to abide by their wishes.

Traditionally, British MPs are representatives, acting on behalf of their constituency. However, the advent of strong political parties has pushed MPs nearer to being party delegates. Most MPs follow the party whip in the House of Commons (see page 70).

their constituents, not merely those who voted for them. MPs are not delegates – they should use their own judgement when deciding how to vote in the Commons.

In the Commons the views of individual MPs, along with 650 others, allow a government to be drawn from the house with the support of the majority of the electorate's representatives. Therefore, say supporters of first past the post, the government must, surely, represent the electorate as well and has a mandate (see page 24) to govern.

Responsibility

Usually, the government has a clear, overall majority in the House of Commons, so not only is it representative, it is responsible. Those in favour of FPTP argue that the government's overall majority leaves it free to act responsibly and to do the 'right thing' while in office. Thus it is not tied to taking the most popular course solely to preserve a Commons majority. It can follow a strong policy line, even though it might be unpopular in the short term.

In addition, the government is easily held accountable for its 'responsible' policy line. At the time of the next election the electorate can assess the quality of the government's performance and may vote for one of the opposition candidates in the constituencies in order to displace their MP and the sitting government.

Responsibility is often seen as the predominant characteristic of the British electoral system. Supporters of FPTP tend to concentrate on the benefits it brings to the workings of government rather than 'fairness' of the House of Commons, i.e. the government takes a responsible course for which it is then held accountable.

Opposition to first past the post

Public opinion

Opponents of first past the post believe that representation should extend beyond every constituency having an MP to act on its behalf. They argue that the composition of the House of Commons should reflect public opinion and that the electoral system should not distort the result. In other words, the result should be proportional – if the Conservative Party receives 42 per cent of the votes cast, then it should win 42 per cent of the seats in the Commons.

The results of the 1983 general election clearly show that the composition of the House of Commons does not reflect the votes cast in the country (see Table 2.1).

Table 2.1 Results of the 1983 general election

Year	Votes cast (% of votes)				No. of seats (% of seats)			
	Con.	Lab.	Alliance	Other	Con.	Lab.	Alliance	Other
1983	13.0m (42.2)	8.5m (27.6)	7.8m (25.4)	1.4m (4.6)	397 (61.1)	209 (32.2)	23 (3.5)	21 (3.2)

On the basis of only 42.2 per cent of the popular vote the Conservative Party gained 61.1 per cent of the seats; while the Liberal–Social Democrat Alliance gained 25.4 per cent of the vote but won only 3.5 per cent of the seats in the assembly. In terms of reflecting opinion, the Conservative Party was overrepresented in the Commons while the Alliance was even more seriously underrepresented.

Winner take all

This is possible because first past the post is a **winner-take-all system** under which parties are only rewarded if they win a constituency. It does not matter how many votes are accumulated across the country, only that enough votes are amassed in certain areas in order to win constituencies.

The Conservative and Labour Parties have their support concentrated in the south and the north respectively. Therefore, the Labour Party wins seats in the north and the Conservatives win in the south. The Liberal Democrats do not have concentrated support, except in south-west England. Their support is considerable, but it is spread evenly across the country. Therefore, they can only amass enough votes to beat the two leading parties into second and third place in very few constituencies. In fact, in 1987 the Alliance came second in 261 constituencies. As a result of these anomalies, in 1983, 300,144 votes were needed to elect an Alliance MP, compared to the 41,811 needed to elect a Conservative (see Table 2.2).

Concentrated support

Table 2.2 Results of general elections, 1945–92

Year	Votes cast (% of votes)				No. of seats (% of seats)			
	Con.	Lab.	Lib.	Other	Con.	Lab.	Lib.	Other
1945	9.6m	11.6m	2.2m	0.7m	213	393	12	22
	(39.8)	(48.3)	(9.1)	(2.8)	(33.3)	(61.4)	(1.9)	(3.4)
1950	12.5m	13.3m	2.6m	0.4m	299	315	9	2
	(43.5)	(46.1)	(9.1)	(1.3)	(47.9)	(50.4)	(1.4)	(0.3)
1951	13.7m	13.9m	0.7m	0.2m	321	295	6	3
	(48.0)	(48.8)	(2.5)	(0.7)	(51.4)	(47.2)	(1.0)	(0.5)
1955	13.3m	12.4m	0.7m	0.3m	345	277	6	2
	(49.7)	(46.4)	(2.7)	(1.2)	(54.8)	(44.0)	(1.0)	(0.3)
1959	13.7m	12.2m	1.6m	0.3m	365	258	6	1
	(49.4)	(43.8)	(5.9)	(0.9)	(57.9)	(41.0)	(1.0)	(0.2)
1964	12.0m	12.2m	3.1m	0.3m	304	317	9	–
	(43.4)	(44.1)	(11.2)	(1.3)	(48.3)	(50.3)	(1.4)	(–)
1966	11.4m	13.1m	2.3m	0.5m	253	363	12	2
	(41.9)	(47.9)	(8.5)	(1.7)	(40.2)	(57.6)	(1.9)	(0.3)
1970	13.1m	12.2m	2.1m	0.9m	330	287	6	7
	(46.4)	(43.0)	(7.5)	(3.1)	(52.4)	(45.6)	(1.0)	(1.1)
1974 Feb.	11.9m	11.6m	6.1m	1.8m	297	301	14	23
	(37.8)	(37.1)	(19.3)	(5.8)	(46.8)	(47.4)	(2.2)	(3.6)
1974 Oct.	10.5m	11.5m	6.3m	1.9m	277	319	13	26
	(34.8)	(38.0)	(20.8)	(6.3)	(43.6)	(50.2)	(2.0)	(4.1)
1979	13.7m	11.5m	4.3m	1.7m	339	269	11	16
	(43.9)	(36.9)	(13.8)	(5.4)	(53.4)	(42.4)	(1.7)	(2.5)
1983	13.0m	8.5m	7.8m	1.4m	397	209	23	21
	(42.2)	(27.6)	(25.4)	(4.6)	(61.1)	(32.2)	(3.5)	(3.2)
1987	13.8m	10.0m	7.3m	1.4m	376	229	22	23
	(42.3)	(30.8)	(22.6)	(4.3)	(57.8)	(35.2)	(3.4)	(3.5)
1992	14.2m	11.6m	6.1m	1.2m	336	271	20	24
	(42.9)	(35.0)	(18.4)	(3.6)	(51.6)	(41.6)	(3.1)	(3.7)

Note: In 1983 and 1987 the Liberal Party contested elections in partnership with the Social Democratic Party – together they were known as the Alliance. In 1988 the two parties merged to become the Social and Liberal Democratic Party. This became the Liberal Democrats in 1989.

Wasted votes

In addition, under a winner-take-all system the size of a candidate's majority in a constituency is ignored. If a candidate wins by 20,000 votes or only 2,000, the reward is still one seat in the Commons. This results in **wasted votes** because the large majorities are votes that could have been better used in other constituencies where they would have gained more seats. In other words, all votes other than those required to secure a simple majority do not contribute to the election of an MP.

Obviously, the ability to place voters strategically around the country is every party's desire. However, the wasted votes can lead to serious electoral anomalies. In 1951 the Labour Party polled 13.9 million votes compared to the Conservative's 13.7 million, but the Labour Party lost the election because the Conservatives won 26 seats more than Labour.

These electoral anomalies also affect the extent to which a British government can be held accountable for its actions. It is true that under a winner-take-all system one party is likely to control government, with an overall majority in the House of Commons, and, therefore, is in a position to act 'responsibly'. However that government is not always held accountable for its actions.

In 1979 the Conservative Party gained 13.7 million votes (43.9 per cent of votes cast) and as a result, it won 339 (53.4 per cent) of the seats in the Commons. In 1983 it polled only 13 million votes (42.2 per cent) and so may be considered less popular than four years earlier. However, its reward was 397 (61.1 per cent) of the seats. The increase in the seats won by the Conservative Party was largely due to the revision of constituency boundaries by the Boundaries Commission. However, it seems surprising that a party which has lost support should form a government with an even larger majority.

Proportional representation

While first past the post embodies the winner-take-all principle, the alternative system would be based on **proportional representation** (PR). PR is not a system in itself, but a characteristic of a number of different systems, all of which will give an election result in which the composition of the assembly reflects, to a greater or lesser extent, the way the votes were cast.

For those who favour an assembly that reflects public opinion PR is obviously a preferred method of election. Table 2.3 shows how a different system of election would have affected the result of the 1992 election (the results from Northern Ireland have been excluded).

Table 2.3 Number of seats 'won' by the parties in the 1992 general election according to proportional representation

	Con.	Labour	Lib. Dem.	Nationalist	Green
FPTP	336	271	20	7	0
PR systems:					
Alternative Vote	325	270	30	9	0
Additional Member System	268	232	116	18	0
Single Transferable Vote	256	250	102	20	6

Source: Dunleavy, Margetts and Weir, *LSE Public Policy Paper 3*, London School of Economics, 1992, quoted in Conley, *General Elections Today*, Manchester University Press, 1994

The Additional Member System

The Additional Member System has two different types of MP: those elected under the FPTP system and an additional 'top-up' member chosen from lists of party nominees. The former MPs are the constituency representatives. The top-up MPs are used to build up each party's representation to reflect fully the proportion of votes cast for that party. Usually a 5 per cent threshold operates and parties are not given 'top-up' MPs until they have reached this level of voter support. This is the basis of the system used in Germany. Its great advantage is that it combines the assets of PR with those of FPTP.

The **Alternative Vote** system is not founded on the principle of proportional representation, rather it tries to ensure that a winning candidate gains at least 50 per cent of the vote in the constituency. Therefore, it would change the election result relatively little. However, either of the two systems of PR that have been considered for Britain, **Additional Member System (AMS)** and the **Single Tranferable Vote (STV)**, would dramatically reduce Conservative seats and redistribute most of them to the Liberal Democrats, the nationalists and, in the case of STV, to the Green Party.

Under a system of PR, the distribution of seats would certainly reflect the votes cast and in that sense would be fairer. However, Table 2.3 also highlights a criticism of PR – it would allow a multi-party system to develop in the House of Commons.

Single Transferable Vote

The Single Transferable Vote (STV) is used in the Republic of Ireland. Voters are divided into multi-member constituencies and they register their preferences for candidates 1, 2, 3, 4, etc. Candidates are elected when they receive a certain quota of the votes. The quota is determined by the Droop formula:

$$\frac{\text{Number of votes cast}}{\text{Number of seats} + 1} + 1$$

Any candidate receiving the quota on first preferences is elected. If not all of the seats are filled in this way, the candidate with the least votes is eliminated and their second preferences redistributed. Any candidate receiving in excess of the quota has their surplus redistributed also. Ultimately, the required number of candidates will be elected.

Multi-party politics and coalitions

Traditionally, the British party system has been viewed as a two–party system, with the House of Commons dominated by the Conservative and Labour Parties. As we have seen, a system of PR would reduce the representation of the two largest parties and increase the number of seats held by smaller parties. Therefore, seats would be more evenly distributed between the parties, to such an extent that no single party would have an overall majority in the Commons. This is known as a 'hung Parliament'.

Hung Parliament

The problem of a hung Parliament can be solved in two ways – either by a minority government or a **coalition government**. The former happens when the largest single party decides to govern alone, despite the fact that if all of the other parties in

Minority government

23

> **Minority and coalition governments**
>
> Minority and coalition governments both stem from 'hung' Parliaments, in which no single party has an overall majority of seats. **Minority governments** are formed when the largest single party decides to govern alone. The Labour governments of February–October 1974 and in 1978 were minorities. In the latter case, Prime Minister James Callaghan governed with the support of the Liberals through the Lib–Lab Pact. A coalition government involves two or more parties forming the government together and sharing seats in cabinet, forming policy jointly and sharing responsibilities for policy. Coalition governments are common in Germany, Italy and Sweden.

the House of Commons combined against the government it would lose every vote. To achieve any success in the assembly, the government needs to win the support of individuals or parties on the floor of the House of Commons. Therefore, it needs to form a coalition of support around each proposal.

James Callaghan's government of 1976–9 became a minority government as its small overall majority was gradually whittled away by a series of by-election defeats. In order to maintain a majority in the house the Labour government formed a pact with the Liberals, known as the Lib–Lab Pact. Both parties were keen to make such a pact because each wished to avoid a general election. It gave the Labour government time for the state of the economy to improve and the Liberals a voice in the determination of government policy.

The Lib–Lab Pact did not give the Liberal Party any seats in cabinet. A government in which two or more parties share seats in cabinet is known as a coalition government. Under these circumstances the coalition partners jointly determine policy and take responsibility for those policies. During World War II Britain was governed by a coalition of the Conservative and Labour Parties, under the leadership of Winston Churchill. Given the special circumstances, this was called a government of 'national unity'. The period between World Wars I and II saw coalitions led by Lloyd George and Ramsay MacDonald, but coalitions have never been considered 'normal' under the British system. They would be much more likely to be so if Britain adopted a system of proportional representation.

> **The electoral mandate**
>
> A mandate is an instruction to carry out a proposal or a set of proposals. An electoral mandate comes from the people to a political party through a general election. When people cast their vote they are assumed to be endorsing the policies of a particular party. If that party then gains an overall majority in the House of Commons, it is regarded as having a 'mandate' to carry out the policies in its manifesto.
>
> The type of electoral system in Britain has caused some commentators to question the existence of an electoral mandate. FPTP exaggerates the support of large parties, taking a minority of the vote and turning it into a majority of the seats. In the general election of 1992 the Conservative Party received the approval of 42.9 per cent of voters, but of only about 30 per cent of electors. Also most voters do not read manifestos, but vote on the basis of their *perception* of a party's policies. Finally, a government often departs from its manifesto during its term of office for which it can be said to have no mandate, although it may refer to the 'Doctor's Mandate', which allows it to take any steps it considers necessary.

Coalitions and representation

Coalition governments have a number of implications for representation and responsibility. Usually, parties do not announce their intention to form a coalition prior to a general election in the hope that they might win an overall majority. Therefore, voters do not have an opportunity to approve or disapprove of the idea of a coalition.

Once the need for a coalition has been established by the election result, the voters are again excluded from the process as politicians negotiate, behind closed doors, to find a bargain that will suit both parties. Therefore, while proportional representation produces an assembly that reflects public opinion, the government is decided without any reference to public opinion. As a result, some commentators argue that the coalition has not been given a mandate to govern by the electorate.

If two or more parties combine to form a government, a significant proportion of the voters ought to be satisfied. For example, if the Labour Party had formed a coalition with the Liberal Democrats after the 1992 election, 17.7 million voters would have been satisfied that their party was in government – as opposed to the 14.2 million who were happy with a Conservative victory. However, this assumes that people vote for a party solely to see it enter government. Perhaps it is more likely that people vote for a party in order to see its policies implemented. Participation in a coalition government is not a guarantee of this.

Compromise

When two or more parties join together in a coalition, the policies that result are likely to be compromises between those of all the players. In the example above, they would be neither Labour nor Liberal Democrat but a third set of hybrid policies that were never presented to voters and so could not be representative of public opinion. It is also possible that the junior partner wielding influence over policy making is a small party representing a tiny proportion of voters. Their influence in government would be far beyond their popularity in the country and in no way a reflection of public opinion.

In Britain coalition government is often considered to be a coalition of the 'centre' with either the Conservative or Labour Parties joining with the Liberal Democrats. In this case the junior partner in the coalition is seen to be a moderating, and so perhaps a desirable, influence. This need not be so, however. Voters might not feel comfortable with a coalition of the right which might include the Conservative Party and the Ulster Unionists or even the British National Party. Similarly, an extreme coalition of the left might include the Labour and Communist Parties.

Coalitions and responsibility

Coalitions can also be difficult to hold accountable. With only one party in government it is clear who should be to blame. In a coalition the question of which party should take responsibility might arise.

Small parties

This is particularly the case when one party holds the balance of power in a parliament. In Germany, for example, the Freie Demokratische Partei (FDP) has held the balance of power between the right-wing Christlich-Demokratische Union (CDU) and the left-wing Sozialdemokratische Partei Deutschlands (SPD). As a result it has been a party in government since 1961 – with the exception of 1969 when the CDU and SPD formed a coalition between themselves. Therefore, the SPD or CDU win or lose elections while the FDP remains in office whatever happens and so is not being held responsible.

25

When the second definition of responsibility – strong leadership – is considered, coalition government can again be criticized. Policies must always be based on compromises, so the government does not have the strength to undertake the policies it might consider necessary.

Instability

Coalition governments can also be affected by instability. The senior partner of the coalition can live in fear of the junior partner withdrawing from the relationship. In Italy governments have been made and unmade with alarming regularity. Between 1945 and 1994 Italy had more than 50 governments. To an extent, this instability has contributed to the Italian government's decision to reform the electoral system along the lines of a winner-take-all system.

However, the appearance of instability can be deceptive. While Italian governments have come and gone, the personnel of government has largely remained the same. Democrazia Cristiana (DC) dominated government from 1946 to 1994 with many of its senior officials circulating between high offices.

Adversary politics

On the other hand, the apparent stability of British government has, at times, also been illusory. Professor Samuel Finer coined the term 'adversary politics' to describe the dramatic swings of policy as a 'strong' Labour government was replaced by an equally 'strong' Conservative government. Perhaps this concept is more useful to describe the situation in the 1970s when the two main parties moved to extremes of the political spectrum and seemed likely to alternate regularly in government.

Constitutional effects of PR

The introduction of a system of proportional representation would not only have effects on representation and responsibility. It would also have a significant impact on many of the institutional relationships of the governmental system.

The monarch

The monarch has two roles concerning elections: the dissolution of Parliament prior to an election and the appointment of a prime minister after the election (see pages 116–7). Both have been considered largely ceremonial given the relative simplicity of the first-past-the-post electoral system: the leader of the party with the overall majority becomes prime minister and then has the power to call a general election at a time most suitable to their party within the next five years.

Dissolution of Parliament

The introduction of a system of proportional representation could create a very different scenario. Consider the following: a Conservative prime minister leads the largest party in the House of Commons, but lacks an overall majority. Reluctant to form a coalition, the prime minister decides that the Conservative Party should govern alone, forming a minority government. The opposition parties unite against the government to defeat the Queen's Speech (see page 65). A vote of no confidence follows and the government is defeated. The prime minister asks the monarch to dissolve Parliament to allow another general election to be held. At this point, the monarch would have two key decisions to make: should the prime minister be given a dissolution and if not, who should be asked to form an alternative government?

Appointment of prime minister

The second question is perhaps easier to answer than the first. Presumably, the alternative prime minister would be the leader of the Opposition who would be asked if they could form a minority or coalition government that could retain the confidence of the Commons. To turn down a prime minister's request for a dissolution of Parliament might be a little more controversial.

In early 1995 Prime Minister John Major technically led a minority government – nine MPs had refused to follow the party line and were no longer covered by the Conservative whip (see page 70) – but both of these issues are more likely to arise under a system of proportional representation and would involve the monarch, an unelected and non-partisan figure, in a politically controversial situation.

The prime minister

Prime ministers who lead a government made up of their own loyal party supporters with a guaranteed majority in the House of Commons are in a very powerful position. The introduction of proportional representation could change this. A coalition government would be highly likely and a prime minister would have to consider the feelings not only of their own party but also those of the coalition partners. The need for compromise would be paramount and the scope for prime ministerial government would be severely reduced.

Prime ministerial power

The House of Commons

If, as seems likely, proportional representation were to lead to a hung parliament, the power of the House of Commons would increase. No longer would governments be able to take the support of the house for granted and like an American president they would have to work to build a secure coalition of support around every piece of legislation. The threat of a vote of no confidence would always hang over them.

Voting behaviour

For much of the post-war period explanations of voting behaviour in Britain were relatively uncomplicated. The way people voted was largely explained by **class** allegiances. Very simply, the Conservative Party was seen as the party of the middle class and the Labour Party that of the working class. Ninety per cent of voters supported one of the two main parties, so third parties and nationalist parties were largely ignored. In addition, the way people cast their votes was relatively predictable because 80 per cent of voters were loyal to their party, in other words, were *party identifiers*.

Party identifiers

In the 1970s analysis became rather more complicated as society underwent fundamental changes. Today the level of party identifiers has fallen; the Liberal Democrats and the nationalist parties have become more popular and the nature of class has changed.

Class voting

Class voting is typical of what sociologists refer to as **expressive voting**. We all tend to identify ourselves as part of a particular group in society which is made up of family, friends and colleagues. As we grow up within this group we are *socialized* to behave in particular ways, and the way we vote in elections is one aspect of this. If we see ourselves as a member of the working class and believe that the Labour Party best represents the interests of our class, then we are likely to vote Labour in a general election. Such trends are reinforced by peripheral factors such as membership of a trade union, living in an industrial community and perhaps living in local authority accommodation.

Socialization

Deviant voting

As the working class accounted for 60 per cent of the population it would seem likely that if individuals voted by class, the Labour Party would be the 'natural' party of government, never being out of office. However, in the post-war period this was not the case because, even in the 1950s, voting along class lines did not always occur: approximately 67 per cent of the working class voted Labour; while 80 per cent of the middle class voted Conservative. The willingness of one-third of the working class to desert their class loyalties allowed the Conservative Party to dominate government for 13 years in the 1950s and 1960s. As a result, much analysis of voting behaviour during this period concentrated on the reasons for this pattern of *deviant voting*.

Embourgeoisement

The *working-class Tory*, as this deviant voter became known, was explained in a number of ways. The term *embourgeoisement* was coined to explain the tendency of the working class to vote Conservative as their standard of living improved. Also some political scientists sought to explain working-class behaviour via deference. According to this view, members of the working class viewed members of the Conservative Party as their 'betters' who were well suited to govern the country.

Partisanship

Since the 1970s explanations of deviant voting have been more than ever called for. Voters are no longer so tied to the two-party model of party competition. Therefore, the Labour and Conservative Parties account only for 75 per cent of the vote. Furthermore, the level of partisanship (those voters who are loyal to a particular party) has declined dramatically from 81 per cent in 1964 to 70 per cent in 1983, with only 23 per cent strongly identifying with a particular party (down from 38 per cent in 1964). Labour's claim to 67 per cent of the working-class vote fell to only 38 per cent in 1983, while the Conservative Party's hold over 80 per cent of the middle class had fallen to 60 per cent.

Some political scientists have attempted to explain the recent changes in voting behaviour by claiming that the traditional methods of stratifying British society have become outdated.

Definitions of social class

Social class categories (Heath et al.)

Salariat	27%
Routine non-manuals	24%
Petit bourgeoisie	8%
Foreman, technicians	7%
Working class	34%

Social class categories (Dunleavy and Husbands)

Manual workers	45%
Non-manual	25%
Controllers of labour	22%
Employees/petit bourgeoisie	8%

Social class categories (British Market Research Society)

A Upper middle	2%
B Middle	13%
C1 Lower middle	24%
C2 Skilled workers	31%
D Semi-skilled and unskilled workers	18%
E Poor	2%

Source: Bill Jones et al., *Politics UK*, Harvester Wheatsheaf, 1994

Most traditional analysis has relied on the classification used by the British Market Research Society which uses categories A, B, C1, C2, D and E. This has been considered inadequate because its categories are largely based on occupation. A teacher would fall into category B – professional and managerial – and would, therefore, be expected to vote Conservative. However, many teachers in state schools feel insecure with Conservative policies towards education and are unlikely to vote Conservative.

Anthony Heath, Roger Jowell and John Curtice (*How Britain Votes*, Pergamon, 1985) have created a new middle-class category, the *salariat*, to take account of the growing number of salaried members of the middle class who might well vote Labour. Erik Ohlin Wright ('Class Crisis and the State', *New Left Review*, 1975) has referred to these voters as 'contradictory' because their status suggests they should vote Conservative, but their occupational circumstances encourages them to support Labour.

Heath et al. have also created a category called the 'petit bourgeoisie', including owners of small businesses. In the British Market Research Society classification these are included in the C1 category with the skilled working class, with whom they share little in terms of ideals and objectives.

Patrick Dunleavy and Chris Husbands (*British Democracy at the Crossroads*, Longman, 1985) have also redefined class boundaries by including a Marxist perspective. Individuals are classified according to their relation to their means of production. This system takes into account not only the traditional divisions between working class and middle class but also an individual's position in 'the system of production and exchange'. In other words, the working class can be further subdivided into those who own their own home or rent from the local authority, work in the public or private sector, are members of trade unions or not, etc. Those who deal mostly with the private sector are more likely to vote Conservative.

Instrumental voting

Instrumental voting behaviour concentrates on the short-term factors that influence behaviour, rather than the long-term factors such as class loyalty. This is sometimes known as the *regency approach*. Issues that might affect voting habits, according to this, might include policy issues, leadership, media coverage and the election campaign. Naturally, as short-term factors, these points can be used to explain the volatility of voting behaviour, particularly in the light of the rise of the independent, or floating, voter.

Such an approach might explain the great swings in popularity of parties and governments as leaders and circumstances change. One of the factors leading to Margaret Thatcher's downfall was her poor standing in **opinion polls** compared to Michael Heseltine and John Major. Also, prior to each of the Conservative Party's general election victories of 1979, 1983, 1987 and 1992, the Conservative government had gone through periods of considerable unpopularity, including the loss of by-elections, before recovering to win the general election.

The difficulty of assessing the importance of such issues in determining electoral behaviour is that research relies on opinion poll data. Polling companies, such as MORI and Gallup, have designed scientific methods to ascertain the way a sample of people feel about particular issues, leaders and parties. They then extrapolate from the sample to predict the way in which the country as a whole will react. Given a margin of error of approximately + or − 3 per cent, opinion polls are quite reliable.

However, pollsters consistently predicted a hung parliament in 1992 with Labour as the largest party. An overall majority for the Conservatives was a great surprise. The misleading poll information may have been due to a poor sample or to voters being able to separate their replies to opinion poll questions from their voting intentions. For example, some commentators believe that a number of voters stated a preference for more funding for the health service and education but, when faced with a ballot box decision, voted for the lower taxes offered by the Conservative Party.

Exercises

Short questions

1 What importance may be attached to by-election campaigns and their results? (ULEAC, June 1992)
2 Briefly describe (a) the Single Transferable Vote (b) the Additional Member System. (c) Which do you prefer and why? (ULEAC, January 1991)
3 a Define the concept of the electoral mandate.
   b Assess its validity as a principle of representative government. (ULEAC, June 1991)

Essay questions

1 State (a) the case for (b) the case against electoral reform. (ULEAC, January, 1993)
2 'Social class remains the significant indicator of voting behaviour.' Discuss. (Oxford and Cambridge, 1992)
3 Did the 1992 general election demonstrate once again that the 'first-past-the-post system' is undemocratic? (Cambridge, June 1994)
4 Why do some voters 'float'? (Oxford, June 1992)

Data response question

The 1987 general election (1983 figures in brackets)

Party	% of votes	Seats	% of seats
Conservative	42.3 (42.4)	375 (397)	57.7 (61.0)
Labour	30.8 (27.6)	229 (209)	35.2 (32.0)
Liberal/SDP	22.6 (25.4)	22 (23)	3.4 (3.5)
Others	4.3 (4.6)	23 (21)	3.5 (3.2)

Overall Conservative majority: 101 (144)
(Speaker not included)

Turnout: 75.4% (72.2%)

From *British Politics Today*, Bill Jones and Dennis Kavanagh, Manchester University Press

Imagine that a general election is to be held tomorrow. The latest opinion polls suggest the result will be: Conservative 38 per cent; Labour 34 per cent; Liberal Democrats 21 per cent; Others 7 per cent. Big swings seem likely in some constituencies and regions. 80 per cent say they are 'certain' or 'very likely' to vote.

What assumptions would you make in estimating the number or proportion of seats each party is likely to win? Suggest the number of seats you would expect each party to hold when the votes have been counted and indicate the factors which influence your prediction. (AEB, June 1993)

3 Political parties

Questions to be answered in this chapter

- What are political parties?
- What roles do they perform and how powerful are they in Britain?
- What is a party system?
- To what extent can the British party system be considered a two-party system?
- How are British political parties organized and where does the power lie within the parties?

Terms to know

Adversarial politics
'Bottom-up'
Electoral role
Extra-parliamentary
Fabians
Governing role
Manifesto
Manifesto Group
Militant Tendency
Monday Club
Multi-party system

Neo-liberal
1922 Committee
One member, one vote (OMOV)
One Nation Toryism
Party discipline
Party whip
Political consensus
'Top-down'
Tribune Group
Two-party system
'Wets'

A definition of party politics

A political party is a group of like-minded people organized as a single unit in order to gain the power necessary to govern the country. The group considers a wide range of issues and seeks to implement its solutions when in government. In a democracy parties seek power by proposing candidates for election.

The development of parties in Britain

Prior to the extension of the electoral franchise in the nineteenth century political parties were merely loose formations of MPs, bound together by anything from political beliefs to friendship and family. However, as the right to vote was extended in 1832, 1867 and 1884 parties began to formalize their organizations in an effort to gain the support of voters and to organize the House of Commons. The parties set up bureaucracies to manage party affairs from the centre, as well as constituency bodies to organize local support.

Electoral reform

This trend towards formal party organization was given an additional boost by the rise of the Labour Party in the twentieth century. As the representatives of the working class, which had been excluded from British politics for so long, the Labour

Organization

Party felt that it would need to be highly organized in order to make an impression on the status quo as represented by the Conservative and Liberal Parties.

Functions of political parties

Electoral and governing roles

Parties perform a wide range of functions, but a definition of what they are varies from one textbook to another. Suggestions include representation, communication and recruitment. All of these tend to concentrate on the participative aspect of party functions. By this, we mean political parties allow citizens to take part in the political process, either by becoming a member, a candidate or even a leader of a political party. This aspect of the role of parties is undoubtedly important; in fact, parties are often identified as one of only three ways to take part in politics: voting, parties and pressure groups. However, the role, or the power, that political parties have in any political system can best be seen by examining their:

- **electoral role**
- **governing role**.

In the former Soviet Union the electoral role of the Communist Party of the Soviet Union was minimal, but its role in government was commanding. In the USA the Republican and Democratic Parties play a limited role in elections because campaigns and voting tend to be centred on the candidates rather than the parties themselves and as a result, the role they play in congressional politics is also narrow. In Britain political parties dominate both elections and the processes of government.

The electoral role

The electoral role that political parties play in elections can be divided into:
- nomination of candidates
- organization of campaigns
- finance of campaigns
- provision of policy
- organization of voters.

Nomination of candidates

Parties in Britain put forward candidates for election at national and local levels. The main unit of party organization away from the centre is the constituency party and in both the Conservative and Labour Parties this unit carries the prime responsibility for the selection of parliamentary candidates.

Conservative method

In the Conservative Party the constituency party selection committee usually puts forward one or two candidates for consideration by the constituency association as a whole. However, the chosen candidate must be on the list of 'approved candidates' put together by Conservative Party Central Office (see page 44). Therefore, the central party keeps a firm grip on who is chosen as a prospective candidate.

Labour method

The Labour Party, too, has a number of 'approved lists' – trade union sponsored, constituency party nominated, Co-operative Society nominated and those recommended by the Women's Section. A shortlist is drawn up by the general management committee of the constituency party and the list must include a female candidate. The Labour Party has committed itself to increasing the number of women in Parliament. Since 1993 it has agreed to the selection of women candidates for all safe Labour seats falling vacant at the time of the next general election. In these constituencies the shortlists will be made up of women candidates only.

Traditionally, the final choice was made by an electoral college made up of all the elements of the constituency party, including individual members, trade unions and other affiliated organizations. However, since 1993 the selection has been on a **one member, one vote (OMOV)** basis.

OMOV

Until 1992 the Labour Party had an additional part to its selection process, i.e. the mandatory reselection of parliamentary candidates prior to a general election. Adopted in 1980, this requirement meant that all sitting MPs were required to go through the reselection process within the lifetime of a parliament. They did not have an automatic right to stand as the party's candidate in the next election. This had the effect of encouraging candidates to pay attention to the wishes of their local party as well as to the national leadership. Today reselection only occurs if requested by the constituency party.

Reselection

The Liberal Democrats also have a list of 'approved candidates', but allow the local party to make the final choice by a ballot of all constituency party members.

Liberal Democrat method

These slightly varying methods of selecting candidates have in common the importance of the party in the choice of candidates. Unlike in the USA, the voters have no voice in the matter at all and so the party, whether local or national, becomes the focus of loyalty.

Organization of campaigns

Once the candidates have been appointed, the election campaign needs to be organized. The pattern of campaigning for much of the twentieth century was set at the end of the nineteenth century – at constituency level. In the Midlothian Campaign of 1879 and 1880 former Liberal leader William Gladstone toured his constituency denouncing the Conservative government. At about the same time the Conservative Party was setting up its constituency organizations with local members and party agents.

Since then local party activists have organized party events, raised money, recruited members and campaigned for their candidates. At election time a small army of party members can be seen in every constituency carrying out the ritual of door-to-door campaigning. They spend hours cajoling, chatting and arguing with voters trying to get them to vote for their party.

Local activists

However, since the late 1950s elections have been increasingly dominated by the national campaign. Initially, this meant the party leaders would travel all over the country meeting and addressing the voters. In 1959, for example, Conservative Prime Minister Harold Macmillan travelled 2,500 miles and spoke at 70 public meetings. More recently, party leaders have used the media to gain access to the electorate.

National campaigns

Party political broadcasts, television and radio interviews, stage-managed media events, 'photo opportunities' and 'sound bites' now dominate election campaigns. Highlights of recent campaigns have included Labour leader Neil Kinnock's broadcast of 1987 and the Conservative Party leader John Major's 'soap box' in 1992. In the former case the Labour Party commissioned a party political broadcast from the director of the film *Chariots of Fire*, Hugh Hudson. The broadcast concentrated solely on Neil Kinnock's background and beliefs and ended by inviting the electorate to 'vote Kinnock'. In 1992 John Major began the eletion campaign with a series of highly stage-managed meetings with supporters. However, poor opinion poll ratings

Media

persuaded him to abandon this presidential style in favour of being amongst the people on the street, speaking to them from a soap box. All of these events are elements of the national party campaign, not constituency activism. Therefore, the national parties dominate the organization of campaigns.

Finance of campaigns

Election spending

As the campaign is dominated by national party activity, it follows that much of the money for the campaign is raised and spent at a national level. In 1987 the

Election funding

'Britain is unusual among Western democracies in not providing large-scale funding for political parties. It is also unusual in fixing no limit to what parties may spend at national level in general elections, and having no requirement at all for party accounts to be meaningful to outsiders.

In America, taxpayers can tick a box on their tax forms to opt to pay $1 towards federal funding for presidential elections. This provides payments to match money raised privately by candidates in primaries, as well as grants for presidential candidates and party conventions. Candidates are required to disclose any contribution over $200.

In Japan, political parties receive a monthly subsidy of about £47,000 per member of parliament. Under current rules, donations to individual politicians are theoretically limited to £9,735 a year, but this has not prevented widespread corruption.

In Germany, about £100m a year is paid to parties represented in the Bundestag, according to a formula based on their electoral success. Parties must publish accounts including the names of anyone giving them £8,000 or more.

In Spain, parties receive £8,000 for every seat they hold in the Cortes plus 31p for every vote they win. Details of private donations – which must not exceed £50,000 – have to be published and party funds audited.

In Italy, generous state financing of political parties was introduced in 1974. But a national referendum last year ended it. Italian parties are required by law to publish details of donations.

In Sweden, Finland, Denmark and Norway state subsidies relate to numbers of votes or MPs. Parties are required to publish accounts and list large donors.

In Belgium, each party receives an annual subsidy of £100,000, plus £1 for every vote it won in the previous election. Accounts must be submitted to an independent audit commission. Political donations by companies or trade unions are illegal.

In Canada, voters are entitled to a tax credit for political donations. The scale of the credit is geared to encourage small donations. There are strict limits on electoral spending. Parties are reimbursed 22.5 per cent of their electoral expenses, individual candidates up to 50 per cent.

Should Britain follow suit? Already the so-called short money, £2m a year, is provided to opposition parties for their work in Parliament. But sceptics will note that neither state funding nor regulation stops abuse – as the examples of Italy, Spain and Japan demonstrate.'

Source: *The Economist*, 16 April 1994

Conservative Party spent over £17 million on its election campaign (not including 'benefits in kind', i.e. free postage and television broadcasts). Of this total, £9 million was spent at national level (£5 million on national advertising). In fact, British campaign finance law encourages expenditure to be controlled from the centre because there are no limits on the level of election spending at national level. In the 1987 general election individual candidates were restricted to a campaign budget of £5,000–£6,000.

Thirty-three per cent of the Conservative Party's national election spending in 1987 was financed by a levy on local parties. The remainder came from donations to the party's Central Office, mainly from industry.

In 1994 the Parliamentary Home Affairs Select Committee reported on political funding. The eleven-member committee was split along party lines, with Labour members submitting a minority report that was highly critical of Conservative Party funding, which was described as 'one of the great mysteries of British politics'. Between 1987 and 1991 half of the £38 million donated to the party could not be traced to any source, although Major General Sir Brian Wyldebore-Smith, a former chairman of the Conservative Board of Finance, confirmed that about £7 million came from abroad before the 1992 election. It is believed that Polly Peck, owned by Asil Nadir who fled Britain to avoid fraud charges, donated £440,000 without declaring it, as required by law.

Conservative funds

Provision of policy

Immediately prior to a general election, each party publishes its election **manifesto** which outlines the policies it will seek to enact if elected to government. As well as giving voters a choice, the manifesto also fulfils an educational function as the electorate learns more about the political, economic and social issues of the day and alternative approaches to them (see Table 3.1 overleaf).

Manifesto

The policy themes of an election are all determined by the national parties with little room for local variations or freedom of expression for candidates. Certainly, national media coverage, national advertising and party political broadcasts are all focused on national party policy. Therefore, individual candidates and even constituency parties have little or no voice in the making of party policy, but they are expected to follow the party manifesto during the election campaign.

Organization of voters

By offering candidates for election grouped around sets of policies, parties allow the electorate to make a choice between different approaches to the governing of the country. Their freedom to do this is a fundamental characteristic of truly democratic elections.

However, 55 million individual voters could have 55 million attitudes to each issue confronting the country. It is impossible in a representative democracy to give all of these views a fair hearing. Therefore, they need to be consolidated into a smaller, more manageable range of views. Parties do this by uniting voters behind their respective banners as people vote for the party that most closely suits their own attitudes.

Between 1945 and 1965 once voters had decided on a party affiliation they were unlikely to lose it. In fact, it was likely to grow stronger as they grew older. Since 1965 the level of voters identifying themselves with a particular party has declined

Party identification

Table 3.1 Selections from the 1992 election manifestos

Issue	Conservative	Labour	Liberal Democrat
The economy	Tax reductions Membership of Exchange Rate Mechanism (ERM) Fight inflation Reduce public spending	Recovery programme Reform tax system ERM membership	Recovery programme ERM membership Independent Bank of England Tax reform
Employment	Vocational qualifications	Skills fund Work and train scheme	Reduce business rates Training scheme
Europe	Maastricht agreement No social chapter Broaden European membership	Maastricht agreement and social chapter Central part in EU	Maastricht agreement and social chapter Membership of European Monetary System (EMS) Democratize EU institutions
Health	Hospitals trusts Reduce waiting times More resources	No opt-out hospitals Increased resources Repeal marketization policy in National Health Service	More resources No internal market Repeal GP fundholding Free eye tests, dental check-ups and prescriptions
Education	National curriculum Testing Opt-out schools League tables Opt-out further education colleges	More resources No opt-out Reform A levels Repeal student loans	More resources No opt-out Review charitable status of independent schools Guaranteed nursery education
Industry	Privatization Marketization reforms Trade union reform	Return water and electricity to public sector Restore unions to Government Communications Headquarters (GCHQ) Minimum wage	Strong anti-monopoly laws Profit-share schemes No more privatization

from 81 per cent to 70 per cent. Over the same period those voters *strongly* identifying themselves with a political party has fallen from 38 per cent to 23 per cent. This means that there are more floating voters to be captured by the parties at general elections and that they can no longer take the votes of many of the electorate for granted.

American campaigns

In the USA the decline of partisanship has meant that individual candidates have taken control of their own campaigns, promoting *themselves* more than the party. As a result, the party tends to be a label to hang on a particular candidate. However, it does not mean that the influence of political parties has disappeared. The party label continues to be important as a foundation on which to build one's personal appeal.

In Britain individual candidates have not been able to base campaigns on their own appeal. The campaign at the constituency level is relatively insignificant because general elections are so dominated by the campaign at national level. Most voters will decide whether to switch their vote according to the appeal of a national party leader, a particular set of national issues or even the effectiveness of a national advertising campaign. They do not do so according to the personality of their local candidate or their policies. Therefore, elections in Britain remain party-orientated rather than candidate-orientated.

The governing role

Once elections are over, parties move into office, whether as the government or as one of the opposition parties in the House of Commons. When installed parties perform three further functions:
- provision of policy
- allocation of office
- organization of the assembly.

Provision of policy

We have already seen that provision of an election manifesto is the responsibility of the party. According to the concept of the mandate, the next step is to carry through these policies in government, having received the permission of the electorate to do so. However, political, economic and social circumstances change during the lifetime of a parliament and so governments have always reserved the right to depart from manifestos if necessary. On these occasions, decisions are taken by the party leadership in the cabinet rather than by the party as a whole.

Within the Conservative Party such a decision-making process is expected and even demanded because the party looks for strong leadership and gives decision-making power to its leaders. This reflects the origins of the party – a collection of constituency organizations designed to support the party in the Commons.

Conservative Party

The Labour Party originated outside Parliament in order to gain parliamentary representation for the Labour movement as a whole, led by the trade union movement. This is most clearly illustrated by the original title of the modern Labour Party – the Labour Representation Committee, which was abandoned in 1906. As a result, decisions regarding Labour Party policy are, according to the party's constitution, the responsibility of the annual conference or, when the conference is not in session, the responsibility lies with the National Executive Committee. Therefore, the focus of decision making in the Labour Party is at odds with the focus of decision making in the British political system as, theoretically, a Labour government and Labour MPs would be required to consult with **extra-parliamentary** bodies before departing from stated party policy.

Labour Party

In fact, Labour leaders in government have paid more attention to the British Constitution than to that of their party. In 1928 Ramsay MacDonald told the Labour Party Conference: 'As long as I hold any position in the Parliamentary Party – and I know I can speak for my colleagues also – we are not going to take instructions from any outside body unless we agree with them.' In recent years, Harold Wilson and James Callaghan both ignored conference decisions by claiming a greater responsibility to the country than to the party.

37

Labour Party Conference

When the Labour Party is in opposition its leaders have found it more difficult to ignore the extra-parliamentary elements of the party. Hugh Gaitskell, James Callaghan, Neil Kinnock and John Smith all had battles with the Labour Party Conference over issues such as unilateral disarmament (Hugh Gaitskell), the expulsion of Militant Tendency (Neil Kinnock), internal democracy (James Callaghan, Neil Kinnock and John Smith) and rewriting Clause 4 (Tony Blair). Unable to resort to the argument of government, that they must consider the interests of the nation as a whole, party leaders have tended to use the carrot of electoral success as the means to restrain the extra-parliamentary party.

In government and opposition, therefore, most policy is party policy. However, the focus of the decision-making power within the party varies between the Conservatives and Labour.

Allocation of office

Ministerial positions

In a parliamentary system the party that commands a majority in the assembly is usually asked to form the government because it has the confidence of the Commons. Once installed, the party leader as the prime minister has the power to allocate around 120 ministerial offices, from cabinet ministers to a range of junior ministers.

Patronage

The power of patronage lies solely with the prime minister and so is not the responsibility of the wider party, in terms of MPs or the extra-parliamentary party. However, the prime minister usually bears in mind the wishes of the party when making appointments. Therefore in the British system of government the rewards of office are within the gift of the party and its leader and so there is a great incentive for members of the parliamentary parties to 'toe the party line' in the hope of achieving promotion into the executive branch of government.

Shadow cabinets

Again, the situation differs slightly between the Conservative and Labour leaders. In the Conservative Party the leader has the power to appoint government or shadow spokespeople, when in opposition. In the Labour Party the members of the shadow cabinet are elected by MPs as a whole and the leader must create the shadow cabinet from those chosen. When in government, however, the Labour leader has the freedom to choose the cabinet.

Organization of the assembly

Party discipline

The House of Commons and, to a lesser extent, the House of Lords are organized along party lines. In 1994 all of the members of the House of Commons were members of a political party and no constituency was represented by an independent MP. In the House of Lords most peers are affiliated to one party or another. However, some choose to be 'crossbenchers' – not taking the whip from any of the main parties.

Not only is membership of political parties predominant in the House of Commons but parties also organize the work of the Commons. The majority of time available for debate is allocated along party lines with most time set aside for government legislation and opposition supply days (see page 69). The few days that remain are available for private members' bills (see pages 65–6). In addition, places on Commons committees are allocated according to party strength on the floor of the house. Finally, and most importantly, most votes are taken along party lines with the overwhelming majority of MPs voting according to their **party whip**.

MPs have strong incentives to 'toe the party line' because parties have such a firm grip of the electoral process and on the allocation of offices. Therefore, MPs are aware that their present jobs, as MPs, are dependent on continued party support and any future promotion depends on their own ability to impress the leaders of their party.

The result of such strong **party discipline** is that the business of the Commons is highly organized. Only occasional backbench revolts disturb the predictability of the procedures of the House of Commons. In the modern British system of government political parties are the oils that lubricate the constitutional system, providing candidates, policies and organization.

The party system

When examining the roles that political parties perform in the British system of government we tend to concentrate on the Labour and Conservative Parties. This is because Britain has what is commonly referred to as a **two-party system**. However, in practice Britain has far more than two political parties. So, what exactly does two-party system mean and is it an accurate description of the state of affairs in the UK?

A two-party system

A party system is a way of describing not only the number of political parties in a country but also the relative power of the parties and the issues around which they are formed. Britain is referred to as having a two-party system because the House of Commons is dominated by two parties – Labour and Conservative. After the 1992 election the two major parties held 93 per cent of constituencies, a percentage which was one of the lowest since 1945. During the 1950s and 1960s it was more typical for the two major parties to hold 98 per cent of the seats in the Commons. As a result, every post-war government has been formed by one of these parties alone, with its rival forming the official Opposition.

Multi-party system

The two-party system looks less convincing when looking at election campaigns and voting. It is very easy to assume that the look of the House of Commons reflects the nature of party political activity across the country. It does not.

The two-party division in Britain has its roots in the class system. Even though in the 1960s and 1970s the relationship between class and voting behaviour weakened, the Conservative Party is still perceived as the party of the middle class and the Labour Party as that of the working class. However, such a view of the party system is Anglocentric. The English party system may be dominated by class divisions, but those of Scotland, Wales and Northern Ireland are not.

Parties and class

According to Lipset and Rokkan ((eds) *Party Systems and Voter Alignments: Cross-national Perspectives*, Collier-Macmillan, 1967), political parties form around four main divisions in society, known as 'cleavages' – they are class, centre-periphery (nationalism), religion and urban-rural (agricultural interests). In Britain only the first three of these cleavages are present.

In Scotland and Wales Conservative–Labour competition is complicated by the nationalist parties. The Scottish Nationalist Party and Plaid Cymru in Wales have arisen from the desire of many people in these countries to have greater

Scotland and Wales

39

independence from central government. However, the Conservative and Labour parties remain the dominant players in elections in Scotland and Wales.

Northern Ireland

Northern Irish politics offers a completely different party picture. The dominant cleavage in the province is religion with party affiliations being drawn around the division between Catholic and Protestant. Here the Conservative and Labour Parties, as they are known in England play no role at all, although the Conservative Party is allied to the Unionist Parties. (For a fuller discussion of Northern Ireland, see Chapter 15.)

North and south

In fact, a simple contest between the Labour and Conservative Parties is not even the case in England. Support for each of the two main parties has a geographical aspect. In the south, with the exception of London, the Conservative Party is dominant, while the Labour Party is dominant in the north of England. In each of these areas the main challenger has been the centre party, in the form of the Liberals, the Liberal–Social Democratic Alliance and most recently, the Liberal Democrats. Therefore, it might be said that a **multi-party system** exists since straight contests between Labour and Conservative are rare.

Votes

The strength of the Liberal Democrat vote across the country confirms that Britain does not in practice have a two-party system. The renaissance of the Liberal Party began in the election of February 1974, under the leadership of Jeremy Thorpe, when its share of the vote rose to 19.3 per cent from 7.5 per cent in 1970. The centre party's fortunes reached a high point in 1983 when the Alliance polled 7.8 million votes (25.4 per cent), only 0.7 million votes behind the Labour Party. Since then Liberal Democrat support has fallen to 6.1 million (18.4 per cent), but this remains sufficient to warrant talk of a three-party system, at least in the minds of many voters.

Preservation of the two-party system

Despite pressure from the Liberal Democrats and the nationalist parties, the two-party system in the House of Commons has remained in place. The main reason for its survival can be found in the anomalies of the British electoral system.

First past the post

The first-past-the-post system (see page 18) rewards winners only. A candidate wins a constituency by accumulating more votes than their nearest rival. With their support concentrated in geographical areas, the Labour and Conservative Parties are able to win seats in the north, for the former, and the south, for the latter. This leaves the Liberal Democrats to accumulate a considerable number of votes, but to be placed second in many constituencies. Therefore, the centre party is unable to convert its widespread support into seats in the Commons.

Duverger

Another interpretation of the survival of the two-party system has been offered by Maurice Duverger. The French political scientist has argued that the Labour and Conservative Parties can be placed at each end of a political spectrum with the Conservatives on the right and Labour on the left, reflecting their political ideologies. At times, both parties slide along the spectrum as their policies become more moderate or more extreme.

Consensus

For much of the postwar period, the two main parties were not seriously divided on key policy issues. Both were agreed on a Keynesian approach to economic management (see page 172), the importance of the National Health Service, the desirability of full employment and the need for a British nuclear deterrent. The period of British politics from 1945 to 1970 has often been called the postwar

political consensus or Butskellism, after Rab Butler (Conservative) and Hugh Gaitskell (Labour) whose economic policies were virtually indistinguishable. This can be represented on Duverger's spectrum as the two main parties sitting near the centre (see Figure 3.1)

Figure 3.1 Duverger's spectrum: political consensus

```
                    Labour    Conservative
              L      < >          < >        R
```

As the two main parties were so close together there was little room for the Liberal Party to make an impact on electoral politics and they polled less than 3 million votes in every general election except 1964.

In the 1970s the Conservative and Labour Parties began to move further apart. First the Conservative Party under Edward Heath confronted the trade unions, then the Labour Party embarked on a series of nationalizations that lacked cross-party support. The adversarial nature of party competition was intensified when Margaret Thatcher became leader of the Conservative Party in 1975 and Michael Foot was elected leader of the Labour Party in 1980. Margaret Thatcher moved the Conservatives to the right with radical policies such as privatization, the sale of council houses, trade union reform and monetarist economic policies (see pages 179–80 and 185). Michael Foot committed the Labour Party to renationalization, unilateral disarmament, full employment and higher public spending.

As the postwar political consensus crumbled, the two main parties moved to **adversarial politics** and towards more polarized positions on the left–right spectrum. This left the middle ground free for the centre party to capture (see Figure 3.2). The Liberal Party was revitalized under the leadership of first Jeremy Thorpe and subsequently David Steel. It formed the Alliance with a group of moderate Labour MPs who had broken away to form the Social Democratic Party.

Adversarial politics

Figure 3.2 Duverger's spectrum: the centre party captures the middle ground

```
              Labour    Alliance    Conservative
         L     < >       < >           < >        R
```

Under these circumstances, Duverger argues, the two main parties will adjust their policies in order to recapture the middle ground, crushing the centre party as they do so. To support this argument, we can point to the election of John Major as the Tory leader with a more moderate image and approach than his predecessor and the Labour Party's gradual move towards the centre, or even the right, of the spectrum under the leadership of Neil Kinnock, John Smith and Tony Blair.

According to Duverger, the two-party system is maintained as the two main parties take back the centre ground, leaving the Liberal Democrats to be a party of protest unable to break the mould of traditional two-party politics.

A one-party system

The idea of a two-party system implies that the two main parties alternate in power on a fairly regular basis. For much of the twentieth century this has not been the case. Since 1918 the Conservative Party has participated in government for 54 of 76 years and by the time of the next election, assuming the Conservative government

Conservative dominance

remains in office until 1997, the party will have been in power continuously for 18 years.

However, Conservative dominance has been in the House of Commons alone. Voting patterns show that in the four elections between 1979 and 1992 the Conservative Party never polled more than 44 per cent of the vote, so its 'dominance' in terms of votes has never taken it beyond 50 per cent of the popular vote. Its dominance of the House of Commons has been based on the tendency of the British electoral system to exaggerate the popular support of the Conservative Party by over-representing it in the house.

Of course, the over-representation of large parties in the House of Commons also contributes to the possible one-party system because the victorious party usually has an overall majority. Therefore, the party in government is virtually in an unassailable position and can govern almost without reference to the opposition parties.

Party organization and structure

Most people are only aware of political parties when they fulfil the roles of government or opposition. However, parties are organizations in their own right outside the governmental structures of Parliament and cabinet and have their own constitutions, bureaucracies and members. All British parties consist of:
- the parliamentary party
- the extra-parliamentary party
- the party's bureaucracy.

The Conservative Party

Origins

The Conservative Party originated as a loose grouping of Tory MPs in the House of Commons in the nineteenth century. As the electoral franchise was extended, they set up a system of constituency associations which were intended to give MPs the support they needed to be re-elected in a more democratic environment. The extra-parliamentary party was set up in support of the parliamentary party. The distribution of power within the party reflects these origins.

The parliamentary Conservative Party

The parliamentary party is the focus of power inside the party with all other branches being subordinate to it. Although party discipline is as strong in the Conservative Party as in any other party, perhaps stronger given the Conservatives' respect for authority, it is by no means absolute. It would be a mistake to imagine that the party would always follow its leader no matter what the issue.

One Nation Tory

The modern Conservative Party has two wings. The first is commonly associated with the **One Nation Toryism** of Disraeli. The second is the **neo-liberal** wing of the party associated with Margaret Thatcher.

The One Nation Tories dominated the party until the 1970s. Neville Chamberlain, Winston Churchill and Harold Macmillan all believed that their main aim was to unite the country behind policies that would allow prosperity, while also taking care of the needs of the poor. Traditionally, the MPs supporting this view were from the landed gentry who saw it as their duty to govern in the best interests of all classes. As their wealth was usually inherited, their comfortable position was due to luck and in their eyes, poverty was often the result of bad luck. Both were, therefore, two sides

Election of the Conservative leader

Traditionally, the Conservative leader 'emerged' as the natural leader. It was not until 1965 that the leader, Edward Heath, was elected.

A sitting Conservative leader can only be challenged within a period three months before and fourteen days after the opening of Parliament. The support of ten per cent of MPs is required for the 1922 Committee (see page 72) to grant a ballot.

To win on the first ballot a candidate needs an overall majority and a lead of 15 per cent over their nearest rival. If a candidate does not achieve this, a second ballot is required. In 1990 Margaret Thatcher was four votes short of the required majority.

At the second ballot stage candidates can enter or leave the contest. To win a candidate needs an overall majority. In 1990 Margaret Thatcher withdrew after the first ballot. Michael Heseltine was left to compete against John Major and Douglas Hurd in the second ballot. John Major gained 49.7 per cent of the vote and the other candidates conceded defeat.

If no candidate gains the majority, a third ballot is needed, but only the two leading candidates go forward. A fourth ballot is only required in the event of a tie.

of the same coin and so the poor should be supported, not judged. Hence the state should be used to provide benefits, the National Health Service, employment and security for everyone in society. This is sometimes referred to as the paternalist wing of the party.

Recently, members of this wing have become known as **'Wets'**. This is a derogatory term applied to them by the Thatcherite or neo-liberal wing.

Thatcherites

The Thatcherites believed in the free market with the forces of supply and demand allocating resources, individual effort determining success or failure and state intervention doomed to failure because it interferes with the delicate balance of capitalism (see page 180).

Tendencies

Traditionally, the Conservative Party is a party of loosely organized grouping, 'tendencies', rather than the more formal groupings, 'factions', associated with the Labour Party. However, as conflicts over ideological issues intensified in the 1970s and 1980s, so have the conflicts between groupings within the party.

Monday Club

The right of the party has a number of groupings which promote their views. The **Monday Club** was formed in 1961 in response to fears of some MPs that Harold Macmillan's government was moving too far to the left, particularly on issues concerning the empire and immigration. In recent years this group has gained considerable notoriety as a rather extreme right-wing group, possibly infiltrated by far-right groups from outside the party, such as the National Front, which were attracted by its strong line on immigration.

Right-wing groups

The Selsdon Group was formed in 1973 to keep alive the ideas that Edward Heath had adopted in the late 1960s but seemed to have abandoned in a dramatic U-turn in 1972. Similar groups have been formed more recently in order to keep alive the legacy of Thatcherism. The No Turning Back Group (1985) and the Conservative Way Forward (1991) are pledged to promote Thatcherite ideals in economic and social policy, while the Bruges Group (1988) concentrates its energies on an anti-federalist approach to Europe.

Party left

The left of the party, or the 'Wets', includes the Tory Reform Group (1975) and the One Nation Group. They provide a counterbalance to the right-wing groups and allow the left to discuss ideas.

Within Parliament, the Conservative Party has a series of committees that examine specific policy areas. However, the most important one is the 1922 Committee which is made up of all of the party's backbench MPs. The executive committee of 'the 1922' is a powerful force within the party and both wings compete for control of it.

Conservative Central Office

Central Office is the bureaucracy of the party and is staffed by full-time party officials. It is responsible for fundraising, research, assisting in selecting candidates and organizing election campaigns.

Party chairman

It is headed by the party chairman and vice chairman, both of whom are appointed by the party leader. The appointments are of vital importance to ensure that the central bureaucracy will be loyal to the leader and also to ensure that the wheels of the party machine will be well oiled in the run up to a general election.

The National Union of Conservative Associations

The National Union was set up by Disraeli following the 1867 Reform Act. It is made up of all of the constituency associations and headed by an executive committee. As an extra-parliamentary body its role is to support the leadership, by offering advice and organization, rather than to regulate the leaders in any way.

Conservative Party Conference

The executive council is also responsible for organizing the party's annual conference. This has long been criticized as a party rally designed solely as a promotional exercise for the party, and more specifically, the leader. It is true that the Conservative Party Conference is highly stage-managed and open warfare, so associated with the Labour Party, rarely breaks out there. However, the conference can provide a forum for serious debate and offers members an opportunity to influence policy, although it does not have the power to make policy. Also the conference raises the morale of the party and sends party activists out into the country to campaign with a new vigour and enthusiasm.

The Labour Party

Origins

The Labour Party originated outside Parliament with the broader Labour movement. Trade unions, co-operative societies and Fabian organizations (see below) decided to set up the Labour Representation Committee in 1900 in order gain a voice for the workers in the House of Commons. Its first success came in 1906 when 29 Labour MPs were elected. It was at that time that the committee became the Labour Party.

'Bottom-up'

The fact that the party originated outside Parliament means that the parliamentary party was created as an extension of the extra-parliamentary party, not the other way round – as was the case with the Conservative Party. As a result, the extra-parliamentary sections of the party have considerable power and constitutional authority flows upwards from the grassroots to the leadership. The party is described as a **bottom-up** party, as compared to the Conservative Party which is **top-down**.

Election of the Labour leader

Prior to the rule changes in 1981, the Labour leader was elected by a ballot of Labour MPs. Since then it has been opened up to the whole party.

The leader or deputy can only be challenged with the support of 20 per cent of Labour MPs. Candidates must win the support of 12.5 per cent of MPs.

The subsequent ballot is via an electoral college which weights the votes of the three components of the party: the MPs and MEPs (Members of the European Parliament), the trade unions and the constituency parties. Since 1993 each component has had 33⅓ per cent of the votes.

In July 1994 Tony Blair was elected Labour leader after the death of John Smith. He gained 57 per cent of the vote, winning the votes of 61 per cent of the MPs and MEPs, 58 per cent of constituency members and 52 per cent of trade unionists.

The Parliamentary Labour Party

The Labour Party was created from a number of diverse groups, so it is perhaps natural that these divisions should be evident in the parliamentary party. In fact, one of the most well-known groups, the **Fabians**, were established in 1884 and were involved in the creation of the Labour Party. Its influence on party policy was probably at its greatest in the 1920s when the Fabian Society was headed by Beatrice and Sydney Webb. Today the Fabians provide a forum for debate about new policy ideas and constitutional reform for the party.

Fabians

Other groups within the party tend to be clustered around the division between those seeking rapid and radical reform as opposed to those promoting a more gradual approach. This division between left and right has often been personified by conflict between senior figures in the party, perhaps most famously between Hugh Gaitskell and Aneurin Bevan; Harold Wilson and Michael Foot; and James Callaghan and Tony Benn.

Left and right

On the left are the **Tribune Group** and the Campaign Group. Tribune was set up in 1966 in an effort to push the policies of Harold Wilson's government further to the left on issues such as unilateral disarmament and nationalization. Michael Foot, a leading member of Tribune, became leader of the party in 1980 and the Tribune's line on policy began to soften as Michael Foot moderated his policies. This trend was continued when he was replaced by another member of Tribune, Neil Kinnock, in 1983.

Left-wing groups

In view of the softening of Tribune's line, the hard left set up an alternative group known as Campaign. This has proved a rallying point for the left-wing allies of Tony Benn, promoting greater links with the trade union movement, fundamental reform of the constitution, including abolition of the monarchy and reform of the House of Lords.

Groups of the hard left have been retreating in recent years as first Neil Kinnock, then John Smith and Tony Blair, moved the party further to the right. A high point of the conflict between the moderates and the hard left occurred in 1986 when Neil Kinnock confronted members of **Militant Tendency** at the Labour Party Conference. Militant, a Trotskyist group, had infiltrated many constituency associations and had taken control of Liverpool City Council. The moderates objected to such a revolutionary group within their ranks and many members of Militant were expelled from the party in 1987.

45

Right-wing groups

The main groups on the right of the party are the **Manifesto Group** and Solidarity. The former was formed in 1974 in order to fend off the advance of the left. This was also the motive behind the creation of Solidarity in 1981 by Roy Hattersley and Peter Shore.

The extra-parliamentary party

The Labour constitution of 1918 and the reforms of the early 1980s have given considerable power to party groups outside Parliament. This is most clearly illustrated in the annual conference and the National Executive Committee (NEC). Constitutionally, the annual conference is the policy-making body in the Labour Party.

Trade union role

This body is dominated by the trade union movement whose members account for 70 per cent of the votes cast at conference, with constituency parties holding the remaining 30 per cent. The unions have been further strengthened by the block vote. This was a type of winner–take–all system which enabled a trade union leader to cast all of a union's votes in one direction, either for or against a proposal, regardless of how close the division of opinion might be inside the union. This system gave the five biggest trade unions an enormous amount of power as they commanded the vast majority of votes at the conference. The system was abolished in 1993 when John Smith persuaded the conference to adopt the One Member, One Vote (OMOV) proposal, which means that the union block is now divided between the 'yes' and 'no' groups on a proportional basis.

Labour democracy

As the Labour Party was created by extra-parliamentary bodies the power, constitutionally, lies with the institutions of the whole party rather than the parliamentary party – it is a 'bottom-up' party.

However, the broader party has often criticized the leadership for ignoring NEC and annual conference decisions. Therefore, in 1981 there was a move to make the party more democratic through changes to the election of the leader, the selection of parliamentary candidates and the formulation of the manifesto (the latter was unsuccessful). This move was largely initiated by the left of the party.

Since then the right has responded by pushing internal democracy further by adopting the OMOV proposal which removes the power of the block vote.

NEC

As the conference is only in session once a year the day-to-day running of the party is the responsibility of the National Executive Committee (NEC), which is elected by conference. Here, too, the trade unions have a great deal of power. Twelve members of the 30-strong NEC are elected by the trade unions alone, but they also have a substantial voice in the election of the party treasurer and the five women members of the NEC who are elected by the conference as a whole. The remaining members of the NEC are elected by the constituency parties (seven), the Young Socialists (one), the socialist societies (one), with the exception of the leader, deputy leader and party secretary who are automatically members by virtue of their office (*ex-officio* members).

Despite the constitutional fact that the conference, and in its absence the NEC, has policy-making power its impact on party leaders has been variable. Harold Wilson,

James Callaghan and Neil Kinnock all ignored conference decisions at times, helped by the distinction between the party programme and the party manifesto. Although any proposal carried by a two-thirds majority at conference automatically becomes part of the party programme, that is not the same as the party manifesto. The latter is officially the responsibility of the cabinet and the NEC when in government or the Parliamentary Labour Party Committee and the NEC, when in opposition. However, the party leader wields the main influence on the manifesto.

In view of the tendency of the leadership to ignore the wishes of the conference, the party initiated a number of notable rule changes in the early 1980s. First, the election of the Labour leader was thrown open to the whole party, rather than simply the parliamentary Labour Party. Second, MPs were required to face mandatory reselection before every general election. However, the left, which was pushing for these reforms, was unable to achieve its aim of giving control of the manifesto to the NEC.

Reform

The constituency Labour Parties, as we have seen, have a role in the work of conference and the NEC, although they tend to be overshadowed by the trade unions. The 1993 conference went some way to rectifying this situation with regard to the selection of parliamentary candidates. Traditionally, candidates had been chosen by an electoral college in which the trade unions controlled 40 per cent of the vote. This system has now been replaced by the OMOV principle which allows constituency members only the right to vote. Trade union members are required to pay an additional levy if they wish to participate.

OMOV

Many of the candidates chosen to fight elections are sponsored by various sections of the party. In 1992 the trade unions sponsored 173 candidates, while the Co-operative Society sponsored another 26. Sponsorship money, which is about £2,000–£3,000, is used as a contribution to election expenses.

Sponsorship

Central headquarters

The Labour Party bureaucracy is based at John Smith House, Walworth Road in south-east London and is headed by the party's General Secretary who in 1994 was Tom Sawyer. Under Neil Kinnock and John Smith 'Walworth Road' became responsible for co-ordinating the various policy reviews, launched to 'update' socialism and make the party more electable.

Walworth Road

Like Conservative Central Office, Walworth Road is responsible for party finance and the organization of election campaigns, but it has often been considerably weaker than its Conservative counterpart because of the Labour Party's relative shortage of funds. However, since the 1992 election roles have been reversed and the Conservative Party has experienced cash-flow difficulties.

The Liberal Democrats

At the end of the nineteenth century the Liberal Party was the main rival to the Conservatives. However, it consistently lost support after World War I and was eventually surpassed by the new Labour Party. Its fortunes did not improve after 1945 as the Conservative and Labour Parties occupied the centre ground of British politics and squeezed out the Liberals.

Third party

The renaissance of the party occurred in the 1970s under the leadership of Jeremy Thorpe and subsequently David Steel. As the two main parties took up more

1970s revival

extreme positions the centre ground was left vacant for the Liberals and as a result their level of electoral support increased.

The Alliance

In 1981 the Liberal Party joined with the Social Democratic Party (SDP), formed by a group of breakaway MPs from the Labour Party, to create the Alliance. The SDP was headed by the 'Gang of Four' (David Owen, Roy Jenkins, Shirley Williams and Bill Rodgers). It put forward many of the policies associated with the right of the Labour Party and aimed to displace Labour as the main party of opposition.

In 1983 the centre parties polled their highest proportion of votes (25.4 per cent) of the post-war period. However, the first-past-the-post electoral system prevented them converting these votes into seats in the House of Commons. After a similar election result in 1987 the Liberals and SDP merged to form the Social and Liberal Democratic Party, which changed its name to the Liberal Democrats in 1989.

Devolution

The Liberal Democrats, like the Liberals before them, are committed to greater devolution of power in the UK. This aim is reflected in the structure of their party. Local constituency parties are run by three 'state' organizations in England, Wales and Scotland. Each state body is responsible for local organization, including the selection of local candidates and finance. Above the 'state' level are three federal bodies, the Federal Executive, the Federal Policy Committee (FPC) and the Federal Conference.

Policy making

The FPC is made up of the leader, the president, four MPs, one peer, three local government councillors, two Scottish and two Welsh representatives, plus thirteen members elected by the conference. It is responsible for drawing up the party's manifesto and circulating proposals for changes to party policy. The FPC can also call a ballot of party members on any issue that threatens to question fundamental party values.

The Federal Executive manages the party at national level. It is made up of the president and three vice presidents; the leader, two MPs, one peer, two councillors and fourteen members elected by the conference.

The Green Party

Origins

The Green Party was formed in 1985 from the Ecology Party. Its policies are concerned with the preservation of the planet and the need to switch our focus from continuous economic growth in favour of greater spiritual fulfilment. As such, it is breaking the traditional pattern of UK politics and its own internal organization reflects this new approach. It is committed to decentralized decision making and emphasizes the local parties as the main units of organization, responsible for policy ideas and overall leadership.

Speakers

The party conference elects a national council which is responsible for day-to-day administration and six 'speakers' who speak on behalf of the party on particular issue areas. However, these officials are not considered 'leaders'.

Euro-election success

In 1987 the party gained only 90,000 votes in the general election and seemed doomed to be a peripheral force in UK politics. However, in the 1989 Euro-elections the party won 15 per cent of the vote and appeared set to take advantage of the growing concern for green issues.

After the 1989 success the party was unable to capitalize on this breakthrough. The main parties put forward their own environmental policies and so squeezed the Greens out of mainstream politics. In the popular imagination they moved still further from the mainstream when a well-known Green spokesman claimed to be the Son of God. Perhaps the worst setback for the Greens came as a result of the advent of the economic recession in Britain in 1990. As the electorate became more concerned about jobs, prosperity and security, environmental issues fell from the political agenda.

In the 1992 general election the party's 253 candidates polled a total of 171,000 votes, compared to 2 million in 1989.

Exercises

Short questions

1 a How do the Conservative and Labour Parties replace their leaders?
  b Which of the two procedures is the more effective? (ULEAC, January 1993)
2 a Explain how the Labour Party selects parliamentary candidates.
  b How democratic is this selection process compared with those used by other parties? (ULEAC, June 1994)
3 What is the role of parties in a democracy? (ULEAC, January 1994)
4 a Describe two factions in the Conservative Party.
  b Explain their origins. (ULEAC, June 1991)
5 What is meant by:
  a One Nation Toryism
  b neo-liberal Conservatism? (ULEAC, January 1994)
6 To what extent have the constitutional changes in the Labour Party since 1987 made it more democratic? (ULEAC, January 1991)

Essay questions

1 To what extent has Britain a two-party system? (ULEAC, June 1992)
2 Does Britain now have a permanent party of government? (ULEAC, June 1994)
3 To what extent does party competition contribute towards democracy? (ULEAC, January 1992)
4 To what extent is there consensus politics in Britain today? (ULEAC, January 1993)
5 What are the main functions performed by parties in the British political system? (Cambridge, June 1993)

Data response question

Changing the prime minister
'27–8 October 1990
Margaret Thatcher, the British prime minister, is isolated at the Rome European Council meeting. Opinion polls show Labour 16 per cent ahead.

30 October
In the Commons, the prime minister accuses the European Commission of "striving to extinguish democracy".

1 November
Sir Geoffrey Howe resigns as deputy prime minister and Leader of the House on the grounds that he can no longer support the prime minister's approach to Britain's role in Europe.

13 November

In his resignation speech Sir Geoffrey Howe concludes by saying: "The time has come for others to consider their response to the tragic conflict of loyalty with which I have myself wrestled for perhaps too long."

14 November

Heseltine announces: "I intend to let my name go forward."

16 November

Opinion poll claims that a Labour lead of 6 per cent would become a Conservative lead of 10 per cent under Heseltine.

20 November

Result of first ballot announced: Margaret Thatcher 204 votes, Michael Heseltine 152. The prime minister, just four votes short of the necessary majority, announces she will fight on.

22 November

Margaret Thatcher decides to step down. Douglas Hurd and John Major enter the fray before nominations for the second ballot close.

24–5 November

The candidates are interviewed on television and present "manifestos", all of which include a review of the poll tax as a high priority; opinion polls suggest that John Major would win more votes than Michael Heseltine.

27 November

The result of the second ballot is announced: John Major 185 votes; Michael Heseltine 131; Douglas Hurd 56. Although John Major is two votes short of the winning figure, Cranley Onslow, Chairman of the 1922 Committee, declares him elected when both other candidates state they will vote for him on a third ballot.'

Adapted from John Benyon, 'The Fall of a Prime Minister', *Social Studies Review*, Vol. 6, No. 3, January 1991

1 Why did the Conservative Party decide to change its leader?
2 Describe the formal process for removing a Conservative Party leader.
3 How acceptable is this process as a means of changing the prime minister?

(ULEAC, June 1992)

4 Political ideologies

Questions to be answered in this chapter
- What is ideology?
- What are the main beliefs behind liberalism, conservatism and socialism?

Terms to know

Consent	Limited government
Conservatism	Meritocratic
Equality	Order
Evolutionary change	Rational
Freedom	Revolution
Ideology	Rule of law
Individualism	Socialism
Liberalism	Toleration
Liberty	

What is ideology?

Traditionally, the terms **ideology** or ideological have been used in a derogatory way, most commonly by politicians against their opponents. As a result, the accuser believes they know the true way while the opponent merely follows an 'ideology'. For example, the view from London is that British courts are non-political and trials are 'fair'; while courts in the People's Republic of China are ideological, political and unfair. In Beijing the opposite is true.

A more open-minded definition of ideology is that it is a system of ideas and beliefs that offer a means of understanding the world. The ideas allow the believer to interpret the past as well as providing a programme for shaping the future. Thus, to politicians ideology provides a framework within which to analyse issues and to prescribe future action.

System of ideas

Liberalism

Liberalism has probably contributed more to the development of the British political system than any other ideology. John Locke, Jeremy Bentham, John Stuart Mill and Adam Smith can all be considered the founding fathers of liberal thought and their ideas lie at the centre of British politics. Indeed, a great deal of Western constitutional thinking is based on liberalism, and the demise of communism has left it with no real ideological rival.

Importance

When examining liberalism we are looking at an ideology that was developed in the eighteenth century and which has a life of its own, independent of the Liberal Party, now known as the Liberal Democrats. In fact, many liberal ideas are to be found in **conservatism** and, indeed, many commentators have viewed Margaret Thatcher as a nineteenth-century liberal rather than a Conservative. Therefore, even though the Liberal Democrats are faring poorly in British electoral politics, liberal ideology is flourishing.

Human nature

John Locke (1632–1704) believed that human beings were **rational** and that they made decisions according to analysis rather than emotion. Therefore, they sought proof and evidence to support theories while retaining a healthy scepticism.

Toleration

The scepticism of liberal thinkers encouraged political **toleration**. Liberals do not claim to have sole access to the truth and so encourage open debate. They strongly defend freedom of speech for all, including minority groups. They tend to be opposed to censorship of any sort. For the early liberal thinkers toleration was particularly important given the background of conflict between Catholic and Protestant and between the monarch and Parliament.

Individualism

Individualism is at the heart of liberalism. John Locke believed that in their natural state people were independent individuals capable of making their own decisions. If they decided to come together in society, they would do so as equal individuals. Therefore, individuals would **consent** to government. In return the government's duty is to preserve the rights and liberties of individuals.

The individual's rights are political, economic and legal. Politically, individuals have the right to participate in the political system through voting, forming political parties and pressure groups. Economically, individuals have the right to private property and to pursue their own happiness. This liberal view of individualism is perhaps best expressed by the American Declaration of Independence, written by Thomas Jefferson:

'We hold these truths to be self-evident, that all men are created equal, that they are endowed by their Creator with certain unalienable Rights, that among these are Life, Liberty and the pursuit of Happiness. That to secure these rights, Governments are instituted among Men, deriving their powers from the consent of the governed . . .'

John Stuart Mill and liberalism

'. . . the sole end for which mankind are warranted, individually or collectively, in interfering with the liberty of action of any of their number, is self-protection. That the only purpose for which power can be rightfully exercised over any member of a civilized community, against his will, is to prevent harm to others. His own good, either physical or moral, is not a sufficient warrant. He cannot rightfully be compelled to do or forbear because it will be better for him to do so, because it will make him happier, because in the opinions of others, to do so would be wise, or even right. These are good reasons for remonstrating with him, or persuading him, or entreating him, but not for compelling him, or visiting him with any evil in case he do otherwise. To justify that, the conduct from which it is desired to deter him, must be calculated to produce evil to someone else. The only part of the conduct of anyone, for which he is amenable to society, is that which concerns others. In the part which merely concerns himself, his independence is, of right, absolute. Over himself, over his own body and mind, the individual is sovereign.'

Source: J S Mill, *On Liberty*, 1859

Legally, all people should be treated equally before the law and the judiciary should be free from political interference; in other words, liberals support the **rule of law** (see page 123). John Locke stated: 'Where there is no law there is no freedom. For liberty is to be free of restraint and violence by others, which cannot be where there is no law.' This view is in line with the liberal view of the role of the state. Government should be **limited** and subject to checks and balances to prevent power being concentrated in the hands of one individual or institution. This was a means of preventing government infringing on the freedom of the individual.

Rule of law

Liberals have traditionally conceived **freedom** in a negative way. This means that the individual is best placed to determine their own interests. Therefore, they should be free from government interference in order to pursue those interests. This is clearly seen in the economic philosophy of Adam Smith (1723–90). Smith believed in the free market and that if individuals pursued their own best interests, society as a whole would benefit.

Freedom

In line with this thinking liberals define economic **equality** not in terms of equality of outcome but equality of opportunity. They believe that everyone should have the same opportunities in life and should have the freedom to make whatever they will from those opportunities. Therefore, they believe in a **meritocratic** society, rather than a class society based on privilege.

Equality

Conservatism

Conservative thought has its roots in the eighteenth century as philosophers, such as Edmund Burke, responded to the French Revolution at the end of the century. Conservatives are conservative by nature and are opposed to **revolution**, preferring incremental, **evolutionary change**. Radical change, according to the conservative view, is rather like jumping from the frying pan into the fire. The revolution is usually painful without any guarantee that the end result will be any better than before. They believe that politicians who pursue radical change to create a grand scheme are arrogant and foolish and that their designs will flounder on their own inadequacies. As a result, the people will be worse off. Therefore, the Conservative Party has generally seen itself as the party of pragmatism, i.e. making policy to suit the circumstances, rather than coming to office with a programme designed to take the country to a clearly defined target.

Origins

Margaret Thatcher was, however, an exception to this. Her approach to politics was based on conviction, was radical and there was a distinct aim in mind – a free market system in which individual enterprise could flourish (see page 180). Margaret Thatcher's divergence from traditional conservative thought on this point accounts for some of the criticism she received from within the party during her leadership.

Conservatives believe that the economy, the political system and social structure change gradually over time in order to adjust to changing circumstances. This, they believe, is the reason behind the success of the British Constitution which has evolved, in its unwritten form, as the nature of British society has changed (see pages 8–9). Therefore, conventions are an important part of the British constitutional arrangement. They are a major source of the constitution's flexibility and to remove them in favour of a codified document would be to create system that would be more likely to break than bend as society changes.

Evolution

The idea of evolutionary change is linked to the conservatives' view that society is a living organism, not a constructed machine. It has grown through numerous

> ## Edmund Burke and conservatism
>
> *'It is a presumption in favour of any settled scheme of government against any untried project, that a nation has long existed and flourished under it. It is a better presumption even of the choice of a nation, far better than any sudden and temporary arrangement by actual election. Because a nation is not an idea only of local extent, and individual momentary aggregation; but it is an idea of continuity, which extends in time as well as in numbers and in space. And this is a choice not of one day, or one set of people, not a tumultuary and giddy choice; it is a deliberate election of the ages and of generations; it is a constitution made by what is ten thousand times better than choice, it is made by the peculiar circumstances, occasions, tempers, dispositions, and moral, civil, and social habitudes of the people, which disclose themselves only in a long space of time . . . The individual is foolish; the multitude, for the moment, is foolish, when they act without deliberation; but the species is wise, and, when time is given to it, as a species it always acts right.'*
>
> Source: Edmund Burke, *Reform of Representation in the House of Commons*, 1792

transformations to reach its present state. Therefore, all parts of the organism are important and play a function. This is as true of the older as well as the more modern institutions. Traditional institutions, such as the monarchy and the House of Lords, contain wisdom because they have developed over such a long period of time. Therefore, they should be preserved.

Nationalism

Institutions also bind society together. They are part of the common heritage and experience of the nation and, therefore, help to build the identity of the nation. Nationhood, patriotism and unity are major principles of conservative thought. This can be clearly seen in the unwillingness of the Conservative Party to devolve power to Scottish and Welsh parliaments. The nation is also important on the world stage. Conservatives tend to see the nation as the basic unit of currency of international politics and one of the roles of government is to be guided by the national interest at all times.

Institutions

It is not only political institutions that are important in society. Marriage, the family, the church and the education system are all important means of maintaining social control. For conservatives social control is particularly important because their view of human nature is generally pessimistic. They believe that people are basically greedy, selfish and imperfect. Given the state of human nature, it is important to control that nature rather than to try to reform it. The conservative's emphasis on law and order also reflects their belief in the wicked nature of humankind.

Order

Within society, conservatives believe in a natural **order** that is hierarchical. Everyone has their place in society, performs a useful function and it is damaging to upset this structure. Included in this natural order is rule by an elite or a ruling class. Only a few are blessed with the qualities required of a leader and so the mass of people will be prepared to follow such an individual or group. Such authority could be derived from natural charisma or from tradition. Often leaders of the Conservative Party have been drawn from the aristocracy where there is a tradition of public service. Furthermore, leaders should have been trained in the correct methods of leadership and conservatives turn to the traditional institutions of public schools and the universities of Oxford and Cambridge for that preparation.

Liberty

In public life conservatives believe that the power of leaders should be limited. If power is concentrated in the hands of a few people, there is a danger that the **liberty** of the people will be infringed. The conservatives' view of liberty tends to be negative, in that they tend to emphasize freedom from government interference. Therefore, conservatives believe in balanced government with the power of one institution checked by the power of another.

Another method of diffusing power within a society is to encourage property ownership. This is a fundamental principle of conservatism. However, property ownership is also a means to educate people in the benefits of stability. Individuals can only keep their possessions in a stable society in which public order is maintained. This is linked to the conservatives' view that the rule of law is the basis of all freedom. Everyone must be subject to the law and the law must be applied equally.

Socialism

Socialists differ from both liberals and conservatives in their view of human nature. To a socialist individuals are inherently good but can be made wicked by the society in which they live. Capitalism brings out the worst characteristics of human beings. It encourages them to be selfish, competitive and greedy and in order to survive in the system those characteristics are necessary. However, if people can be made wicked by a system, then logically, the reverse must be true. Therefore, **socialism** seeks to build a society in which individuals can *co-operate* with other human beings.

While liberals and conservatives believe that people shape the environment, socialists believe that individuals are *influenced* by the environment in which they live. This can be clearly illustrated by a socialist's views on crime which often identify poor social conditions as a cause of crime. Poor housing, unemployment, alienation from the political system all contribute to the frustration that a large section of the society feel and so they turn to crime as a means to escape and as a method of drawing attention to their plight. Again, if society could be improved the individual within that society would be so much better.

Methods to change that society range from reform to revolution. Socialists believe that capitalism divides people, while their natural inclination is to come together in a co-operative and fraternal manner. Therefore, society must be transformed into one in which everyone is free to work together, where each is rewarded according to their effort and their function, rather than by the forces of supply and demand.

A fundamental requirement for a future society is greater equality. While conservatives and liberals stress political equality, socialists emphasize economic equality. Without greater economic equality, they argue, true political equality cannot be achieved. The wealthy will always have more political power and better access to the protection of the rule of law. Therefore, they advocate redistribution of income via a progressive tax system, in which the wealthy pay a greater proportion of their income in tax. The tax revenue can then be used by the government to create a network of services such as social security, universal health care and public education, so that everyone may benefit from the country's wealth.

Some socialists also argue that considerable public ownership of the means of production is also necessary to ensure that production is properly planned for the good of the whole society and that industrial life is not dominated solely by the demands of the market place. Under its 1918 constitution, the British Labour Party is committed to the nationalization of the 'means of production, distribution and exchange'. This is known as *Clause 4*. The recently elected Labour Party leader,

Human nature

Society and individuals

Co-operation

Equality

Tony Blair, sparked some controversy within the party in the autumn of 1994 when he recommended that Clause 4 be replaced by a more modern version of what many saw as a sacred commitment of the party.

It is clear then that socialists place much emphasis on the well being of the group rather than the individual. In socialist ideology the needs of the individual are combined with the needs of society as a whole in an effort to create more freedom for everyone, rather than just for those who can afford it.

Exercises

Short questions

1 How do the Conservative and Labour Parties differ in their understanding of
   (a) freedom (b) justice? (ULEAC, June 1994)
   How do the Conservative and Labour Parties differ in their understanding of
   (a) authority (b) equality? (ULEAC, June 1992)

Essay questions

1 How accurately and in what ways may the Labour Party be regarded as 'socialist' and the Conservative Party as 'individualist'? (AEB, June 1991)
2 How radical has Thatcherism been? (ULEAC, June 1990)
3 Is the Labour Party a socialist party? (ULEAC, January 1991)

Data response question

'Under the Conservative administration of the 1980s, the emphasis has ben on unrestrained individualism, consumption and private property. Public life has deteriorated, standards of behaviour have declined and our shared environment has become at best down at heel and at worst downright dangerous. People are encouraged to prize chiefly what can be owned exclusively, hoarded or displayed in their homes. Status depends on money and possessions. Private greed has been elevated to the status of a public virtue . . .

There is a paradox at the heart of the Conservative government's vision of society. They proclaim the enterprise culture yet their policies trap people in dependency. They promote adaption to change, yet they have created real fear of change among the most vulnerable. Instead of 'rolling back the frontiers of the state', the Conservatives have rolled over the safeguards which protect the citizen. That is why they have to spend so much more . . . on crime, on police, on punishment, on officialdom, on surveillance.'

Source: Paddy Ashdown, *Citizens' Britain: A Radical Agenda for the 1990s*, Fourth Estate, 1989

How accurately does the extract describe the contemporary political values of Conservatives? To what extent and in what ways is it possible for a government to influence or change the long-term, underlying political values of society?

(AEB, 1992)

5 Parliament

Questions to be answered in this chapter
- What are the functions of Parliament?
- How effectively is Parliament performing its functions?
- How could Parliament be reformed to improve its performance?

Terms to know

Backbench revolts	Life peers
Backwoodsmen	Parliamentary sovereignty
Crossbenchers	Referendum
Delegates	Representation
Guillotine	Representatives
Hereditary peers	Select committees
Investigation	Separation of powers
Judicial review	Standing committees
Legislation	Vote of no confidence
Legitimization	Working peers

The composition of Parliament

The Queen-in-Parliament

Parliament was formed in medieval times as a forum of 'great men' to be summoned by the king to discuss the state of the kingdom. It was divided into two houses: the Lords and the Commons. The former consisted of the aristocracy and senior figures from the Church. The latter was made up mostly of gentry.

Origins

The third branch of Parliament was the monarch, referred to as the King-(or Queen)-in-Parliament. This reflected the fact that it was originally formed by the king and remained at his disposal. Parliament could be summoned by him, existed to consider royal business, looked to him for the solutions to problems and could be dissolved by him.

However, the balance of power between the monarch and Parliament began to change when it became generally accepted that the king needed the consent of Parliament to raise new taxes and to pass new laws. Gradually, the power and stature of Parliament began to grow until it attempted to usurp the power of the monarch, Charles I. The result was the Civil War of 1642–5 which ended in defeat for the royalists, the beheading of Charles and the subsequent abolition of the monarchy by Oliver Cromwell.

Civil War

The monarchy was reinstated in 1660, but with greatly diminished power. This was particularly so after the 'Glorious Revolution' in 1688 – the Bill of Rights was

Glorious Revolution

accepted in 1689 which limited the power of the monarchy and laid the foundations of the 'constitutional monarchy' we know today.

Constitutional monarchy

Queen Elizabeth II has a largely ceremonial role in Parliament with most of her powers, or prerogatives, having passed to the government of the day, often to the prime minister. The opening of Parliament, signing a bill into law and the dissolution of Parliament are largely ceremonial functions. (For a full discussion of the monarch's powers, see Chapter 8.)

Therefore, when we discuss the role of Parliament it will be confined to an examination of the workings of the House of Lords and the House of Commons.

The House of Lords

Composition

Traditionally, the House of Lords is made up of **hereditary peers**, archbishops and bishops and the law lords. In 1995 those who had inherited their titles accounted for 742 peers; the clergy 26 peers; and the law lords 23.

The remainder of the 1,199 peers are either hereditary peers of first creation (15) or **life peers** (378). Of the life peers, 64 are women. Hereditary peers of first creation are appointed by the prime minister. However, only four have been created since 1964 – they include Lord Whitelaw and Lord Tonypandy (the ex-Speaker of the House of Commons, George Thomas).

The unrepresentative House of Lords

Backgrounds

The Life Peerages Act of 1958 allowed the government to appoint peers for life, i.e. the peerage cannot be passed on to a son or daughter. The aim of the act was to broaden the composition of the House of Lords, both in terms of the social background and the political attitudes. Traditionally, the House of Lords was composed of male (hereditary titles cannot normally be passed to female heirs, although some Scottish titles are exceptions to this rule and 17 hereditary peers are women), landed aristocrats whose political views were largely Conservative. Even today, of the hereditary peers 81 per cent were educated at public school, of which half attended Eton. This led to the common criticism that the House of Lords was unrepresentative of the nation as a whole, both socially and politically.

Labour

The range of peers includes ex-politicians, actors, trade union leaders and businesspeople. Perhaps, more importantly, the representation of the Labour Party has increased since 1958. During the Labour governments of 1964–70 and 1974–9, 160 Labour life peers were created as compared to 28 from the Conservative Party.

The creation of so many Labour peers has gone some way to correct the balance between the Conservative and Labour Parties in the House of Lords. It has also contributed to the distinction between **working peers** and **backwoodsmen**.

Working peers

Of almost 1,200 members of the House of Lords, only 400 attend more than 33 per cent of its sittings. In fact, less than 67 per cent of the eligible peers have ever attended the Lords. Those that attend on a regular basis are known as working peers because it is these members that conduct most of the business. Life peers account for 56 per cent of the working peers.

Backwoodsmen

Despite the creation of a number of Labour life peers, the Labour Party, with only 120 peers, is outnumbered among the Lords as a whole and even among the life peers. The Conservative Party can often rely on a majority among working peers, but when backwoodsmen attend a majority is almost guaranteed.

Some 284 peers choose not to take the whip (see page 70) of either party. They are known as **crossbenchers**. Theoretically, crossbenchers are considered independent. However, the majority have tended to vote with the Conservative government on most issues. Also, their attendance has been poor.

Crossbenchers

The undemocratic House of Lords

A second criticism of the House of Lords is that it is undemocratic. Until the nineteenth century the fact that the Lords was not elected had not aroused disquiet. In fact, it had long been acknowledged that the voice of the elected chamber would hold sway over the upper house. However, constitutionally, the House of Lords held a veto over all **legislation** and the Conservative majority was keen to quell the tide of liberalism from the House of Commons.

Unelected

As the electoral franchise was widened in 1832 and 1867 the power of the unelected house seemed increasingly untenable. The constitutional crisis came to a head under the Liberal government, elected with an overwhelming majority in 1906. In 1909 the Lords rejected Lloyd George's 'Peoples' Budget' and a bill to reduce the powers

Electoral reform

Suggested reform of the Lords

Attitudes to the Lords are often summarized as 'retain, reform, replace or remove'. To retain the Lords in its present form is favoured by Conservatives who wish to avoid radical reform. Currently, it is a mild check on the Commons, it can help save the Commons' time, it has time for debate and it is not hamstrung by strong party discipline.

Reform of the Lords has been undertaken throughout the twentieth century but has never attacked the very basis of the Lords. In 1969 the Labour Party proposed the gradual phasing out of hereditary peers, but this was defeated by Labour left-wingers who believed it did not go far enough and right-wing Conservatives who thought it went too far. Alternative ideas might be to allow only life peers or only working peers to vote.

Replacing the Lords with a democratically elected senate is a more radical proposal, suggested by the Liberal–SDP Alliance in 1987. Problems, though not insurmountable, would include the constituencies to be drawn in order to prevent a replica of the Commons and the electoral system to be used. Adopting a system of proportional representation would make the senate more democratic than the Commons, in many people's eyes. The creation of a senate would also remove the need for the limits on the powers of the second chamber. Therefore, the veto could be restored, possibly leading to deadlock between the senate and the house.

Removing the Lords in favour of a unicameral chamber, the most radical solution of all, was proposed by the Labour Party in 1983. This would remove the second chamber as a check on the Commons, which might be considerd foolhardy given the workload that the Commons faces and the extent to which the executive dominates the work of the Commons. However, the logic behind this view is that if the Commons is the voice of the people, why should it be checked at all?

Project

Draw up your own plans to reform the House of Lords indicating the powers that the reformed house would have and the advantages and disadvantages of such a scheme.

> ### The Lords in 1867
>
> *'When we come to look at the House in which I have now the honour to address your Lordships, I ask how it will be affected by this great democratic change? So long as the other House of Parliament was elected upon a restricted principle, I can understand that it would submit to a check from a House such as this. But in the presence of this great democratic power and the advance of this great democratic wave . . . it passes my comprehension to understand how an hereditary House like this can hold its own. It might be possible for this House, in one instance, to withstand a measure if it were violent, unjust and coercive; but I do not believe that the repetition of such an offence would be permitted. It would be said: "The People must govern, and not a set of hereditary peers never chosen by the people."'*
>
> Source: Lord Shaftesbury during the debate on the 1867 Reform Act

of the Lords quickly followed. The Lords opposed the bill, but after two further election victories for the Liberals in 1910 and a threat to create enough Liberal peers to end Conservative control of the house, permanently, the Lords backed down and accepted reform.

Reform

The 1911 Parliament Act removed the Lords' veto power over public legislation and replaced it with the power to delay a bill for two Parliamentary sessions. The act also removed the Lords' power to amend, veto or even delay any 'money bills', i.e. those bills relating to national finance. The power of the Lords was further restricted by the 1949 Parliament Act which reduced the delaying power to one session of Parliament.

The House of Commons

The lower house of Parliament is elected. The right to vote in parliamentary elections was gradually extended throughout the nineteenth century. The 1867 Reform Act was one of the most significant extensions of the franchise as the male, urban, working class was allowed to vote for the first time. In 1884 the franchise was widened further and in 1918 women were allowed to vote for the first time. In 1969 the voting age was reduced from 21 to 18.

> ### The Speaker
>
> The office of Speaker developed in the Middle Ages as an agent of the monarch. This link was not broken until 1642 when Speaker Lenthall told Charles I: 'I have neither eyes to see, nor tongue to speak in this place but as the House is pleased to direct me, whose servant I am here.'
>
> Since the mid-nineteenth century the Speaker has been seen as a neutral figure. Elected by MPs, the Speaker resigns from their party on taking office. Although traditionally chosen from the governing party, in 1992 Betty Boothroyd was elected, with considerable cross-party support, from the Opposition.
>
> The Speaker has four main functions:
> - chair of the house
> - referee of proceedings
> - administration of the Commons
> - ceremonial duties.

At present there are 651 Members of Parliament, each representing a constituency of approximately 65,000 voters. Since the 1911 Parliament Act the lifetime of a Parliament has been limited to five years, so the prime minister must ask the monarch to dissolve Parliament, i.e. call a general election, before the five-year limit is reached.

By convention, members of the government are drawn from either the House of Lords or the Commons. It is the composition of the latter that dictates the colour of the government in that a government depends on the support of the Commons only. Hence, under normal circumstances, the largest party, often with an overall majority of seats, due to the first-past-the-post electoral system (see page 18), forms the government. As the House of Commons is set up on adversarial lines, the second largest party forms the official Opposition.

Parliamentary sovereignty

The impact of political party organization on the Commons

'During this period [1832–67], Parliament and primarily the Commons came to form what was effectively part of the decision-making process. It did not itself govern – it has never done so – but it did exercise an effective negative (checking) and sometimes positive (initiating) power in the decision-making process ... Members could and did replace one Government with another without suffering a dissolution (as, for example, in 1852, 1855, 1858 and 1866), and could and did remove individual Ministers who had erred (as, for instance, Lord John Russell in 1855 and Lord Ellenborough in 1858). Members collaborated in the shaping of various Government measures as well as in amending or rejecting legislation on the floor of the House ... ministerial policy on various occasions was overruled; the Ministry was sometimes forced to divulge information (for example, about negotiations with foreign powers); and debate really counted for something ... The golden age was to be short-lived. It came to an end essentially in consequence of the effects of the Reform Act of 1867.

The Act [1867] itself put into practice the principle recognized by the 1832 Act, that of the extension of the franchise, and increased the electorate by 88 per cent ... For the political parties, such an enormous and sudden growth of the electorate meant that 'a system of centralization became inevitable'.' Political leaders realized that they would have to make efforts to cater for the political aspirations of middle-class and some working men, and to attract their support, through constituency-based organizations and through legislation in Parliament. This could be achieved only by the development of large-scale party organizations ... with Members united in the House of Commons to ensure the passage of promised measures.

... The result of a large electoral role, the growth of party competition, and the development of large, centralized party organisations all modified the position of Members of Parliament. The parliamentary action of an individual Member was no longer his own concern or that of a limited few – it was now that of his constituents and party, electors no longer identified with Members as individuals but increasingly with a party, and it was on the strength of their party labels that Members were elected. The dominant force of British political life became the political parties, a development which was gradual but sure. As mass parties assumed positions of dominance, the effect on Parliament and parliamentary life was profound.'

Source: Philip Norton, *The Commons in Perspective*, Basil Blackwell, 1985

Dicey

The main principle of the British Constitution is **parliamentary sovereignty**. This means that Parliament holds the supreme authority in the UK. According to A V Dicey, this meant Parliament 'has under the English constitution, the right to make or unmake any law whatever; and further, that no person or body is recognized by the law of England as having a right to override or set aside the legislation of Parliament.'

Since 1885, when A V Dicey wrote those words, the nature of parliamentary sovereignty has changed. Inside Parliament, as we have already seen, the power of the House of Lords has been reduced through the Parliament Acts of 1911 and 1949. As a result, the balance of power has shifted towards the House of Commons and to some extent, practical sovereignty lies here rather than with Parliament as a whole.

Party control

The impetus for reform of the House of Lords came from electoral reform. However, the Reform Acts also had an impact on the organization of the House of Commons. With more people eligible to take part in elections and the introduction of the secret ballot in 1872, MPs could no longer rely on corruption or contacts to ensure their re-election and so they developed political parties. Since the turn of the century, political parties have dominated elections and the organization of the House of Commons. MPs are organized into tightly disciplined parliamentary groups that make the business of the House of Commons relatively predictable. Some would argue that parliamentary sovereignty has moved towards the political parties and away from a house of MPs with independent voices.

Executive sovereignty?

Executive dominance

The strength of political parties, combined with an overall majority of seats in the Commons, has augmented the power of the executive branch of government. The British government is determined by the composition of the House of Commons and so, given the workings of the first past-the-post electoral system, it usually has an overall majority. The strong party discipline makes that majority reliable and almost guarantees the government victory in Commons votes. When the fact that the executive is backed by the civil service is taken into account, it is easy to see why sovereignty might actually be considered to lie with the executive not Parliament.

Popular sovereignty?

At least once every five years the House of Commons is elected and so, in political terms, at those times, sovereignty could be said to lie with the people. However, once the general election has taken place, sovereignty passes to Parliament with the people having no power to change governments, although they are occasionally given the opportunity to voice opinions in a **referendum**.

European sovereignty?

Perhaps the most fundamental change to the concept of parliamentary sovereignty occurred in 1973 when Britain joined the European Economic Community (EEC), now known as the European Union (EU). By joining this supranational organization, Britain accepted that decisions regarding British society could be made by European institutions, on which Britain would be represented.

European law

By becoming a signatory of the Treaty of Rome, which set up the EEC, Britain accepted that European law has superior status to British law. This means that British

The referendum

A referendum involves the electorate being asked for their opinions regarding a specific issue. This is usually done by the government posing a question and asking the voters to cast a 'yes' or 'no' answer.

Only three referenda have been held in Britain. The first, in 1975, was initiated by Harold Wilson's government over Britain's membership of the European Economic Community (EEC; now the European Union). The second and third were held in 1979, under James Callaghan's administration, over the devolution of power to a Scottish and a Welsh parliament.

All these referenda were justified by the seriousness of the constitutional decision facing the government, making some element of popular participation desirable. However, constitutionally, they are more difficult to justify because MPs are elected to make decisions on behalf of their constituents, not to refer them back to the electorate.

Often a referendum is organized in order to help the government out of a difficult political situation. The 1975 referendum was held because the Labour cabinet was split over membership of the EEC. The 1979 referenda were held because James Callaghan's government hoped to be kept in power by offering devolution proposals in return for continued Liberal suport of the Lib–Lab Pact.

Problems of referenda include the over-simplification of issues into 'yes'/'no' responses, the cost and the fact that the electorate may be ill-equipped to make an informed choice. Advantages include popular participation, the education of the electorate on an issue and the resolution of a difficult problem.

law must be in line with the provisions of European law and British courts have the power of **judicial review** over acts of Parliament. This means courts can scrutinize acts of Parliament, refer them to the European Court of Justice and even suspend those acts (see pages 130–1).

R. v. Secretary of State for Transport ex parte Factortame Ltd (No 2) (1991), the so-called Factortame case, was the first example of a British court reviewing an act of Parliament. In this case, the Merchant Shipping Act (1988) was suspended by the British courts and referred to the European Court of Justice, where it was found to contravene European law.

Judicial review

Although membership of the EU has affected Parliamentary sovereignty on a day-to-day basis, it has not brought it to an end. Parliament is free to withdraw Britain from the EU at any time, although the Treaty of Rome does not explain how it could be done. (For a fuller discussion of the EU, see Chapter 11.)

The functions of Parliament

Parliament has four main functions:
- **representation**
- legislation
- control of the executive
- financial control.

Most are performed by both the Lords and the Commons. However, the lower house is undoubtedly the senior partner.

Representation

Britain is a representative democracy. Since 55 million people cannot participate in political decision making on a day-to-day basis, the voters elect a small group of others to make decisions on their behalf.

Burke

Since members of the House of Lords are not elected, they have no role to play with regard to the representative function. This falls entirely on MPs in the House of Commons. To what extent members of the Commons actually represent their constituents depends on the type of representation being sought. The Commons is representative in that the whole country is divided into constituencies of approximately equal size (65,000 people) with one member elected for each one and the MPs should act on behalf of all of their constituents, not merely those who voted for them. MPs speak on behalf of their constituents, but they are not mouthpieces for their views. They are **representatives**, not **delegates**, and do not have to vote or speak as instructed by their constituents (for Edmund Burke's distinction between representatives and delegates, see page 19).

MPs and constituents

In this role MPs promote the interests of their constituency, trying to foster commerce in the area, taking care of the environment and the infrastructure. They will also help individual constituents with problems relating to government. Common areas of difficulty include the bureaucracies of the National Health Service and the social security system. MPs can put forward oral and written questions on behalf of constituents (see page 69) and can refer problems to the Ombudsman.

The 1992 election result

Party	Votes	Seats
Conservative	14.2m	336
Labour	11.6m	271
Liberal Democrats	6.1m	20
Others	1.2m	24

Electoral reform

However, critics of the electoral system argue that constituents are not adequately represented in that the system distorts election results by exaggerating the popularity of the Labour and Conservative Parties and understates that of the Liberal Democrats. In 1992 the Conservative Party won 42.9 per cent of the vote, but was rewarded with 51.6 per cent of the seats. The House of Commons is, therefore, unrepresentative in that it does not reflect public opinion and critics have suggested that the electoral system should be changed to one of proportional representation (see pages 22–7).

Members of the House of Commons are also unrepresentative of the public in terms of social background: 65 per cent of Labour and Conservative MPs are from professional or business background, while 10 per cent are drawn from manual workers. Ethnic minorities, who make up 5 per cent of the population are seriously under-represented, but perhaps the most striking anomaly in the Commons is the low number of women MPs – only 60 after the 1992 election.

Party delegates

As well as their constituents, MPs also represent their party. As a result, they are expected to follow the party line by voting with the party whip on key issues. MPs' responsibilities to their party have now grown to such an extent that some observers have labelled MPs 'lobby fodder' – meaning that they are merely party-voting robots needed to feed the voting lobbies.

Outside interests

Over recent years considerable attention has focused on the conflict between MPs' responsibility to represent their constituents and their willingness to act on behalf of pressure groups and businesses. This came to a head in 1994 when two Conservative MPs, Tim Smith and Neil Hamilton, were accused of failing to declare in the Register of Members' Interests that they took money in return for asking questions on behalf of Mohammed Al-Fayed, the Egyptian-born owner of Harrods. However, concern over divided loyalties in the Commons encompasses MPs who are company directors outside Parliament, those who are sponsored by pressure groups, as well as those who accept payments from professional lobbyists.

Nolan Committee

Currently, the Register of Members' Interests is supervised by the Committee on Members' Interests, but this lacks the power to investigate allegations of corruption. Therefore, the prime minister set up the Nolan Committee to look into standards of behaviour in public life. The report, published in May 1995, proposed that MPs undertake no paid parliamentary services for lobbyists, that former cabinet ministers, for two years after leaving office, be subject to vetting before taking jobs in industry and the creation of an independent Parliamentary Commissioner for Standards to monitor the arrangements.

Legislation

Parliament is the legislative branch of government and, as its name suggests, one of its key functions is to make law. Both houses have a law-making function, but the main responsibility lies with the Commons. The legislative function also incorporates a secondary function of Parliament, i.e. a forum for debate.

The passage of a bill

Most bills originate from the government and are first introduced in the House of Commons. This is known as the *first reading* and involves no debate. The *second reading* takes place on the floor of the house and involves debate about the principles lying behind the bill. This is followed by the *committee stage* at which point the bill is considered, clause by clause, by a standing committee. Amendments can be suggested at this point and are then considered on the floor of the house at the *report stage*. There follows the *third reading* on the floor of the house and MPs vote on the final stage of the bill.

Bills follow much the same path through the House of Lords. If the Lords suggest amendments, these must be reconciled with the Commons' version of the bill. Once a final version is agreed, the bill becomes law with the *royal assent*.

The majority of bills are sponsored by the government and the most important are announced in the Queen's Speech at the opening of the parliamentary session. Most bills take a few months to be passed and controversial legislation can take even longer. However, no bill may be carried over from one session to the next allowing about a maximum of eleven months for consideration.

Private members' bills

MPs who do not hold ministerial office can introduce private members' bills. However, their opportunities to do so are limited because the schedule is so packed with government bills. Private members' bills are rarely successful without government support at least in terms of time. The government often chooses to support private members' bills in order to legislate on controversial issues of social morality. Such a strategy allows bills to be debated and voted on without bringing them into the centre of party political conflict. Votes on these bills are usually free votes, i.e. MPs may vote as they choose, without having to follow the party whip (see page 70). Well-known private members' bills have dealt with abortion, homosexuality and the abolition of the death penalty.

Control of the executive

In the British parliamentary system the executive is drawn from Parliament and is responsible to it. The structure of British government creates another set of major and minor functions for Parliament. Both houses are responsible for training and cultivating recruits for ministerial ranks and for checking government and individual ministers once in office.

Growth of the executive

The scrutinizing function has become particularly important in the twentieth century as the role of the executive has grown. Government is expected to take responsibility for all of society's troubles. The 'Peoples' Budget' of 1909 pushed government responsibilities into unemployment benefit and pensions. The end of World War II saw the government adopting the ideas of Keynesian economics (see page 177), which identified the need for government intervention to solve the problems of inflation and unemployment, and in 1948 launching the National Health Service.

Increased government intervention requires greater government initiation of policy programmes and their implementation. Therefore, it is important that Parliament is able to scrutinize the government's policies and the effectiveness of their implementation.

Foreign policy

The government is also the centre of foreign policy activity. Summit meetings, the technology of war and the advanced telecommunications that have made the world a global village have also reinforced the government's command of foreign policy. The role of Parliament is limited to scrutinizing the work of government.

Public perception

The world outside Parliament also focuses on the government. The majority of the public understand the British system of government only through the personalities of the government. Therefore, the prime minister, in particular, takes the credit and criticism for government policy. Of course, this is reinforced by the media which tend to concentrate on personalities as much as issues. The fact that the government is the focus of political attention adds to the need for parliamentary scrutiny.

Both houses of Parliament are responsible for the **investigation** and scrutiny of the government. This takes place through debate, oral and written questions to ministers and the select committee systems in both houses (see page 75).

Financial control

Control of the purse strings has been a function of Parliament since the assembly was convened in order to approve the monarch's plans to raise revenue. Today the government presents Parliament with its budgetary proposals and seeks the approval of the House of Commons only. In fact, the Commons only considers requests for funds from the government. It does not initiate spending plans itself. For example, in November 1994 the Commons defeated the government's plan to increase value added tax (VAT) on domestic fuel to 15 per cent, but did not suggest alternative methods of raising the revenue. The House of Lords' involvement in financial matters has been restricted since the 1911 Parliament Act.

Until 1994 the government traditionally presented its spending plans and revenue expectations in two separate procedures. Its estimates of public spending were given in November and its approach to the raising of the necessary revenue in the budget in March. Since 1994 both elements have been combined into a single budget presented in November.

Budget

Once requests for funds have been made, they are incorporated into a finance bill which is debated by the house. The committee stage of the bill is undertaken by the *committee of the whole house*. This means that the finance bill is examined clause by clause on the floor of the house, rather than through the usual standing committee.

Committee of the whole house

In addition to debate, the Commons scrutinizes the ways in which the money is spent through the Public Accounts Committee and the departmental **select committees**. The Public Accounts Committee is probably the hardest working select committee in the Commons. It is usually headed by a member of the Opposition and is served by the National Audit Office which provides financial information.

It should be clear that the Commons' financial role is one of scrutiny, rather than full responsibility. The government is responsible for finance and it alone can initiate financial proposals. The Commons does not have the power to usurp the function of the government by putting forward its own budget.

The interaction of Parliament's main functions

Functions of Parliament

- Representation
- Legislation
- Investigation
- Finance

A frequently asked question is 'Which of Parliament's main functions is the most important?' Representation is a popular choice because in Britain's representative democracy parliamentary elections are the chief form of political participation for the public and so the House of Commons becomes the voice of the people. However, if the voice of the people has no power the system is not truly democratic. Therefore, the legislative, investigative and financial powers are also of vital importance.

Some commentators argue that in the twentieth century the government has become more dominant and so the investigative and financial functions are the most significant because they might enable Parliament to check the power of government. However, this power is closely linked to the legislative function because debate of government policy is a means of checking the executive.

Therefore, all of Parliament's key functions are interlinked. They are dependent upon each other and they reinforce each other. Without any one of its functions Parliament would be a significantly weaker assembly.

Perhaps the best way to draw all of Parliament's main functions together is under the heading **legitimization**. As the House of Commons is composed of the elected representatives of the people, the government must put financial and legislative proposals before MPs for their approval and MPs are able to criticize the

Legitimization

government. In doing so, they are indirectly putting the people's seal of approval, or veto, on government actions. As a result, the people are expected to obey laws and so public order is maintained.

Factors affecting Parliament's performance

We have already questioned the extent to which Parliament is representative of the country. Now we turn our attention to the extent to which Parliament fulfils its other functions.

Given the importance of the executive branch of government in the twentieth century, the chief determinant of the effectiveness of Parliament is the degree to which it is dominated by government.

The structure of government

Parliamentary
government

British government is characterized as parliamentary. This means that the government is drawn from Parliament and depends upon the support of the House of Commons for its survival. This is in contrast to the presidential system of the USA in which the president, who heads the executive branch, is elected separately from Congress, the legislature.

Presidential government

The distinction between these two styles of government illustrates an important factor influencing the effectiveness of Parliament. The American president is not drawn from Congress and therefore is not sustained by a congressional majority. The British government depends on a majority of support in the Commons, without which it may be brought down.

Control of the assembly

The first-past-the-post electoral system has created an overall majority of seats for all but one government since 1945 (the Labour government of February 1974 was a minority government). Therefore, all but one government, since 1945, has had the benefit of its own supporters controlling the House of Commons. The bigger the majority, the more control the government is likely to have. This contrasts sharply with the experiences of post-war American presidents. Only three, John Kennedy, Lyndon Johnson and Jimmy Carter, have faced a Congress controlled by their own party throughout their term of office.

As well as having an almost guaranteed majority in the lower house, the parliamentary system also allows the executive considerable scope to interfere in the affairs of the legislature. In a parliamentary system members of the government are drawn from the assembly so the members of the executive are also members of the legislature. Strictly speaking, this is an infringement of Montesquieu's **separation of powers** (see page 6) and it allows government ministers to introduce their own bills, to take part in the debates and even to manipulate the time available for consideration of legislation.

Guillotine

A **guillotine** motion is a mechanism available to the House of Commons to curtail debate of a bill. It is usually proposed by the minister concerned with the bill and the whole house is required to vote on the motion. The guillotine has only been defeated once since 1945.

Despite the opportunities available to a government to dominate Parliament, the parliamentary structure does create openings for the Commons to check government. The ultimate censure for a government that loses the support of the house is a **vote of no confidence**.

The Opposition

Normally, the second largest party in the Commons forms Her Majesty's Opposition. The leader of the Opposition, the chief whip and two deputies are paid a salary by the state.

The Leader of the Opposition expects to be consulted on issues that are a matter of the national interest and which might require bipartisan support.

Twenty Opposition days are set aside for the use of the second party (17) and the third party (3). On these days the opposition parties can chose the subject for debate.

If the government has a majority and party discipline is strong the Opposition is in a very weak position. Therefore, it tends to concentrate on appearing as a government in waiting, criticizing the government and airing important issues.

Vote of no confidence

A no confidence motion can be tabled by the Opposition. Typical phrasing of such a motion would be: 'This house has no confidence in Her Majesty's Government.' A government losing a vote of confidence should resign or call a general election. Since 1945 only one government has lost such a vote, the Labour Government of James Callaghan in March 1979. The Labour Party lost the subsequent general election.

Questions

Question time is the aspect of parliamentary procedure that has most caught the public imagination since the house was televised in 1989. The first 45 minutes of the sitting from Monday to Thursday are occupied with oral questions to ministers. Oral questions to the prime minister are allocated 15 minutes on Tuesday and Thursday.

MPs must table their question ten days in advance if they are to have a chance of being called. The initial question tends to be bland in order to disguise the topic of the supplementary question that follows for which no notice is required and which usually contains the main point.

MPs can also ask written questions. Ministers' replies are published in *Hansard* (the record of Parliamentary business).

Question time

The parliamentary system also allows question time to take place. This most famous of Commons occasions takes place every afternoon from Monday to Thursday and involves ministers, on a strict rota, answering questions regarding departmental business. On a Tuesday and Thursday Prime Minister's questions attract the most attention.

Even though the time available is short, question time gives backbenchers the opportunity to ask ministers difficult and searching questions. Prime ministers and departmental ministers are judged critically on their performance on these occasions and prime ministers, in particular, are very conscious of the need for good performances. Harold Macmillan believed:

'You have to know who is your questioner . . . like a prep school, there are boys who are popular, whom you must never slap down, even if they are asking a silly question . . . then there are the unpopular, the tiresome, and the House rather enjoys their being slapped down . . . You must remember that, like a school, on the whole it dislikes the front bench (the

masters) . . . often you can turn an enemy into a friend, by some slight recognition. Always keep your temper . . . and always have a good control of questions and supplementaries . . . in many ways it is the most anxious work; I would never have lunched out on question day.' – quoted in Andrew Adonis, *Parliament Today*, Manchester University Press, 1993

In the American system cabinet members can be asked to answer questions before congressional comittees, but the president is never questioned by members of Congress and is only required to appear in Congress once a year to deliver the State of the Union Address. So, in the USA, the separation of powers is much stronger than in Britain and, while it does release the President from some duties, on balance, this tends to strengthen Congress and prevent it being dominated by the executive. In Britain the parliamentary structure gives Parliament a great deal of potential power, but few opportunities to use that power.

Possible reforms

- Electoral reform to reduce the size of a government's majority and possibly create a 'hung parliament' and a coalition government
- Abolition of the guillotine to prevent the curtailment of debate
- Removal of the notice period for oral questions

Party discipline

A majority in the House of Commons is not sufficient to allow government to dominate the house. The majority must be cohesive and the government must be relatively confident that its supporters will stick together.

We have already seen that since the late nineteenth century political parties have been a powerful force in British politics. As a result of this development, parties have forged two clear roles in the political system:
- an electoral role
- a governing role.

The whips

Most MPs are members of a political party. As such, they are subject to the party whip. This means that when a vote is due to be taken MPs receive voting instructions. This comes in the form of a *three-line whip* if the issue is of crucial importance; a *two-line whip* if it is very important and a *one-line whip* if it is quite important. A vote without an instruction is known as a *free vote*'.

MPs who ignore a three-line whip are in danger of retribution from their party. In November 1994 nine Conservative MPs had the whip withdrawn after abstaining in a confidence vote over Britain's financial contributions to the EU.

When the whip is withdrawn, MPs are effectively ostracized from the party. They are not allowed to vote in party elections, to represent the party on parliamentary committees and ultimately, they may be deselected before the next election.

Strength of parties

At election time parties control the nomination of candidates, the organization of the campaign, the finance of the campaign, the provision of policy and they command voter loyalty. Therefore, MPs are aware that their electoral success is largely due to their party, rather than their own candidature. As a result, when pressed to vote for the party line, MPs often do so, aware that the withdrawal of their party's whip could mean the threat of deselection as a candidate before the next election.

The parties' governing roles include the provision of policy for government, the staffing of government offices and the organization of the assembly. Therefore, MPs know that if they have ambitions to gain promotion into the ranks of government ministers they must meet the approval of the party leader and the party whips. They are unlikely to gain this promotion if they persistently vote against the party line.

So, MPs depend on the party for their present job and for any future job. These are strong weapons in the hands of the party whips who are employed to keep the MPs in line with party policy.

Promotion

The strength of the party whips means that party discipline in the British Parliament is almost certain and governments can usually rely on their supporters to vote with them. In 1969 the political writer Samuel Beer described party discipline as 'so close to 100 per cent that there was no longer any point in measuring it'. Beer expressed amazement at the level of party loyalty:

Discipline

'In the House of Commons were two bodies of freedom-loving Britons, chosen in more than six hundred constituencies and subject to influences that ran back to an electorate that was numbered in the millions and divided by the complex interests and aspirations of an advanced modern society. Yet day after day with a Prussian discipline they trooped into the division lobbies at the signals of their whips and in the service of the authoritative decisions of their parliamentary parties. We are so familiar with this fact that we are in danger of losing our sense of wonder over them.' – Samuel Beer, *Modern British Politics*, Faber, 1969

Between 1945 and 1970 this high level of party loyalty can be clearly seen. For example, between 1950 and 1959, 97 per cent of all votes in the Commons showed absolute party cohesion. So confident were parties of their supporters' constancy, that a government defeated on a major issue, not necessarily a vote of confidence, would resign.

Backbench dissent

However, since 1970 the level of party loyalty has begun to slip, as backbenchers have found their voice. Between 1970 and 1979 only around 75 per cent of votes witnessed absolute party loyalty. Edward Heath's Conservative government (1970–February 1974) was defeated six times and the Labour government of October 1974–9 was defeated 23 times as a result of backbench dissent (quoted in Philip Norton, 'The Pattern of Backbench Dissent', *Parliament in the 1980s*, Basil Blackwell, 1985). These defeats contrast sharply with the record of no defeats at all for previous post-war governments.

Conservative governments since 1979 have also experienced backbench defections. The 1979–83 government saw at least ten Conservative backbenchers voting against it, or abstaining, on 16 occasions, while at least 40 did so on four occasions. The 1983–7 government also experienced backbench dissent. In 1986, despite a majority of 144, the government was defeated in the Commons on proposals to legalize Sunday trading. In 1990 32 Conservative backbenchers, including Michael Heseltine, voted against the government's poll tax proposals.

Rebellions

John Major's government weathered a series of **backbench revolts** over the Maastricht Treaty in 1992 and 1993 and the treaty was finally passed only when John Major made the vote an issue of confidence – a defeat would have led to the resignation of the government.

Maastricht

71

Communication and the whips

Of course, government defeats at the hands of its backbenchers gain considerable publicity, but to be effective a backbench revolt does not need to result in a government defeat. Party whips are not merely party enforcers. A good whip will be the eyes and ears of the party leadership, reporting on the mood of backbenchers and counting likely party support. An astute government will take account of backbench feeling and move to head off a rebellion before it reaches the voting stage.

The Conservative governments of 1979–92 made a number of tactical retreats, including dropping the sale of the car manufacturer British Leyland to an American company and the Police and Criminal Evidence Bill. More recently, John Major's government withdrew proposals to privatize the Post Office from the Queen's Speech in the autumn of 1994. This resulted from objections to the proposal from about a dozen MPs. The Conservative Party's majority at this time was so small that even the dissent of just a few Conservative backbencher could have meant defeat in the Commons.

Party committees

In addition to the party whips, the leaders can also gauge backbench opinion via party committees. The major parties form specialist committees that are made up of backbenchers only, when the party is in government, and backbenchers and shadow cabinet spokespersons when in opposition. Party committees provide a voice for backbenchers on specific issues and can provide a counterweight to leadership policies.

1922 Committee

Political parties also form larger committees consisting of all of their MPs. Perhaps the most famous is the Conservative Party's 1922 Committee, which consists of backbench Conservative MPs. The executive committee of the 1922 is an extremely powerful force within the party, particularly at times of crisis. The chair of the Committee, in early 1995 Sir Marcus Fox, is one of the most influential figures in the party.

Parties in the Lords

Party discipline in the House of Lords is not as strict as in the lower house. This is because its members are not elected and so owe less to their party. Some are crossbenchers, others adopt no affiliation whatsoever. Relative independence, combined with a higher degree of regular attendance, due to the advent of working peers, has made the behaviour of the Lords much more unpredictable over the last twenty years. Conservative governments have been as susceptible to House of Lords defeat as have Labour governments. In fact, during the Conservative government of 1983–7, the House of Commons majority was so great (144) that many considered the Lords the only practical opposition to government policies.

It is easy to exaggerate the importance of the Lords' independence. The Conservative Party has a majority of both working and voting peers, including a majority of crossbenchers who usually vote with the government.

The Lords has suggested numerous amendments to government legislation, but once an amendment has been defeated in the Commons, the Lords has not taken up the fight and on only one occasion since 1979 has it voted against a bill outright, the War Crimes Bill (1990), which was finally passed without the approval of the Lords in 1991.

Time

Since 1945 the workload of Parliament has grown beyond recognition. This has resulted from the government taking responsibility for society's problems, technological advance, greater pressure group activity, membership of the EU and more letters from constituents. While the amount of work that an MP is expected to do has risen, the time available for debate and investigation has barely increased at all.

Parliament's timetable has often been criticized as inefficient, with sessions starting in the afternoon and often continuing late into the night. The original intention of this schedule was to allow MPs to hold other jobs in the morning, particularly barristers who could attend court before coming to the Commons after lunch. It still serves that purpose today, although there is growing controversy about whether MPs should be allowed part-time jobs. With salaries of £31,000 some argue that there is no need for second jobs and MPs should devote all of their time to their parliamentary and constituency business. On the other hand, defenders of the practice argue that it broadens their perspective and better equips them for their parliamentary duties.

The unsociable hours of parliamentary business are also believed to discriminate against female members of the house and are likely to discourage more women from coming forward as parliamentary candidates. All-night and late-night sittings, in particular, may be difficult for women MPs who often shoulder the responsibilities of family life alongside their parliamentary duties.

Parliamentary reform in 1980 introduced a 9 a.m. start for Friday sittings to allow MPs more time to travel home to their constituencies for weekend surgeries.

A series of reforms have been passed in the 1980s aimed at preventing government

Workload

Outside interests

Women

Opposition days

Pressure on MPs

'The pressure on Members of Parliament has increased dramatically in recent years, and it continues to increase. There is legislation to scrutinize, Select and Standing Committees to take part in and a flood of European Community directives to take note of and to follow through. At the last count, about two years ago, I found that I had dealt with about 6,000 individual constituency cases in a year. I hold five surgeries a month, each lasting for five or six hours. The flow of correspondence from constituents gets greater and greater every year.'

Source: Chris Smith in a House of Commons debate on allowances, 1992

business completely dominating parliamentary time. In 1983 it was agreed that three days would be set aside as estimates days to allow discussion of specific items of expenditure. Furthermore, 20 Opposition days have been set aside since 1985 to allow the leader of the Opposition and leader of the third largest party to choose the topics for debate.

Jopling Report

More recently, the Jopling Report on Parliamentary procedure, published in 1992, recommended that more time should be set aside to debate private members' bills. As a result, in January 1995 the House of Commons' procedure was changed to allow Wednesday mornings to be set aside for private members' bills.

A traditional strength of the House of Lords has been the amount of time it has at its disposal compared to the Commons. This perhaps results in a relatively high level of debate, particularly when the quality and experience of many of the peers is considered, and allows the Lords to introduce a great deal of non-controversial legislation, so saving the Commons time.

Possible reforms

- Reduction of the workload of the Commons by devolving more power to Scottish, Welsh and Northern Irish parliaments
- Greater use of morning sittings and a fixed time of adjournment to prevent anti-social hours
- MPs could be prevented from taking other employment, thus creating full-time, career politicians

Information and facilities

Any deliberative chamber is only as good as the information available to it and there is concern in Britain that Parliament is starved of information. The government has the backing of over 500,000 civil servants who draft bills, brief ministers and prepare them for parliamentary scrutiny.

Staff

Parliament, on the other hand, has very limited facilities. In 1988 MPs employed 1,344 members of staff – equivalent to 2.1 each – and many engaged unpaid researchers. Since 1991 and the opening of new offices, most MPs have an office of their own. In addition, MPs make use of the Commons library as a research facility.

The lack of facilities available to British MPs contrasts greatly to those available to members of the American House of Representatives, each of whom represent approximately 450,000 constituents. On average, a member of the House of Representatives has 25 staff, access to the Library of Congress and to the Congressional Budget Office which prepares information on financial matters.

Possible reforms

- Civil service back-up for the Opposition
- A Freedom of Information Act to improve the availability of information to MPs, the media and the public
- More staff for MPs

Committees

In order to save time and to improve the flow of information, assemblies throughout the world set up committee systems. Parliament has two main types of committee:

- standing
- select.

The role played by the former in the legislative process has been outlined above.

The House of Commons has had a select committee system for some time, including the Public Accounts Committee. The committees are made up of personnel selected from the house and their main purpose is to scrutinize the work of government.

In 1978 the system of select committees was reviewed and the need for a new system was made clear by the Procedure Committee's report:

'The House should no longer rest content with an incomplete and unsystematic scrutiny of the activities of the Executive merely as a result of historical accident or sporadic pressures, and it is equally desirable for the different branches of the public service to be subject to

Standing committees

Select committees

Select committees

'A quiet revolution has transformed Parliament. Its real work is no longer done on the floor of the House of Commons, where debate, save for set-piece occasions such as the budget, is confined to ritual partisan abuse. The action has moved upstairs, to the all-party select committees, where MPs now focus their efforts to hold the executive to account...

... the new generation of select committees, introduced in 1979 by Norman St John Stevas, then leader of the Commons, took time to make an impact. Allowing television into the committees' hearings has helped. An MP can make his name by skilfully quizzing a minister before the cameras. This explains why committees have a 70 per cent attendance rate, though attendance in the Commons chamber often drops below a miserable 5 per cent... According to a MORI poll of MPs, 88 per cent rate the committees effective. Only 45 per cent think that questioning ministers in the Commons itself works.

In 1992–3, the departmental select committees published 74 reports. One, from the Trade and Industry Committee, forced the government to modify its pit-closure programme. Another, from the Treasury Committee, exposed the Bank of England's mishandling of BCCI. And yet another, from the National Heritage Committee, lambasted the high price of compact discs.

The committees could do still better ... The committees need more resources. Their outside advisers – crucial to their authority – work for peanuts, and they commission little original research. Their reports should be regularly debated on the floor of the Commons. Then ministers who lost their arguments in front of select committees would be forced to justify publicly their all-too-frequent decisions to take their revenge by turning down the committees' recommendations.'

Source: *The Economist*, 12–18 March 1994

an even and regular incidence of select committee investigation into their activities and to have a clear understanding of the division of responsibilities between the committees which conduct it.'

In 1979 Margaret Thatcher's government set up a new select committee system. Each committee is responsible for scrutinizing the work of a government department, but has the remit to stray beyond departmental boundaries in pursuit of an issue. Each is made up of eleven backbenchers with the balance between the parties reflecting the distribution of seats in the Commons. In 1992 the Conservatives had a majority of one on each committee.

The role of chairing the committees is divided between the two parties, depending on their relative strengths. Traditionally, the Public Accounts Committee is chaired by a member of the Opposition.

Composition

Members of the committees are chosen by the Committee of Selection. Traditionally, the selections are made without any intervention from the party whips. However, in 1992 there was controversy over the omission of Nicholas Winterton from the chair of the Health Committee. He had held positions on the Social Services and Health Committees since 1979 and there was some suspicion that he had not been reappointed because of his failure to toe the party line.

Many members of the government feared that select committees would swing the balance of power from the government to the Commons. With this in mind, their powers were curtailed: they are unable to force ministers to come before them; there is no obligation to find the time to debate committee reports on the floor of the house; and there is no time limit within which departments must respond to reports.

Suggested reforms
- Select committees could be given the power to force ministers to attend
- An end to government majorities on select committees
- Time could be set aside to debate select committee reports on the floor of the house
- The functions of select and **standing committees** could be combined and carried out by permanent committees on each issue area. This would increase the expertise of committee members

Summary of factors affecting performance
- Structure of government
- Party discipline
- Time
- Information
- Committees
- Financial powers

... And as for Parliament, parties and government ...

'The whips, the party policemen who press members to vote for the government have a long history and MPs exchange horror stories of rough treatment by former chief whips. They hold the keys to promotion and favours, ranging from free trips to knighthoods or jobs in the government. And as fewer members have independent means or jobs, still fewer can resist the lures of office. The Tory whips became much dreaded and effective under Thatcher; they could compel MPs with their three-line whips to stay up at night, to prevent the opposition laying an ambush to deprive the government of a majority.

When Major took over, Members of Parliament hoped for a freer regime, but the whips are even tougher under their chief, Richard Ryder, Major's close ally; and when they lost patience with the rebel MP, Nicholas Winterton, they sacked him from his chairmanship of the Select Committee on Health – a new degree of vengeance. The whips faced a greater challenge from the 63 new Tory MPs elected in 1992 who were cockier and less respectful than earlier intakes; many of them were "Thatcher's children" with a strong dislike of Europe.

But they were also even more ambitious to join the government; and the whips' real secret is that their side of Parliament, after thirteen continuous years, has become an annexe or waiting room to the government and once in office Parliament looks much less important. "It wasn't until I joined the government," said one just-retired minister, "that I realized just how irrelevant Parliament was."'

Source: Adapted from Anthony Sampson, *The Essential Anatomy of Britain*, Coronet, 1993

Exercises

Short questions

1 Distinguish between the role of an MP and a member of the House of Lords. (ULEAC, January 1993)
2 a What is the role of Her Majesty's Opposition?
  b How effectively is it carried out? (ULEAC, January 1991)
3 Distinguish between the power and authority of (a) the House of Commons (b) the House of Lords. (ULEAC, June 1991)

Essay questions

1 Read the extract, 'And as for Parliament, parties and government'. To what extent do parties make unreasonable demands on their MPs? How far and in what ways can the claim that Parliament is 'irrelevant' be justified? (AEB, June 1994)
2 In what ways could government be made more accountable to Parliament? (ULEAC, June 1991)
3 Is there any realistic sense in which Parliament controls the Government? (ULEAC, January 1993)
4 How much power and influence do backbenchers have in Parliament? (Cambridge, June 1994)
5 'Reform of the House of Commons is not urgent; reform of the House of Lords is.' Discuss. (Oxford and Cambridge, June 1992)

6 Evaluate the importance of the whips in the Parliamentary process. (Cambridge, June 1993)

7 'The government controls Parliament but cannot always rely on getting its way, though it is virtually impossible in normal circumstances to bring the government down and, in practice, very difficult to engineer any defeat in the House of Commons.' – Adapted from Coxall and Robins, *Contemporary British Politics*, Macmillan.
To what extent and in what circumstances may the wishes of the government be thwarted by Parliament? How far could the claim be justified that MPs of all parties have become more assertive and less disciplined in recent years? (AEB, June 1992)

8 Recent political debate has revealed considerable support for proportional representation, referenda and the replacement of the House of Lords by an elected second chamber. Consider the likely impact of such changes on the House of Commons. If Parliament were no longer dominated by a party majority, what roles might it usefully fulfil? (AEB, June 1993)

Data response question

'The evidence for arguing that by the mid-twentieth century Parliament has become little more than a rubber stamp for whichever of the two major parties was in power is compelling ... In some respects this paints too stark a picture ... Nevertheless, backbench MPs were not particularly well equipped to keep a check on the government.

There can be no doubt that significant changes have taken place in the role of the House of Commons. That role has changed dramatically – the British parliamentary system remains executive-dominated, but it has changed nonetheless. Parliament in general and the Commons in particular is more assertive, more critical, more demanding and significantly less subservient.'

Source: M Rush, 'Recent Parliamentary Developments', *Developments in Politics*, Vol. 2, 1991

1 What is the case for and the case against the view that 'by the mid-twentieth century Parliament had become little more than a rubber stamp'?
2 According to the author, how has the role of Parliament changed?
3 To what extent are MPs now 'well equipped to keep a check on the government'?

(ULEAC, January 1994)

6 The prime minister and the cabinet

Questions to be answered in this chapter

- What is the traditional and constitutional role of the cabinet? Where do concepts such as collective and individual ministerial responsibility fit into the system?

- To what extent is a prime minister able to dominate the cabinet and how far are these factors under the prime minister's control?

Terms to know

Agreement to differ	Patronage
Bilateral meetings	Policy Unit
'Bottom-up'	Politicization
Cabinet committees	Presidential government
Cabinet government	Press Office
Coalition government	Prime ministerial government
Collective ministerial responsibility	*Primus inter pares*
Efficiency Unit	Reshuffle
'Kitchen cabinet'	Thatcherite
Minority government	'Top-down'
Party discipline	'Wets'

Cabinet government

Composition

The cabinet is the committee that heads the executive branch of British government. It has around 18 to 26 members, drawn from either house of the legislature. In cases where the governing party has an overall majority in the House of Commons, the members of the cabinet are all likely to come from the majority party. In the case of a **coalition government**, members would be drawn from two or more parties – this is currently the case in Italy and Germany.

Most cabinet ministers head a department of state, for example, the Department of Trade and Industry or the Department for Education. Traditionally, the senior ministers in the cabinet, other than the prime minister, are the chancellor of the exchequer, the foreign secretary and the home secretary. Beneath them, most cabinet ministers have a number of junior ministers who have specific responsibilities within the department, but do not have cabinet rank. The exception is the first secretary to the Treasury who usually has a seat in cabinet.

The cabinet provides the collective leadership of the executive branch of government. As such it oversees the work of government, planning legislative proposals for Parliament, co-ordinating the work of government departments and confirming government policy.

Collective decisions

Decision making within cabinet should be collective, rather like the board of a company. This means that all members of the cabinet have a right to be present when decisions are made and have the right to make their views known at that time, but the view of the majority on the committee prevails.

Collective ministerial responsibility

The concept of collective decision making is supported by the idea of collective cabinet responsibility or **collective ministerial responsibility**. According to the convention of collective ministerial responsibility, decisions should be made collectively and once a decision has been made, all ministers must publicly support the decision. If they cannot back the decision, they should resign. The doctrine is intended to ensure that the cabinet stands or falls together. All members are responsible for government policy and so they should all unite behind it.

Agreement to differ

However, collective ministerial responsibility is a constitutional convention and how vigorously it is applied depends on the attitudes of the prime minister and cabinet colleagues. In 1975 Harold Wilson found his Labour cabinet divided over membership of the European Economic Community (EEC; now European Union). Afraid that he would not be able to enforce collective cabinet responsibility without mass resignations, Harold Wilson decided to allow the people to decide via a referendum. He then permitted his cabinet to adopt an **agreement to differ** which allowed ministers to speak either for or against EEC membership during the referendum campaign.

John Major

More recently, John Major's Conservative government has been divided, also over Europe. Government policy stated that Britain might decide to return to the European Monetary System (EMS) with a single European currency if the circumstances were right. In a speech in 1994 secretary to the Treasury Michael Portillo interpreted this policy to mean that Britain would never return to the EMS and would never subscribe to a single European currency. As a result, observers looked to John Major to reinforce cabinet responsibility.

Time

The doctrine of collective responsibility has also come under some pressure as the nature of cabinet's work has begun to change. As the workload of government has grown, it has become impossible for every decision to be discussed in full cabinet. Traditionally, cabinet met twice a week, on Tuesdays and Thursdays, for approximately three hours. A committee of around 25 ministers could not cover all of the work on every issue in such a short time. The pressure on cabinet became even greater during Margaret Thatcher's term of office, as cabinet meetings were reduced to only once a week.

Cabinet committees

As a result of this workload, an elaborate system of **cabinet committees** has developed. These committees examine particular issues in depth, allow discussion between the ministers most closely concerned and then make the final decisions. Cabinet committee decisions carry the weight of full cabinet decisions and need only be referred to the full cabinet if there is disagreement on the committee.

The cabinet committee system has been a closely guarded secret for much of the post-war period. This was an attempt to preserve collective cabinet responsibility across the cabinet system by giving the impression that decisions were being made by the government as a whole. However, since 1992 John Major has pledged to make more details of the committee system open to the public.

Cabinet committees

Before 1992 the system of cabinet committees had been a moderately well-guarded secret, but after the general election, John Major decided to make the system public.

Cabinet committees fall into three categories:
- *Standing committees* are permanent during the prime minister's term of office. They have specific terms of reference. Key committees include Northern Ireland, Economic and Domestic Policy and Intelligence Service.
- *Ad hoc committees* are set up when needed by the prime minister who has the power to shape their terms of reference. Perhaps the most well known is the 'Star Chamber' or MISC62, which determines the allocation of funds to spending departments.
- *Ministerial committees* are made up of civil servants only. They help to co-ordinate the work of government departments.

The prime minister

The head of the cabinet is the prime minister. As such they are the dominant figure, chairing meetings, summing up discussions and often acting as the chief government representative. However, they are only one member of the committee and so can be outvoted by their colleagues. This position has been variously described. For example, the constitutional lawyer Sir Ivor Jennings (1903–65) termed the prime minister as 'the sun around which the planets revolve', but perhaps best known is Walter Bagehot's phrase *primus inter pares* or 'first among equals'. To this day, his description probably sums up the prime minister's special position most accurately.

Primus inter pares

The prime minister is only one member of Her Majesty's Government, but as the leader of the government has a very special position. The functions of the prime minister include providing leadership for the government and, indeed, for the country as a whole; appointing, and dismissing, members of the government; organizing government and requesting a dissolution of Parliament from the monarch.

Prime ministerial government

Richard Crossman

In 1964 the Labour Minister of Housing Richard Crossman wrote that British government had moved away from **cabinet government** towards **prime ministerial government** or even **presidential government**. By this he meant that decision making at the top of the executive branch of government was becoming increasingly dominated by one person – the prime minister.

Richard Crossman was describing prime ministerial government at the time of Harold Wilson's first Labour government (1964–6) and the idea gained a new lease of life during Margaret Thatcher's eleven years of office. However, the concept of dominant prime ministers was not a new one, even in the 1960s. David Lloyd George, Neville Chamberlain and Winston Churchill were all considered dominant prime ministers.

Presidential government

While there is perhaps some merit in describing the British government as prime ministerial government, we must be much more careful about using terms like 'presidential' because they bring with them a whole new set of specific constitutional rules and relationships.

The president

A presidential system of government usually involves a chief executive being elected separately from the legislature, directly by the people. This is the case in the USA where the president is elected every four years, the House of Representatives every two years and the Senate every six years (33 per cent of members every two years). The president is not allowed to be a member of the legislature while holding a position in the executive. He is not allowed to introduce bills into Congress, he cannot take part in Congressional debate and he cannot be removed by Congress, unless he is to be impeached – for which he must be formally charged.

British government is not presidential; it is parliamentary. The House of Commons is elected by the people and its composition determines the government. The prime minister is usually the leader of the largest party in the House of Commons and normally remains in office only as long as they are leader of the party. Cabinet ministers are also chosen from Parliament. Government ministers introduce bills to the floor of either the House of Lords or Commons; they take part in parliamentary debate; and they answer questions on the floor. Furthermore, the House of Commons has the power to bring down the government which it has done on many occasions through a vote of no confidence.

The British prime minister does not have the constitutional independence of an American president. This was clearly illustrated by the fall of Margaret Thatcher in 1990. Few post-war prime ministers have been so closely associated with the 'prime ministerial/presidential thesis' of British government. Many commentators saw her as the 'Iron Lady' subjecting the cabinet to her will. However, it was this same cabinet that finally convinced her that she should resign. Without the support of the cabinet, her party and, therefore, of the House of Commons Margaret Thatcher had little choice but to go.

However, the idea of presidential government in Britain should not be dismissed completely – prime ministers have given the *impression* of being presidential. The media focus on the prime minister and now, for their part, prime ministers employ image-makers and advertising agents to ensure that the public gaze remains on them. But it is more than merely image. Some prime ministers have gathered about them a great deal of political power. In many cases such a concentration of power would be the envy of an American president.

Richard Crossman's arguments

Efficient and dignified

Walter Bagehot's interpretation of the British political system, *The English Constitution* was written in 1867. Since then, it has become a classic text on the constitution and indeed has become part of Britain's unwritten constitution. In it, Bagehot distinguished between efficient and dignified parts of the constitution, i.e. those parts that are working elements of the constitution and those that play a largely ceremonial role in British politics. At the time, the cabinet was considered to be an efficient part of the constitution; since then some might argue, it has been relegated to dignified status.

Richard Crossman was asked to write a new introduction to *The English Constitution* in 1964 and used the opportunity to argue that Bagehot's analysis had been superseded by events almost immediately after its publication. In the spirit of Bagehot's original analysis, Richard Crossman offered a new analysis of British government, centring on the role of the prime minister.

His analysis of the growth of the power of the prime minister rests on three points:
● the power of political parties
● the development of a unified civil service
● the growth of the prime minister's private office and the cabinet secretariat.
Richard Crossman's ideas still offer a comprehensive framework in which to assess the power of a prime minister and the first part of this chapter concentrates on his arguments.

The power of political parties

Until the latter half of the nineteenth century, British political parties were little more than clubs for MPs. Bagehot stated: 'At present the member is free because the constituency is not in earnest; no constituency has an acute, accurate doctrinal creed in politics.' As we have seen in Chapter 5, this began to change as the electoral franchise was widened and organized political parties developed.

This trend moved a stage further with the development of the Labour Party. This new party of the working class was intended to break the middle class stranglehold on the House of Commons. It did so by being well funded and highly disciplined.

Today political parties have two broad roles in the political process: an electoral role and a governing role. In elections parties nominate candidates, organize their campaigns, finance their campaigns, provide manifestos and command voter loyalty. As a result, MPs know that their position in the Commons is dependent on the continued support of the party because without party backing few potential MPs secure a seat.

The parties' governing role includes provision of policy, the organization of the assembly and the allocation of government offices. In Britain provision of policy is largely the function of the party, via the election manifesto and there are few opportunities for MPs to depart from the party line. The strong electoral role of British parties is a further incentive to party cohesion in Parliament because MPs rely on party backing to retain their seat. Furthermore, if they harbour ambitions to be promoted into government or to the opposition front bench MPs would do well to vote as instructed by the party.

Party strength

This combination of strong electoral and governing roles for British political parties has strengthened the position of the prime minister. As the head of the party, the disciplinary machinery of whips is at prime ministerial command and, therefore, a prime minister with a majority in the House of Commons is unlikely to lose a vote in the house.

Patronage

Appointments

The prime minister has an additional means of control over the party in the form of **patronage**. Traditionally, the monarch held the power of patronage, i.e. the power of appointment, but this has now passed to the prime minister. Therefore, an MP's future in government depends on the prime minister. It is the prime minister who

83

has the power to appoint ministers and junior ministers. At the turn of the twentieth century, appointments would have involved around 20 ministers; today about 120 ministers are appointed. This accounts for almost one-third of government MPs and so is an extremely powerful weapon. It not only gives the prime minister a great deal of power over MPs but also over ministers.

To be appointed to government office is only part of the aim of many MPs. Once the status of junior minister has been achieved, an ambitious MP seeks promotion into the cabinet. Once in cabinet, a minister will be anxious to at least hold their position and possibly to advance in the cabinet hierarchy, with the top jobs of home secretary, chancellor of the exchequer and foreign secretary the ultimate goals. Every minister knows that hiring and firing; promoting and demoting is the responsibility of the prime minister and falling out of favour with your leader can mean the end of your career.

This power of patronage gives prime ministers, at least theoretically, the opportunity to shape the composition of the cabinet to suit their own needs. In other words, the balance of cabinet could be tilted towards their own supporters in an effort to bolster their own power.

Composition of the cabinet

Margaret Thatcher used her power of patronage to move her cabinet gradually away from the 'well-balanced' cabinet of 1979 to the more right-wing versions of later years. Her first cabinet included ministers who were from the left of the party, such as Norman St John Stevas, Lord Soames, Mark Carlisle, James Prior and Ian Gilmour. These ministers were soon to be labelled **'Wets'** – a derogatory term, coined by Thatcher supporters, to show their lack of resolve in the face of difficult policy decisions. Within two years, all four ministers had been removed from cabinet and James Prior had been moved from the Ministry of Employment to Northern Ireland. At the same time, younger, **Thatcherite** ministers, such as Cecil Parkinson, Leon Brittan and Nigel Lawson had been moved into cabinet.

However, the successful use of the power of patronage is not merely a question of numbers. It is not just the prime minister's desire to have more allies than critics. The ministerial portfolios allocated to supporters is also of vital importance. In Margaret Thatcher's 1979 cabinet 'Wets' or moderates almost out-numbered Thatcherites. In addition to those already mentioned, they included William Whitelaw, Lord Carrington and Peter Walker. However, Margaret Thatcher ensured that the key economic ministries, the Treasury and Trade and Industry, were held by her supporters – the chancellor of the exchequer was Sir Geoffrey Howe and the secretary of Trade and Industry was Keith Joseph, who many considered to be the high priest of Thatcherism.

A unified civil service

Although the British civil service has been permanent since the Northcote-Trevellyan Report of 1854, it has only been unified since 1919. Lloyd George circulated a paper in September 1919 that outlined the new powers of the Treasury. In it he stated that the permanent secretary to the Treasury would also be the head of the civil service, particularly with regard to appointments. This meant that from then on all appointments to the civil service would be made centrally rather than departmentally. In Richard Crossman's words: 'Instead of a cluster of departments, each with its own traditions, characteristics, and standards of recruitment, there has emerged a new horizontal stratification, with the heads forming a single, like-minded group of super bureaucrats.'

As a result of centralization, individual ministers have lost a great deal of control over the personnel of their department. When senior civil service appointments are due to be made in any department, the prime minister is given a short list prepared by the Senior Appointments Selection Committee. Hence, the prime minister has accumulated the power to influence the composition of staff in ministerial departments. In doing so, the prime minister can influence the advice and cooperation ministers receive.

Appointments

'Politicization'

Margaret Thatcher has often been accused of 'politicizing' the higher civil service by seeking to appoint and promote civil servants who are, in her words, 'one of us'. She certainly had the opportunity to do so because in the first six years of her premiership, there was virtually a complete turnover of permanent and deputy secretaries. However, observers have only been able to point an accusing finger at one instance of her interference leading to the promotion of one of her 'favourites'. This was Peter Middleton, who succeeded Douglas Wass as permanent secretary to the Treasury in 1983. Douglas Wass was thought to have been a believer in Keynesian economics, while Middleton was a devout monetarist.

The Cabinet Secretariat and the prime minister's staff

The Cabinet Secretariat

In 1916 Lloyd George was responsible for another major reform of the British cabinet system when he created the Cabinet Secretariat. Today this group of around 35 civil servants is responsible for servicing the system of cabinet government. Headed by cabinet secretary Robin Butler (in 1995), the Cabinet Office plans cabinet business in advance, draws up the agendas for full cabinet and cabinet committees, writes and circulates the minutes of these meetings and co-ordinates and supervises the implementation of decisions made in cabinet and its committees.

A number of ministers, including Richard Crossman and Barbara Castle, have drawn attention to the dangers of a close relationship between the cabinet secretary and the prime minister. The ability to control the agendas of meetings and to influence the writing of the minutes would give a prime minister considerable power over cabinet decision making. Both Richard Crossman and Barbara Castle suspected that cabinet minutes were written in consultation with the prime minister, Harold Wilson, although he subsequently denied these accusations.

Ministers

Margaret Thatcher was also subject to accusations of politicizing the Cabinet Secretariat. In this case it was her relationship with the cabinet secretary that was a cause for concern, not only because of the control over cabinet agenda and minutes but also because the cabinet secretary is also head of the home civil service which might give the prime minister added leverage over civil service appointments.

While there is no evidence of Margaret Thatcher, or any other prime minister, influencing the recording of cabinet minutes, it is known that she fought hard to keep issues not to her liking off the political agenda. In the first two years of her premiership many ministers complained of the lack of cabinet discussion regarding the state of the economy. During a period of severe economic recession Margaret Thatcher successfully kept questions of economic strategy within the economic affairs committee rather than in the full cabinet where her support was weaker.

Agenda

Robert Armstrong

Politicization

The cabinet secretary for much of Margaret Thatcher's term of office was Robert Armstrong, a career civil servant, devoted to the traditional civil service characteristics of permanence and neutrality. However, in 1987 David Owen, leader of the Social Democratic Party, described Armstrong as 'damaged goods' and the Liberal leader David Steel stated that 'his credibility is at a very low ebb . . . [he has] become a civil servant who's very much seen as a supporter of the government'. Both leaders were referring to a series of controversial incidents in which Robert Armstrong had appeared not as an anonymous, faceless bureaucrat but as a very public agent of government policy. The incidents included the Ponting case (1985), Westland (1985) and GCHQ (1984) (for a full discussion of these, see chapter 7).

Spycatcher

The Spycatcher case (1986) in particular severely damaged Robert Armstrong's standing in British politics. He was despatched to Australia to defend, in court, the government's decision not to allow former MI5 employee, Peter Wright, to publish his memoirs in Britain. Under cross-examination by an Australian lawyer Robert Armstrong seemed badly prepared and his credibility was severely undermined when, at one stage of the trial, he was forced to change earlier testimony, admitting that he had been 'economical with the truth'.

The result of this was that Margaret Thatcher had appeared to hijack the Cabinet Office by politicizing the cabinet secretary. In fact, Armstrong was not a Thatcherite but did feel that he should work for his government to the best of his ability. As the historian Peter Hennessy (*Whitehall*, Secker & Warburg, 1989) said: 'in so far as he ever let his own political views slip to his friends they were old-fashioned "one nation" Conservative . . . His friends were in doubt that in Mrs Thatcher's terms, he was not "one of us".'

Robin Butler

Perhaps the choice of Robert Armstrong's successor reaffirms that the appointment to the top job was not politicized. On Armstrong's retirement in 1987 Margaret Thatcher appointed Robin Butler, a traditional civil servant, as his replacement and his appointment was widely welcomed without any fear of **politicization**. As Peter Hennessy said: 'Butler, like Armstrong, could have been picked as head of his profession at any time since 1870.'

The historian Anthony Seldon has argued that John Major has been reluctant to manipulate the cabinet agenda and that he is happy for controversial issues to come before cabinet in order to allow discussion and, hopefully, to carry the full cabinet with him. Anthony Seldon has quoted a series of (unattributed) views of John Major's premiership from his colleagues: 'No one would stand up to Mrs Thatcher in cabinet: now it is very different.' 'I can recall few, if any, times when John Major has been beaten in cabinet: the reason for that is that he carries colleagues with him; when he sums up, he does so making people feel they have been consulted.'

The prime minister's staff

A traditional weakness of the prime minister is the lack of civil service support. This remains the case in so far as the prime minister does not have a civil service department capable of implementing policy and for this he must rely on his ministers. However, prime ministers have gradually built up a staff based at 10 Downing Street. This consists of a number of different units, including the **Press Office**, the **Policy Unit**, the **Efficiency Unit** and special advisers.

The Press Office

The Press Office was set up in 1931 to help the prime minister deal with the press. This remains its main brief. Throughout Margaret Thatcher's premiership press secretary Bernard Ingham gained considerable notoriety through his briefings of the press lobby. The lobby system allows the press secretary to brief the lobby correspondents on a daily basis about government policy and the reaction from 10 Downing Street to events. This is done in an 'off-the-record' format which results in media comments being prefaced with phrases such as 'a source close to the prime minister said . . . ' or 'the view from Number 10 is . . .'.

Bernard Ingham was often accused of using the briefing sessions to undermine ministers within the cabinet. News of the prime minister's displeasure with a particular minister would be leaked, either to prepare the media for the minister's dismissal or to encourage the minister to toe the line. In 1985 John Biffen's imminent departure from the cabinet was touted in advance when Bernard Ingham referred to him as 'a semi-detached member of the government'.

John Major chose Gus O'Donnell, a career civil servant from the Treasury, to take over from Bernard Ingham. His approach was much less strident, but his influence was nonetheless significant. However, he was not used to undermine cabinet colleagues and, indeed, bitter rivalries that characterized many of the Margaret Thatcher years have not been apparent in Major's premiership. In 1994 Gus O'Donnell was replaced by Chris Meyer, a former diplomat (he was deputy ambassador in Washington), after some criticism of the administration's presentation skills.

Special advisers

Margaret Thatcher's special advisers also created some cause for concern in the 1980s. Prime ministers appoint individuals on a full- or part-time basis who will provide specialist advice on areas of policy such as foreign affairs and the economy. Margaret Thatcher's appointments included Anthony Parsons, a former British ambassador to the United Nations who acted as her adviser on foreign policy, and Alan Walters, who was a part-time adviser on the economy until 1989.

Conflict between Alan Walters and the chancellor of the exchequer Nigel Lawson led to the latter's resignation in 1989. The issue at the centre of the conflict was membership of the European Exchange Rate Mechanism (ERM). Nigel Lawson favoured membership while Alan Walters was opposed. The chancellor believed that Alan Walter's advice was causing a rift between the prime minister and himself and was also preventing the prime minster fully accepting government policy of membership of the European Monetary System.

At the end of 1994 John Major appointed Howell James as his political secretary. He was ex-director of corporate and government affairs at Cable and Wireless Plc and at the BBC and also former head of press and publicity with TV-am. Given his background in media and public relations Howell James was widely seen as John Major's 'spin doctor', responsible for manipulating media coverage in favour of the prime minister.

Lobby system

Bernard Ingham

John Major

Alan Walters

John Major

The Efficiency Unit

Margaret Thatcher established the Efficiency Unit in 1979 to monitor the use of resources in the civil service. Initially, it was headed by Sir Derek Raynor, managing director of Marks and Spencer. He was succeeded by Sir Robin Ibbs, an executive director of ICI. Derek Raynor made a number of suggestions to save money in the administration, but it was Robin Ibbs who made the most far-reaching suggestions for civil service reform. He proposed that a core of ministerial advisers remain in Whitehall while executive agencies be set up to administer many government functions (see page 111). These reforms continued under John Major's head of the Efficiency Unit, John Oughton.

The Policy Unit

In 1970 Edward Heath set up the Central Policy Review Staff, or 'Think Tank', which was designed to look at government policy in a wider context and to consider alternative options. It was eventually disbanded by Margaret Thatcher in 1983 and its role was absorbed by the Policy Unit which had been set up by Harold Wilson in 1974. The unit is generally made up of staff from outside the civil service who have no pretensions to neutrality.

Sarah Hogg

Usually made up of six to eight people, the Policy Unit is much smaller than anything the White House has to offer, but nevertheless can be extremely influential. Previous heads of the unit have included John Redwood (1983–5), Professor Brian Griffiths (1985–90) and Sarah Hogg (1990–5), who was believed to be so influential that she was sometimes referred to as 'the real deputy prime minister'. Under Sarah Hogg's leadership, the Policy Unit played an important role in a number of areas, including the strategies for non-inflationary growth; an approach to the Maastricht Treaty; an alternative source of local government revenue to replace the poll tax; and many of the ideas behind the 1992 election victory.

Sarah Hogg was succeeded in February 1995 by Norman Blackwell, a senior partner of the management consultants, McKinsey & Company. He was considered by some to be the 'policy fanatic' that John Major needs to sift the good ideas from the bad.

To many observers the development of the prime minister's office at 10 Downing Street has appeared to mark the beginnings of a fledgling prime minister's department. Some, such as Sir Keith Berrill, an ex-head of the Central Policy Review Staff, have argued that such a department would be of great benefit to central government because it would give prime ministers the support they need to speak on behalf of the government on a wide range of issues. The alternative point of view is that it would be a major step towards prime ministerial government. It would strengthen prime ministers to such an extent that they would become more detached from cabinet and be encouraged to make policy in isolation from their colleagues.

Crossman's conclusions

According to Richard Crossman, prime ministers have succeeded in building up a great deal of power in their own hands, at the expense of cabinet government. However, it is also possible to identify other aspects of the changing role of cabinet that have also indirectly strengthened the position of the prime minister.

Crossman's points
- Strong party
- Unified civil service
- Prime minister's staff

The decline of cabinet decision making

We have already seen that since 1945 a considerable amount of cabinet decision making has been diverted towards cabinet committees. This has been largely due to the excessive workload of cabinet. However, while they might be unavoidable, cabinet committees do take power *away* from the full cabinet. As a result, cabinet often does not make key decisions, but merely puts its seal of approval on them.

Cabinet committees

The growth of cabinet committees can also indirectly enhance the power of the prime minister. Prime ministers set up the committee system, appoint the chair of each committee and, indeed, chair the most significant committees themselves. Margaret Thatcher, for example, headed the standing committees covering economic strategy, export policy, public sector strategy, foreign affairs and defence, and the steering committee on the intelligence services.

Since these committees are usually made up of the ministers most directly concerned with the issue, careful allocation of ministerial portfolios can strengthen the prime minister's control over government policy. We have already mentioned that Margaret Thatcher's cabinet in 1979 contained a large number of critics of Thatcherite economic policies. However, Geoffrey Howe and Keith Joseph held the key economic ministries of the Treasury and Trade and Industry. As a result, Thatcherites dominated the cabinet committee concerning economic strategy.

Composition

In fact, Margaret Thatcher did not favour cabinet committees as a method of decision making and she created relatively few of them. Between 1979 and 1987 she set up less than 35 standing committees and 120 ad hoc committees. This compares to Clement Attlee's creation of 148 standing committees and 313 ad hoc committees in just over six years from 1945.

Numbers

Bilateral meetings

Margaret Thatcher's favoured method of doing business was the bilateral meeting with ministers. As issues arose and policy needed to be made, individual ministers, with their advisers, would be invited to 10 Downing Street to make a presentation to the prime minister. If policy ideas did not pass the prime minister's scrutiny, they could not be presented to cabinet. The use of such **bilateral meetings** is another step further away from cabinet government because they are ad hoc and, in constitutional terms, informal for they do not fall under the constitutional arrangements of full cabinet or cabinet committees.

Margaret Thatcher's personal involvement in policy making, such as in bilateral meetings, increased fears about prime ministerial government. These concerns remained undiminished given other elements of her style, for example, her reliance on the Policy Unit, rather than ministers, for initiatives and her tendency to make

89

policy without any consultation with ministers, perhaps on television or during party conference speeches.

'Kitchen cabinets'

Margaret Thatcher

In addition, in later years, Margaret Thatcher relied on a **'kitchen cabinet'** of close advisers, including Charles Powell on foreign policy and Bernard Ingham, her press secretary. Prior to 1987 her range of advisers had been rather wider and included Robert Armstrong (cabinet secretary), William Whitelaw (deputy prime minister), Robin Ibbs (head of the Central Policy Review Staff) and Clive Whitemore (principal private secretary). William Whitelaw, in particular, was instrumental in keeping the prime minister in touch with the feelings of cabinet colleagues and the party as a whole. During the final years of her premiership, she appeared more isolated from colleagues.

John Major

John Major moved away from the use of bilateral meetings back to cabinet committees. In 1993 Lord Wakeham, the Lord Privy Seal, gave his opinion: 'The move towards the use of ad hoc groups appears to have been halted . . . my impression is that the balance has shifted back towards greater reliance on the standing committees'.

It has been reported that John Major relied on an inner cabinet made up of his close colleagues. Kenneth Clarke (chancellor of the exchequer), Douglas Hurd (foreign secretary), Michael Heseltine (president of the Board of Trade), Michael Howard (home secretary), Malcolm Rifkind (defence secretary) and Tony Newton (leader of the House of Commons) have all been part of this grouping of senior colleagues.

The prime minister's personality

Herbert Asquith said: 'The office of prime minister is what the holder chooses and is able to make it.' His remark, much quoted in examination questions, suggests that a great deal, if not all, of a prime minister's power depends on the office holder's personality. After comparing aspects of the premierships of Margaret Thatcher and John Major, it would be all too easy to agree.

Margaret Thatcher

It is well known that Margaret Thatcher was considered a 'conviction politician' who did not suffer fools gladly and opponents hardly at all. Margaret Thatcher's forcefulness also reflected the fact that she came to power with an agenda for change. Her 'conviction' was not based on power for its own sake but rather she felt she had a mission to change Britain's economy, its industrial relations and its patterns of ownership, and she was unwilling to let others stand in her way. Francis Pym, a member of her cabinet, once said: 'The point about Mrs Thatcher is that she was against any suggestion of compromise; which meant that she had a very confrontational style, that was the automatic consequence of it and the idea that someone else might have a valid point of view, which might be a right point of view, wouldn't enter her mind at all.'

Margaret Thatcher was thought to enjoy argument, but Hugo Young quotes two senior Conservative politicians in his biography of her: 'Arguing with her is an extremely unsatisfactory experience . . . She doesn't have discussions, she states opinions.' 'These battles are totally exhausting. They can't be good for government. They're quite unnecessary expenditure of energy. They almost never result in any clarification, mainly because of her habit of going off at a wild tangent and worrying away for half an hour at a minor detail' (Hugo Young, *One of us*, Macmillan, 1989).

John Major has often been described as a consensus politician. Anthony Seldon (Kavanagh and Seldon (eds), *The Major Effect*, Macmillan, 1994) quotes a senior cabinet member: 'John Major's great ability is to get consensus, a position everyone is happy to accept.' According to anecdotal evidence such as this, John Major's approach is more collective and far less dictatorial, but until cabinet papers are released in about 30 years time, this will be difficult to prove.

The atmosphere in cabinet apparently changed following Margaret Thatcher's departure. Anthony Seldon once again quotes a cabinet minister: 'The big difference before and after 1990 is that now if people feel they have something to say, they say it.' In Margaret Thatcher's time ministers were not always encouraged to speak and those who were overly tenacious often received withering rebukes. Former minister Jim Prior has recorded that in 1983 Michael Heseltine's continued opposition to the abolition of the Greater London Council 'led Margaret to deliver him one of the most violent rebukes I have witnessed in cabinet' (James Prior, *A Balance of Power*, London, 1986).

However, it is not only a prime minister's temper and willingness to suffer opposition that is a determinant of their power. One of Margaret Thatcher's legendary attributes was her ability to work harder and to survive on less sleep than any of her ministers. When her phenomenal work rate was combined with her insatiable desire to interfere in all elements of policy, the mixture was potent. Having had only four hours of sleep, she would arrive regularly at meetings better prepared than the minister concerned.

Having briefly compared the personalities and leadership styles of Margaret Thatcher and John Major, it is tempting to conclude that Margaret Thatcher was the more powerful due to her forceful personality. It is probably true that she made greater use of the tools of the prime minister's office in an effort to increase her power and to push through her policies. However, it is important not to confuse consensus politics with weakness. John Major certainly has a different leadership style to Margaret Thatcher, but it is open to debate whether he is a weaker prime minister because of it.

Margaret Thatcher was more dictatorial than John Major, but nevertheless she was defeated on some key issues. John Major's leadership style might lead to his building a better record than his predecessor.

Internal constraints on the prime minister

Whatever the prime minister's personality, there are a number of points about the relationship between the prime minister and the cabinet that need to be considered.

The cabinet agenda

We have seen that a prime minister can attempt to keep certain issues off the cabinet agenda in order to avoid difficult discussions. In some cases, they can be very successful in doing so, particularly if it is not an ongoing issue, for example, Margaret Thatcher made decisions regarding the Americans' use of British air bases from

John Major

which to attack Libya. But if the issue is likely to recur, for example, the economy, sooner or later it has to be discussed by the cabinet.

How long an issue may be left off a cabinet agenda depends partly on the personalities of cabinet ministers. It is possible to argue that had the moderates been more forceful in their objections to Margaret Thatcher's handling of the economy, they would have been able to curb her power.

Primus inter pares

On occasions the prime minister will be defeated in cabinet. As *primus inter pares* the prime minister, unlike the American president, is not able to overrule the cabinet. In 1969 Harold Wilson was isolated in cabinet over trade union reform and in 1986 Margaret Thatcher was defeated in cabinet over the proposed sale of Landrover to General Motors. Also, ultimately, it was Margaret Thatcher's cabinet colleagues who persuaded her that to stand in the second ballot of the 1990 leadership contest would mean ignominious defeat.

Civil service support

Prime ministers are not self-sufficient. They cannot persistently make policy without the support of cabinet colleagues, not least because they do not have the time to master and control every issue and furthermore, cannot implement policy without the backing of ministerial departments.

External constraints on the prime minister

The relationship between the prime minister and the cabinet does not take place in a vacuum. No matter what the relative merits of the cabinet or 10 Downing Street are, neither is immune from outside influence. Events beyond the control of the cabinet room will have as great an effect on the relationship as any of the internal factors.

Parliament

Majority

British government is a parliamentary system (see page 6). This, combined with the first-past-the-post electoral system (see page 18), means that a government is almost guaranteed a majority in the House of Commons. The larger the majority the stronger the government's position and with it the power of the prime minister.

Between 1983 and 1987 Margaret Thatcher's government had a parliamentary majority of almost 150 seats. This made it almost immune from all but the major backbench revolts. John Major, on the other hand, came to power with a majority of only 21. This meant that only twelve government MPs needed to vote with the Opposition in order to engineer a government defeat. Naturally, John Major had to foster his majority most carefully. This situation partly accounts for his difficulties over the Maastricht Treaty in 1994. Eventually, a backbench rebellion was only headed off when he made the vote a test of confidence. A loss would have required a government resignation.

Of course, the prime minister heading a coalition or **minority government** may be in the weakest position of all and would need to compromise either with other parties in cabinet or with parties on the floor of the house. This makes it much more difficult for the prime minister to take a strong line on any policy.

Perhaps the exception to this situation is the leader of a government of national unity. Winston Churchill led a coalition of national unity through World War II and gained considerable strength from the knowledge that the whole of Parliament was behind him.

Party

We have already seen the importance that Richard Crossman attached to the well-disciplined political party with regard to the development of prime ministerial power. However, political parties rarely follow their leader blindly and all prime ministers must nurture their party's support.

Patronage

A prime minister's concern for party support is clear from the way they allocate ministerial office. It would not be prudent to offer cabinet positions to their loyal supporters, hence fashioning a cabinet in their own image. They must consider all wings of party opinion when making their selections.

It was William Whitelaw who advised Margaret Thatcher to include the supporters of Edward Heath in her cabinet. Hence Francis Pym, James Prior, Peter Walker and Lord Carrington all held office in 1979. It was not until 1981 that moderates like Norman St John Stevas, Ian Gilmour and Mark Carlisle were removed from office and replaced by Thatcherites like Norman Tebbitt and Leon Brittan.

Balance

James Callaghan's government of 1976–9 relied on the support of its leading left-wing member, Michael Foot, in order to gain continued co-operation from the trade union movement.

Careful placement of opponents inside the cabinet can also protect a prime minister from criticism in the House of Commons. Harold Wilson included the left-wing MP Tony Benn in both his 1964–70 and 1974–6 cabinets in order to bring him under the banner of collective cabinet responsibility. In this way, Tony Benn was muzzled.

Margaret Thatcher was happy to retain a number of moderates in her cabinet on the basis of the same tactics. She has said: 'Far better to have them with you. even though they tried to slow you down, than it is to have them on the backbenches arguing against you, influencing other people against you instead of accepting the policies.'

Dissent

It is not only all wings of the party that need to be represented in cabinet. Some senior figures within the party expect to be given cabinet positions. Some cabinet positions require a certain degree of familiarity with the issues, for example, the chancellor of the exchequer, and some, like the Scottish and Welsh Offices, require MPs from particular geographical localities. So the prime minister certainly does not have a free hand and an astute one will try to keep the cabinet balanced.

The need to keep the cabinet balanced and to adjust its composition in the light of changing circumstances is clearly illustrated by the cabinet **reshuffle** forced upon Margaret Thatcher in 1989. Nigel Lawson, the chancellor of the exchequer, resigned following conflicts with the prime minister over economic policy and the role of her economics special adviser Alan Walters. This was clearly a blow to the prime minister's standing, but she moved quickly to reinforce her position. John Major, a favourite, was moved from the Foreign Office, after only a few months, to the

Treasury. His place at the Foreign Office was taken by Douglas Hurd, a senior Conservative and a 'safe pair of hands'. Douglas Hurd would probably not have been Margaret Thatcher's first choice, but given her position of weakness, his appointment settled the party's nerves and reinforced her position.

Party structure

Labour Party

A prime minister's ability to control their party does not depend only on the divisions within the party but also on the structure of the party. In the Labour Party power flows from the **'bottom-up'**, while in the Conservative Party power is distributed from the **'top-down'** (see page 44).

Constitutionally, at least, policy-making power lies with the Labour Party conference, i.e. the grassroots. This makes it much harder for the leader to forge a particular path for the party. Neil Kinnock, John Smith and Tony Blair have had, or, in Tony Blair's case, will have, to work extremely hard to persuade the party to follow their particular policy lines – although the task for a Labour leader has been noticeably easier when in government than in opposition.

Conservative Party

Power in the Conservative Party lies at the top. The ministerial personnel, the manifesto and election strategies are all determined by the leadership. Although divisions undoubtedly exist within the party, as the European issue clearly illustrated, the party has tended to unite behind its leader and has largely been content to support their chosen path. A public display of disharmony is relatively rare in the Conservative Party.

Popularity

Whilst the Conservative Party may illustrate the strength a prime minister can gain from the backing of a united party, it also shows the weakness that can overtake the leader of the same party when it is divided. Nothing divides a political party like unpopularity and the fear of electoral losses.

Margaret Thatcher's three electoral victories counted for nothing when her magic touch seemed to have deserted her in 1990. So long as the next election victory seemed assured, her colleagues were prepared to endure her dictatorial style of leadership. When she seemed doomed to lose, she was removed from office.

Similarly, John Major's power in the cabinet suffered in 1993 and early 1994 as his standing in opinion polls slumped. If an election defeat seems likely, the cabinet is much more difficult to hold together as colleagues begin to shape up for a possible leadership contest.

A leader's popularity is likely to depend on the state of the economy, the international prestige of the country or the general mood of the country, all of which are, to a greater or lesser extent, outside the control of the prime minister.

The media

The popularity of a prime minister depends, to some extent, on the media coverage they receive. As leaders, they are subject to more intense scrutiny than any other ministers and they carry the whole of government policy in a way that other ministers do not. As a result, they gain the praise or the criticism that goes with those policies. A prime minister pilloried in the media is likely to be weakened in cabinet.

Which party the prime minister represents can also affect media coverage. The press in Britain is biased in its coverage and editorials, with the *Daily Mirror, The Independent* and the *Guardian* being the only national daily newspapers not to committed to the Conservative Party. Although this does not guarantee a Conservative Party leader a good press, it might seriously disadvantage a Labour leader.

Conclusion

The debate surrounding the growth of prime ministerial power is by no means new. However, the premiership of Margaret Thatcher gave it new life. Throughout her terms of office she gave the impression of prime ministerial or even presidential government, but such an impression was misleading. Even a strong prime minister such as Margaret Thatcher is subject to constraints both inside and outside the cabinet machine.

Perhaps the most important of these constraints are those that act upon the cabinet from outside Whitehall. Parliament, party, popularity and the media all set the context of the prime minister–cabinet relationship and all are, to some extent, beyond the control of the players. Furthermore, the context is in a continuous state of flux – it changes on a daily basis. As it changes, so the fortunes of the prime minister and the cabinet also change. Sometimes the prime minister's star will rise at the expense of cabinet; sometimes all of the players will benefit. So, as with so many constitutional issues, the reality is an ever-changing shade of grey.

A summary of external factors affecting the prime minister's power
- Parliament
- Party
- Popularity
- Media

Exercises

Short questions

1 a Define the convention of collective ministerial responsibility.
   b How effective is this convention in practice? (ULEAC, January 1995)
2 Outline the relationship of the cabinet to the prime minister. (ULEAC, January 1994)
3 What is the role of the cabinet? (ULEAC, June 1993)

Essay questions

1 Discuss the relationship between the office of prime minister and Parliament. (ULEAC, June 1994)
2 How could the power of the prime minister be reduced? (ULEAC, June 1993)
3 Does Britain have prime ministerial government? (ULEAC, January 1994)
4 Compare the relationship between the prime minister and cabinet during the Thatcher and Major administrations. (Oxford, June 1994)
5 Does the fall of Mrs Thatcher indicate that prime ministerial power is not as great as some had argued? (Oxford, June 1993)

Data response question

'The post-war epoch has seen the final transformation of Cabinet Government into prime ministerial Government . . . Even in Bagehot's time it was probably a misnomer to describe the Premier as chairman and primus inter pares. *His right to select his own Cabinet and dismiss them at will; his power to decide the Cabinet's agenda and announce the decisions reached without taking a vote; his control, through the Chief Whip, over patronage – all this had already, before 1867, given him near Presidential powers. Since then his powers have been steadily increased, first by the centralization of the party machine under his personal rule and, secondly, by the growth of a centralized bureaucracy so vast that it could no longer be managed by a Cabinet behaving like the board of directors of an old-fashioned company.'*

Source: Richard Crossman, 'Introduction' to Walter Bagehot, *The English Constitution*, Collins, 1963

1 What was meant by describing the prime minister as *primus inter pares* (first among equals)?
2 Describe recent examples of what 'had already, before 1867, given him near Presidential powers'.
3 Explain how the powers of the office 'have been steadily increased' since 1867.
4 State a case against the view that 'the post-war epoch has seen the final transformation of Cabinet Government into prime ministerial Government'.

(ULEAC, January 1993)

7 The civil service

Questions to be answered in this chapter

- What are the structure, role and characteristics of the civil service?
- What is the relationship between civil servants and ministers and to what extent do civil servants have political power?
- If civil servants do have power, how do they use it?
- How have recent reforms affected the position of the civil service?

Terms to know

Anonymity
Bureaucracy
Continuity and stability
Efficiency Unit
Executive agencies
Individual ministerial responsibility
Interdepartmental committees

Meritocratic
Neutrality
'The Next Steps'
Non-partisan
Permanence
Politicization

The executive branch of government

The executive branch of government can be divided into two parts: the political and the administrative. Ministers form the political part while their officials form the administrative arm.

In the public imagination, the term 'civil servant' means bowler hats, pinstripe suits and tightly rolled umbrellas. This image is associated with the higher civil servants of Whitehall, now immortalized in the television series, 'Yes, Minister'. However, high-level civil servants account for less than one per cent of the total number, and for most people, contact with civil servants is more likely to be in a local tax office or a job centre than in Whitehall.

In this chapter we look at the 7,000 higher civil servants and in particular, at the 600 higher civil servants who are in close contact with ministers at the centre of British government.

Higher civil servants

Functions

Implementation

The tentacles of the civil service reach deep into British society. This is understandable when we consider the main constitutional function of the civil service. As the administrative element of the executive branch of government, it is

97

responsible for executing, or implementing, government policy. Civil servants ensure that statute law and government policy are put into practice.

> ### Providers of continuity
>
> *'Civil servants are servants of the Crown. In today's world, the executive responsibilities of the Crown are carried out by the elected government of the day. The civil service serves that government, irrespective of its political complexion ... It provides continuity through the changes of government ... On policy matters, the Civil Service is responsible for advising Ministers on policy options and ensuring the implementation of Minister's decisions. Ministers must decide on policy issues – and are accountable to Parliament and the public for them. But they expect civil servants to be expert in areas of administration and keep them under review; to analyse and evaluate the options for new approaches; and to provide them with thorough and objective advice on the implications, costs and benefits of alternative courses of action ... Outside the policy area, the Government relies upon the high standards of integrity, fairness and confidentiality of the Civil Service, upon civil servants' commitment to service for every citizen and economy and efficiency on behalf of the taxpayer, and upon the Civil Service's flexibility and sensitivity to changes in Government policy in handling some of the largest managerial and service delivery tasks in the economy.'*
>
> Source: 'The Civil Service: Continuity and Change', Government policy paper, 1994

Advice

At the highest level civil servants have developed an additional function, that of advising ministers. As Charles Trevelyan, in many ways the founder of the modern civil service, wrote in 1854:

'. . . the Government of the country could not be carried on without the aid of an efficient body of permanent officers, occupying a position duly subordinate to that of the Ministers who are directly responsible to the Crown and to Parliament, yet possessing sufficient independence, character, ability and experience to be able to advise, assist and to some extent influence those who are from time to time set over them.'

According to the traditional, constitutional view of the advisory role of the civil service, the 'mandarins', as they are sometimes called, should be available to advise ministers on the decisions that need to be made, to brief ministers on the issues involved and to present options to make the minister's decision making easier.

> ### Functions and characteristics of the civil service
> **Functions**
> - Advise
> - Implement
>
> **Characteristics**
> - Permanence
> - Neutrality
> - Anonymity

However, at no stage should civil servants be responsible for decision making. Constitutionally, there is a clear dividing line between the decision-making role of the minister and the supporting role of the civil servant. As Margaret Thatcher said in 1989: 'Civil servants advise; ministers decide.'

The division of responsibilities between ministers and officials is based on the fact that ministers are the representatives of the elected government of the country and, indeed, most ministers being MPs will have been elected themselves. Of course, some ministers will be from the House of Lords and, therefore, not elected, and the government itself is not directly elected, but at least the government has some democratic credentials as it is drawn from the House of Commons. Civil servants have not been elected and for this reason should not hold political power.

The concept of **individual ministerial responsibility** underlies the division of responsibilities. According to this doctrine, ministers are responsible to Parliament for departmental policy, while civil servants are not. In the case of policy errors or mistakes in implementation, it is the minister who resigns rather than the civil servant. The implication of the doctrine is that civil servants should not be held responsible because they have no role in decision making.

This doctrine was clearly reiterated by the home secretary Sir David Maxwell-Fyfe in 1954 in the wake of the Critchell Down affair. In 1938 the Air Ministry bought a parcel of land under a compulsory purchase order to create a bombing range. Eventually this land was handed over to the Ministry of Agriculture, where it was decided to lease the land back into agricultural use. The original owners of the land were not, however, first given the opportunity to buy back the land – as was required under a compulsory purchase order. It was believed – but this has since been questioned – that the Minister of Agriculture, Sir Thomas Dugdale, was not involved in this error. Nevertheless, Dugdale resigned.

Ministerial resignations

Whether ministers decide to resign or not depends not only on their sense of honour but also on the attitudes of those around them. Probably, the most influential opinions are those of the prime minister and the party's backbenchers. If the prime minister and other members of the party are prepared to give full backing to a minister, then the minister has a chance to survive criticism. However, if the backing of one or both of these bodies is lost the minister's fate is virtually sealed.

If a minister's department has made serious errors or if the minister has been guilty of misconduct, they should be prepared to resign. A number of ministers have resigned over misjudgments over policy. These have included: Lord Carrington, the foreign secretary and his team of foreign office ministers who resigned in 1982 after failing to predict the Argentine invasion of the Falkland Islands; Leon Brittan, the trade and industry secretary, who resigned in 1986 having been blamed for the unauthorized leak of a letter from the solicitor-general to the minister of defence; and Michael Heseltine, the defence secretary, regarding the sale of the Westland helicopter company to a group of European companies.

In the case of Leon Brittan the leak was considered serious because all communications with government law officers are confidential. He later claimed that the release of the letter had been approved by a number of civil servants inside 10

99

Downing Street. Subsequently, civil servant **anonymity** was broken when a number of the civil servants involved were named in Parliament, including Bernard Ingham, Margaret Thatcher's press secretary; Sir Charles Powell, one of her senior advisers; John Mogg, Leon Brittan's private secretary and John Mitchell, an undersecretary at the Department of Trade and Industry.

Staying on

While some ministers have been prepared to resign, in line with the doctrine of ministerial responsibility, many others have remained in office. For example, in 1991 the home secretary, Kenneth Baker, did not resign after two IRA prisoners escaped from Brixton Prison. In 1983 James Prior, Northern Ireland secretary, retained his position after 38 IRA prisoners escaped from the Maze prison in Belfast, killing a prison officer in the process.

Personal misjudgements

In recent years other ministers have resigned for a variety of reasons, all of which came under the heading of individual ministerial responsibility, but involved personal misjudgement rather than departmental errors. David Mellor (1992), Cecil Parkinson (1983) and Lord Lambton (1973) all resigned over scandals in their personal lives that raised doubts about their fitness to hold senior government office. Perhaps the best-known example was the Profumo affair (1963) when John Profumo, minister for war, was forced to resign following an ill-judged affair with Christine Keeler who was also having an affair with a member of the Russian embassy staff.

Characteristics

Northcote-Trevelyan

In order to fulfil its functions the British civil service has three characteristics which were laid down in 1854 by the Northcote-Trevelyan Report:
- **permanence**
- **neutrality**
- **anonymity**.

A review of the civil service was commissioned in 1853 by William Gladstone, the chancellor of the exchequer. The terms of reference for Sir Stafford Northcote and Charles Trevelyan called for the 'revising and readjusting [of] the public establishments as to place them on the footing best calculated for the efficient discharge of their important functions, according to the actual circumstances of the present time'. The result was the permanent, neutral and anonymous civil service that remains at the heart of constitutional theory today.

Permanence

Continuity and stability

While ministers may come and go, civil servants remain. They do not change either when the minister changes or when the government changes. This system ensures that there is some degree of **stability** and **continuity** in government as the political personnel change. Officials are always there to brief an incoming minister on the decisions that have been made and those that need to be made. This enables the minister to take up the reins of office easily and allows the process of government to continue with as little disruption as possible.

In addition to knowledge of the issues and decision making, civil servants build up a sound knowledge of how the department works and how policies can be implemented effectively.

Meritocratic

Once the decision was taken to have a permanent civil service, this had obvious implications for the recruitment of civil servants. Before 1854 civil servants had been

Senior grades in the higher civil service

Grade	Title	Numbers
I	Permanent secretary	36
IA	Second permanent secretary	86
2	Deputy secretary	130
3	Under secretary	487
4	Executive directing bands	280
5	Assistant secretary	2557
6	Senior principal	4569
7	Principal	13,321

Source: Civil service statistics, 1992

appointed through a system of patronage. This meant that jobs could be gained depending on political beliefs, family connections or the whim of politicians. Such a system was no longer appropriate after the Northcote-Trevelyan Report and it was replaced by recruitment based on merit. As the historian Peter Hennessy said: 'It worked. It created the country's first true meritocracy, a genuine aristocracy of talent' (*Whitehall*, Secker & Warburg, 1989).

A **meritocratic** civil service is recruited through a system of examinations and interviews, designed to select the best and the brightest. Today's higher civil servants are usually recruited from universities. Candidates complete a series of written examinations, known as the qualifying tests, and those who are successful take part in another series of interviews, simulations and written papers under the banner of the Civil Service Selection Board. Successful candidates then go forward to the final stage of interviews before the Final Selection Board.

Recruitment stages

The Fulton Report, 1969

The Fulton Report criticized the civil service for its 'amateurism', i.e. the tendency for higher civil servants to be 'generalists' or 'all-rounders', often educated in arts subjects without any prior knowledge of key issue areas. Nevertheless, they had the power to advise ministers on briefings prepared by specialists. This reflected the civil servants' idea that their specialism was administration.

The report also found that management skills were largely ignored in the service and it recommended the creation of the Civil Service College to improve training.

It suggested that recruitment to the service should be broadened and the dominance of Oxbridge arts graduates reduced in favour of a wider range of subjects and candidates with experience in the commercial and industrial sectors.

Finally, it recommended the abolition of the 'class' system in the service to allow greater mobility for talented administrators in the lower ranks.

While some of the report's recommendations were implemented, such as the abolition of the class sytem and the creation of the Civil Service College, the report itself was heavily criticized by the service as simplistic and some of its recommendations regarding recruitment were ignored.

'Oxbridge' predominance

Whether the British civil service is truly meritocratic has been the subject of considerable debate. In 1969 the Fulton Report was highly critical of the predominance of graduates from Oxford and Cambridge ('Oxbridge') among successful applicants. The relative success of Oxbridge applicants is clearly illustrated by recruitment statistics from 1986. They accounted for 15 per cent of the hopefuls at the qualifying tests stage, 38 per cent of the successful applicants who progressed to the interviews and test before the Civil Service Selection Board and 46 per cent of the candidates who went before the Final Selection Board. When the names of the final recruits were announced Oxbridge graduates occupied 55 per cent of the places.

The 'bias' towards Oxbridge would probably not have surprised the initiator of the Northcote-Trevelyan Report, William Gladstone. As his biographer H G G Matthew suggests, his aim was to ensure that 'a civil service appointed by patronage and influence would give way to a non-political administrative class educated in the moral values of a liberal education further developed by a reformed Oxford and Cambridge' (*Gladstone 1809–74*, Clarendon Press, 1986).

At the end of the nineteenth century it was mush easier to justify Oxbridge predominance over other British universities, but today it is more difficult. In any case, some question whether intellectual preeminence is sufficient to merit such success in civil service entrance examinations.

Neutrality

The need for neutrality comes from civil service permanence. If civil servants are to remain in office while governments change, they must be politically impartial. British civil servants should not allow their personal opinions to affect the way in which they serve their minister. They are expected to offer impartial advice and implement ministerial decisions regardless of whether they agree with them or not.

Non-partisan

Civil servants are required to be **non-partisan**; they are not allowed to take part in any party political activity, although they are allowed to vote.

Divided loyalty

There has been some dispute over what the concept of neutrality actually means to civil servants. Some civil servants see themselves as servants of the Crown, which today is a symbol of the state rather than the monarchy. They believe, therefore, that their first loyalty is to the state, not to the government of the day. The danger of such an attitude is that civil servants might regard their professional morals as superior to those of the politicians or might even seek to influence their ministers in the direction of their own views. Indeed, the Labour politician Tony Benn believes that this is already the case: 'The problem arises from the fact that the civil service sees itself as being above the party battle, with a political position of its own to defend against all-comers, including incoming governments armed with their philosophy and programmes' (*Arguments for Democracy*, Penguin, 1979).

Ponting case

The narrow dividing line between the desirability of a civil service conscience and the dangers of civil service independence was illustrated by the Ponting case in 1985. An employee of the Ministry of Defence, Clive Ponting, was tried for breach of the Official Secrets Act after having allegedly leaked information regarding the sinking of the Argentine warship *Belgrano* during the Falklands War to a backbench Labour MP, Tam Dayell. His justification for doing so was that the government had lied to Parliament regarding the circumstances in which the ship was torpedoed and that it was in the interests of the state to make public the information.

State and government

Although Clive Ponting was acquitted by the jury, the secretary to the cabinet and

head of the home civil service, Robert Armstrong, immediately restated the role of
civil servants according to the Cabinet Office:

*'Civil servants are servants of the Crown. For all practical purposes the Crown in this context
means and is represented by the government of the day . . . The duty of the individual civil
servant is first and foremost to the Minister of the Crown who is in charge of the Department
in which he or she is serving . . . The determination of policy is the responsibility of the
Minister . . . In the determination of policy the civil servant has no constitutional*
responsibility *or role, distinct from that of the Minister . . . When, having given all the
relevant information and advice, the Minister has taken the decision, it is the duty of civil
servants loyally to carry out that decision . . . Civil servants are under an obligation to keep the
confidences to which they become privy in the course of their official duties'* – quoted in Peter
Hennessy, *Whitehall,* Secker & Warburg, 1989.

Anonymity

Civil servants are not elected and therefore should not have the power to make
political decisions. Decision making is the responsibility of politicians and it is they
who should take responsibility for the successes or failures of departmental policy.
For this reason, civil servants are said to be anonymous. This might not mean that
their identity is secret, but it does mean that they should not be held publicly
accountable for their advice or for departmental policy.

Power and influence

Despite the constitutional view that civil servants should not wield political power,
politicians from both left and right have accused the civil service of having
considerable influence over policy making. Ironically, the main sources of this power
and influence are the functions and characteristics given to civil servants in the
Northcote-Trevelyan constitutional view of their position. As we saw above, Charles
Trevelyan intended to create a civil service made up of individuals '. . . possessing
sufficient independence, character, ability and experience to be able . . . to some
extent, influence those who are from time to time set over them'.

Advice

Ministers have a large workload and limited time. They are responsible for their
department, general governmental responsibilities in cabinet, parliamentary duties,
constituency business and party matters. As a result, they come to rely on civil
service advice and this puts the civil servant into a privileged and influential position.

Any adviser, in any walk of life, should have some influence. If not, there is little
point in them being there. However, if ministers lack the time to weigh up civil
servants' advice, there is a danger that they may become a mouthpiece for civil
service policies.

Ministerial dependency

Implementation

Once decisions have been taken it is left to the civil service to implement those
decisions. Again, this leaves room for civil servants to interfere in the political process
by delaying or obstructing the implementation of policy. By seeking loopholes,
creating difficulties or simply refusing to co-operate, policies can be undone. Some
Labour ministers were quick to point to an uncooperative civil service when

Obstruction

> ## Bureaucracy
>
> The German sociologist Max Weber believed that the **bureaucracy** would be one of the most powerful political forces in the twentieth century.
>
> According to him, bureaucrats are professional administrators, recruited on merit rather than as political appointees. They work inside a hierarchical structure, following strict rules of procedure and decision making and recording all of the decisions for future reference.
>
> The advantages of bureaucracy are that it is efficient, consistent and gives advice on an objective basis, free from political bias. It also brings continuity to the system of government.
>
> Bureaucracies are criticized for excessive red tape and form filling and the danger that they might use their knowledge and expertise to subvert the governing role of their political masters.

explaining the difficulties of the 1964–70 government. The creation of the Department of Economic Affairs was an attempt to sidestep an uncooperative Treasury. Ironically, the Treasury's refusal to work with that department was also cited as a reason for its demise. In another example, Barbara Castle, the employment secretary, used her diaries published some years later, to accuse her civil servants of ambushing her bill to curb trade union power, a bill known as 'In Place of Strife', by including controversial clauses that she had expressly deleted.

Permanence

Since civil servants are permanent and ministers are not, this potentially gives the former a great deal of power. Civil servants spend a substantial part of their working lives in the service and sometimes even within one department.

Temporary ministers

Ministers, on the other hand, have an average tenure of only two years. After that they can be expected to be promoted or demoted in a cabinet reshuffle. Therefore, they have little time to get to grips with the issues.

Experience

In his diaries the Labour politician Richard Crossman constantly expressed his concerns over his inexperience of housing issues compared to the vast experience of his permanent secretary, Evelyn Sharpe: 'She is really a tremendous and dominating

> ## Departmental knowledge
>
> H E Dale, a senior civil servant before World War II, described the role of a senior administrator:
>
> '[He] knows the construction of the whole machine, the position of his own and other departments as wheels of the machine and their relations to the other wheels, and the general principles of operation which must be observed if the machine is to work smoothly. Finally, and perhaps most important of all ... it is the business of the high official to know the men who for the time being are, like himself, important parts of the central and controlling mechanism'.
>
> Source: Quoted in Clive Ponting, *Whitehall: Tragedy and Farce*, Hamish Hamilton, 1986

character. She has worked with a great many ministers before me . . . [she is] utterly contemptuous and arrogant, regarding local authorities as children which she has to examine and rebuke for their failures. She sees ordinary human beings as incapable of making a sensible decision.'

The former head of the civil service, Edward Bridges, has summed up this advantage as the 'stock of departmental wisdom' that comes from 'the slow accretion and accumulation of experience over the years'.

Of course, such wisdom is relevant not only to the issues but also to the workings of the department. The civil service has developed a great deal of control over the administrative process. Red tape, traditional procedures and set ways of doing things mean that it is very difficult for a minister to get anything done without civil service co-operation.

Administrative knowledge

Civil servants' knowledge of the ways of the bureaucracy is not limited to their own department. Their years in office enable them to make links with civil servants in other departments. The result can be a network of civil servants able to influence ministerial policy right across the civil service regardless of departmental boundaries. For civil servants in spending departments, such as Defence or Health, links with civil servants in the Treasury are particularly useful as the Treasury has a significant voice in decisions over spending plans.

Links

For many civil servants links are built very easily because so many senior members come from similar backgrounds. We saw above that the majority of successful applicants have an Oxbridge background. A H Birch goes further: 'Statistics published in the 1970s showed that most of the successful Oxbridge candidates had been educated at fee-paying schools, and were therefore members of the upper and upper-middle classes' (*The British System of Government*, Allen & Unwin, 1980)). With its culture and traditions which are slow to change, the civil service remains the bastion of the 'old school-tie' network.

Backgrounds

Links between civil servants across departmental lines are institutionalized through **interdepartmental committees**. Their purpose is to co-ordinate the work of government between departments and they shadow the work of cabinet committees. Some observers argue that the committees give civil servants the opportunity to shape policy options before they are presented to ministers. In more extreme terms, they could enable civil servants to run a shadow government from behind the scenes. With this in mind, former Labour minister Peter Shore has referred to civil servants as 'permanent politicians'.

Interdepartmental committees

Neutrality

The constitutional view expects civil servants to have, according to the ex-Conservative minister, Nicholas Ridley, 'a chameleon-like ability to identify with successive governments of quite different political complexion'. There is a danger that the expectation of political impartiality may become a cloak behind which civil servants can hide. If ministers expect civil servants to be neutral, they may be less vigilant regarding the advice they receive.

In 1987, in an interview on Channel 4 News, the former head of the civil service Lord Bancroft said: 'There are occasions when one looks at a manifesto . . . where a balloon comes out of one's head which says "Garbage! God!" and then it is a question of handling matters so that, somehow or other, the garbage is made into

Cloak of neutrality

something edible.' The cloak of neutrality may mean that a minister is not aware that the policies are being made more 'edible'.

Labour politician Tony Benn was nothing if not vigilant during his time in office and he raises similar doubts about civil service neutrality: 'The deal that the civil service offers a minister is this: if you do what we want you to do, we will help you publicly to pretend that you're implementing the manifesto on which you were elected' (quoted in H Young and A Sloman, *No Minister: An Inquiry into the Civil Service*, BBC, 1982).

US appointments

In this sense the shroud of neutrality is a threat to ministerial control. Supporters of this view look to the system of political appointees used in the United States to fill the highest offices of the civil service. President Clinton has the power to appoint around 4,000 civil servants. They can be drawn from any walk of life and are likely to be supporters on whom he can rely.

Anonymity

Theoretically, civil servants do not take responsibility for departmental policy because they are not decision makers. However, the logistics of minister–civil service relations means that this is sometimes not possible. The creation of 'super departments' such as the Department of the Environment has meant that full ministerial control of the department is virtually impossible.

Scale

In his biography of Michael Heseltine, Julian Critchley has pointed out that while at the Ministry of Defence, 'Michael Heseltine was in charge of an organization more than three times the size of the biggest private employer in the country. In 1983 £6 billion pounds were spent on new equipment . . . The scale of the problem facing Heseltine within the ministry can be demonstrated by one statistic: the enterprise was so vast that production orders worth less than £50 million did not go to ministers for approval' (*Heseltine: The Unauthorised Biography*, Coronet, 1988).

Sources of civil servants' power
- Advice
  - time
  - information
- Implementation
  - obstruction
- Permanence
  - knowledge
  - bureaucracy
  - links
  - background
- Neutrality
  - disguise
- Anonymity
  - size

Ministerial weakness?

While the constitutional position of civil servants has obvious advantages, it also carries dangers for the British system of government. Their functions and characteristics give them the opportunity to wield a great deal of influence over ministerial decision making.

However, civil servants and ministers have often claimed that undue civil service influence is largely the fault of weak ministers rather than overly ambitious civil servants. Labour politician Denis Healey has summed this up in the following terms: 'A minister who complains that his civil servants are too powerful is either a weak minister or an incompetent one.' We can also add the words of former prime minister Harold Wilson to this: 'If a minister cannot control his civil servants he should go.'

This view has also been supported by Lord Croham, a civil servant who spent 30 years at the Treasury:

Civil service preference

'Without any hesitation civil servants like strong ministers. They are much easier to deal with for a number of reasons . . . They are more likely to get their own views across and, therefore, if you work hard to do something for a minister it's not wasted. The other point is that if you're dealing with a minister and he doesn't like your advice, you know pretty clearly . . . He decides on his own line..which gives it the maximum chance of succeeding . . . and [he's] most unlikely to turn round and blame the department if it doesn't work. Every civil servant I know likes strong ministers.' – quoted in Peter Hennessy, Whitehall, Secker & Warburg, 1989

Challenges to the constitutional position of the civil service

During Margaret Thatcher's term of office a number of observers, politicians and officials began to voice concern over the constitutional position of the civil service. They argued that Margaret Thatcher's attitude towards the civil service and many of the resulting reforms had seriously damaged the constitutional masonry of the administrative branch of the executive.

Politicization

The first characteristic to come under scrutiny in the 1980s was neutrality. Margaret Thatcher was accused of politicizing the higher civil service by putting her own supporters into key positions. Her famous maxim when considering recommendations for promotion was 'Is he one of us?' – meaning is the candidate on our side? If this were strictly applied, Margaret Thatcher might have seriously undermined the neutrality of the civil service.

One of us?

In the early years of her administration Margaret Thatcher certainly had the opportunity to politicize the higher civil service. Between 1979 and 1985, 43 permanent secretaries and 138 deputy secretaries left the civil service, of their own free will. This represents an almost total turnover of senior civil servants. However, only one example of the alleged **politicization** has ever been put forward to support the case of Margaret Thatcher's critics. In 1983 Sir Douglas Wass retired as permanent secretary to the Treasury and was replaced by Peter Middleton. As the historian Peter Hennessy has commented:

Opportunities

'Certainly, some [civil servants] flew higher and faster because of her patronage. She has her favourites. Peter Middleton . . . was one . . . Middleton was a convinced monetarist who had been crucial in putting together the government's medium-term financial strategy. Mrs Thatcher and those ministers who thought like her (as the Treasury team did) preferred dealing with Middleton rather than the ever-courteous but ever-sceptical Wass.' – Whitehall, Secker & Warburg, 1989

Margaret Thatcher's alleged politicization in civil service appointments was

Investigation

investigated by the Royal Institute of Public Administration in 1985, but no evidence of it was found. However, the report stated:

'To some extent, the appointment process has become more personalized in the sense that at the top level "catching the eye" of the prime minister (in a favourable or unfavourable manner) may now be more important than in the past . . . Downing Street communicates more opinions about the performance of civil servants, even down to quite junior levels, based on impressions made at meetings with the prime minister . . . However, we do not believe that these appointments and promotions are based on the candidate's support for or commitment to particular ideologies or objectives.'

'Catching the eye'

The danger of the need for 'catching the eye' of the prime minister is that ambitious civil servants might sacrifice some of their independence to seek the favour of their ministers. As a result, Margaret Thatcher might not have politicized the civil service, but the impression that she did so was enough to achieve the same effect.

Defence

Individuals who were close to the prime minister at this time have also defended her against critics. Robert Armstrong, who headed the Senior Appointment Selection Committee, has said:

'There is no question of political considerations entering into the choice. The prime minister is ultimately responsible for the appointments of permanent and deputy secretaries, and she takes a keen interest in them . . . She is not concerned with, and I can vouch for the fact that she does not seek to ascertain, the political views or sympathies (if any) of those who are recommended. Nor do I. She wants, as I want, to have the best person for the job.' – quoted in Peter Hennessey, *Whitehall*, Secker & Warburg, 1989

Permanence threatened

Politicization could also undermine the permanence of the civil service because incoming prime ministers might seek to replace the appointees of the previous administration. Indeed, Neil Kinnock, as leader of the Opposition, hinted at his fears of politicization in a 1985 television interview:

'I don't know about the permanent secretaries. We obviously have to examine the degree of enthusiasm and loyalty that they are prepared to demonstrate in support of a Labour government and in the implementation of the policy of that government. I'm prepared to work on . . . the conventional basis, which has stood us in good stead in Britain, about the way in which civil servants are prepared to work.'

Ongoing concerns

Despite Margaret Thatcher's departure from government, the debate regarding civil service neutrality and politicization has continued. In 1994 the minister for open government, William Waldegrave, dismissed one of his civil servants, Peter Kemp, because of difficulties in their working relationship. The minister, often referred to as the minister for the civil service, stated: 'When you put in a new policy which is controversial, it is quite difficult not to appoint people who are sympathetic to you to run it . . . It is crazy to appoint people who are deliberately not going to do what you want.'

Anti-Thatcherite

Despite the fact that Margaret Thatcher was cleared of politicization, it is worth considering why she might have been tempted to make political appointments. She was very critical of some of the civil servants she encountered when she came into office. She felt that a number of senior civil servants did not have the right attitude towards government. She believed that they were negative and obstructive, often standing in the way of her policies. Her views were no doubt partly shaped by the reports of the head of her Policy Unit, John Hoskyns, who stated that joining a civil service team was 'like joining Napoleon's army just before the retreat from Moscow'. He had found that the civil service's approach to Britain's problems was the 'orderly management of decline'.

It could be argued that to Margaret Thatcher's mind, the civil service was insufficiently supportive of her policies and so was not really neutral when she came to office. Having spent their entire working lives in a political environment dominated by Keynesian economic thinking (see page 177) and the post-war political consensus (see page 40), it would be hardly surprising for civil servants to find it difficult to adjust to the new policies of Thatcherism. Therefore, any politicization she might have undertaken, she would have justified as attempts to correct the partisan balance.

Correcting the balance

Anti-Labour

The question of whether the civil service is entirely neutral is certainly not new, but more often it has come from the political left than the right. Richard Crossman, Tony Benn, Barbara Castle and Peter Shore, all members of Labour governments in the 1960s and 1970s, have all accused the civil service of being negative towards Labour policies. Such a bias might be explained, according to Marxist political scientist Ralph Miliband, by the fact that the majority of civil servants are drawn from a privileged background and therefore, they might seek to preserve this privilege against an onslaught by a socialist government committed to the removal of privilege. However, it is perhaps a little unlikely to believe that background should be the major determinant of civil service behaviour.

Backgrounds

An alternative explanation, associated with another Marxist, Nicos Poulantzas, suggests that civil servants are prisoners of the dominant ideology of the state. Britain is a capitalist state, the officials are servants of the state and therefore, if they wish to serve the system, administrators have no alternative but to be servants of capitalism. As a result, they are opposed to the socialism of the Labour Party.

Servants of capitalism

Anti-radical

Many of the criticisms of the civil service have come from the more extreme wings of both of the major political parties. Tony Benn, Richard Crossman and Barbara Castle might all be considered to come from the left of the Labour Party. Of the Conservative critics, Nicholas Ridley and Margaret Thatcher could certainly be said to come from the right of the party.

Radicals

It is possible to argue that the civil service is opposed neither to the Labour Party nor to the Conservative Party, rather it opposes radical change in either direction. This would also explain why Edward Heath, James Callaghan, Denis Healey and Harold Wilson did not have difficulties with civil servants – they were all from the mainstream of their parties.

Moderates

If there was anti-radical feeling in the civil service, this could be in line with its loyalty to the state rather than the government (see page 102). In the best interests of the state civil servants might seek to steer a central course of moderate policies designed, in their opinion, for long-term benefit.

Long termism

Tony Benn has claimed to have identified such 'civil service policies' as civil servants prepare to welcome a new minister:

Civil service policies

'They read the manifestos, then they prepare papers designed to show how part of them could be implemented and how part of them can't be implemented. They dress it up so that an incoming government will feel that there is a sympathetic civil service. In effect, what they do, however, is to write massive briefs, which are the most important documents to be found in Whitehall, in which – and it's the only time it happens – they actually set out civil service policy.' – Tony Benn, *Arugments for Democracy*, Penguin, 1979

On the other hand, the radical government of 1945–51 seemed to be well supported by the civil service.

Civil service morale

Secrets trials

Between 1979 and 1986, 29 individuals were prosecuted for breach of the Official Secrets Acts.

Important cases included those of Sarah Tisdall (1984), Clive Ponting (1985) (see page 102) and the Spycatcher affair (1986–8) (see page 136).

Sarah Tisdall was sentenced to six months in prison after leaking government documents concerning the strategy to head off opposition to the stationing of cruise missiles in Britain. She objected to the government's intention to make announcement to Parliament only *after* the missiles had arrived.

Margaret Thatcher's attitude towards the civil service was sometimes negative. She was concerned that the 'mandarins' (senior civil servants) were opposed to her policies and also were unduly pessimistic about Britain's future. Therefore, she attacked what she perceived as the complacency of the service. Between 1979 and 1992 the size of the civil service was reduced by 23 per cent from 732,000 to 565,000. In 1981 she abolished the Civil Service Department, banned trade unions from Government Communications Headquarters (GCHQ) and held out against a 21-week strike for higher pay. These points, combined with her merciless hounding of those civil servants accused of leaking secret information, served seriously to undermine the morale of the administrators.

Efficiency

Efficiency Unit

Margaret Thatcher was extremely critical of the inefficiency of the civil service. She believed it was ignorant of management techniques, wasteful and showed little concern for the delivery of a public service. To combat these problems, she set up the **Efficiency Unit** as part of her office at 10 Downing Street in order to implant a private-sector mentality in the government administration.

The Efficiency Unit and Derek Rayner

In 1979 the Efficiency Unit was headed by Derek Rayner, who was the joint managing director of Marks and Spencer. He launched a series of investigations into departmental efficiency that resulted in annual savings which averaged £325 million by 1989.

Financial Management Initiative

The unit, in conjunction with individual departments, also launched the Financial Management Initiative (FMI). The aim of the initiative was to foster a greater

Efficiency and effectiveness in the civil service, 1982

A 1982 government white paper outlines the aims of the Financial Management Initiative regarding civil servants:

'... a system in which managers at all levels have:

a   a clear view of their objectives; and assess and wherever possible measure outputs or performance in relation to these objectives;
b   well-defined responsibility for making the best use of their resources including a critical scrutiny of output and value for money;
c   the information (including particularly about costs), training and access to expert advice which they need to exercise their responsibilities effectively.'

business awareness in civil service departments. Civil servants were encouraged to identify their objectives, along with means of measuring success; to accept greater responsibility for the use of resources and to ensure that they had access to the necessary advice and training to enable them to perform effectively.

Individual departments often set up their own versions of FMI. Probably the most well-known was Management Information System for Ministers (MINIS) which was founded by Michael Heseltine at the Department of the Environment.

Management Information System for Ministers

Civil service reform and Robin Ibbs

Derek Rayner was succeeded by Robin Ibbs who pushed the frontiers of civil service reform further than even the Fulton Report had been prepared to go in 1969. His report, 'Improving Management in Government: The Next Steps' was completed before the 1987 general election and recommended the most radical shakeup of the civil service since Northcote-Trevelyan in 1854.

'The Next Steps'

The main element of **'The Next Steps'** was the suggestion that many of the functions of the civil service could be carried out more effectively and efficiently if they were the responsibility of **executive agencies**. These agencies would be discrete units given specific responsibilities under the leadership of a chief executive. The government believed that agencies would be more cost conscious, more responsive to consumers in the delivery of their services and more receptive to new management techniques to improve performance. Peter Kemp, one of the main architects of 'The Next Steps' programme described it as a means of 'getting the best of both worlds, filling a gap in the management armoury of this country . . . it's a public-sector owner, with broad public sector rules with a private-sector approach to running businesses.'

Executive agencies

This was fully in line with the Thatcherite policies of bringing private-sector management principles into the running of government services. Margaret Thatcher believed that the public sector was often wasteful, bureaucratic and unresponsive; whereas, in order to survive and prosper the private sector needed to be efficient, responsive and concerned with the quality of its services. This philosophy also underpinned her other key policies such as privatization of nationalized industries (see page 181) and allowing private firms to bid for the delivery of local authority services (see page 147).

Management principles

The chief executives of the agencies were given a great deal of independence from the traditional departmental structures of the civil service. They were expected to be

Improving delivery

Challenges to the constitutional view
- Politicization
- Bias
- Morale
- Efficiency
- Sir Robin Ibbs

aware of management techniques and to strive constantly to improve the delivery of their services. A 1994 survey showed that chief executives were spending 25 per cent of their time trying to improve cost effectiveness. Indeed, in line with private-sector policies, in 1993, 50 per cent of the chief executives received performance-related pay.

Extension of agencies

The government of John Major continued the Ibbs reforms and by 1994 there were 97 executive agencies including the Employment Service, the Inland Revenue and Customs and Excise and 64 per cent, or 340,000, of civil servants were employed by these agencies. However, there were no plans to delegate any policy-making functions to the executive agencies. The core of around 20,000 higher civil servants remained to work closely with ministers. But even here the government proposed reform. Senior positions in the civil service were opened to public competition with vacancies advertised in the press and candidates from outside the civil service free to apply. It is believed that ministers, including Kenneth Clarke and Michael Heseltine, would like to see senior civil servants put on fixed-term contracts which would lead to greater accountability of civil servants and as a result, might undermine permanence.

Impact of 'The Next Steps'

Although the government concentrated on implementing the efficiency aspects of 'The Next Steps', the recommendations made in the Ibbs Report have serious implications for the traditional constitutional characteristics of the civil service.

Accountability

The aim of the reforms was to make civil servants more aware of service delivery and efficiency. There is a narrow division between becoming more aware and becoming responsible for the implementation of government policy. While there is little wrong with making civil servants accountable for their performance, there is a danger that civil servants will lose their anonymity and be held accountable for government policy. The employment of chief executives and the use of performance-related pay seems to illustrate this problem.

Permanence

When the anonymity of civil servants is threatened, the other characteristics of the service are soon undermined. If administrators are being held responsible, then their permanence is under threat because they might be removed from office if the performance of their agency does not live up to expectations. As a result, their neutrality might also disappear as civil servants, aware of the precariousness of their positions, seek to please their political superiors rather than act in an independent manner. The loss of permanence and neutrality may also be the results of the opening up of senior civil service positions to outside competition and the introduction of fixed-term contracts. The temptation for governments to make political appointments and to dismiss 'unsuccessful' administrators could be greater.

The creation of agencies has also dispersed the administrative functions into many more units. This could make ministerial supervision of the civil service much more difficult. Chief executives, for example, could be required to answer for their decisions before parliamentary committees which would undermine the traditional relationship between ministers and their civil servants.

Exercises

Short questions

1 a What recent changes have taken place in the practice of appointing senior civil servants?
   b What are the implications of these changes? (ULEAC, January 1992)
2 In what circumstances do ministers resign? (ULEAC, January 1993)
3 a Define the convention of individual ministerial responsibility.
   b How does it operate in practice? (ULEAC, January 1995)
4 What principles govern the relationship of civil servants to ministers? (ULEAC, June 1993)
5 Outline the case for the neutrality of civil servants. (ULEAC, January 1994)

Essay questions

1 State a case (a) for and (b) against the view that the civil service has too much power. (ULEAC, June 1992)
2 Has the role of the civil service changed in recent years? (ULEAC, June 1994)
3 Has the notion of a politically neutral civil xervice come under threat? (ULEAC, June 1991)
4 'Civil Servants may be civil, but do they serve?' Discuss this comment respecting the political relationship between ministers and civil servants. (Cambridge, June 1994)
5 'The reforms of the 1980s have made the civil service more effective but less accountable.' Discuss. (Oxford, June 1994)
6 Explain why permanence, political neutrality and anonymity are regarded as important characteristics of the civil service. (Oxford and Cambridge, June 1993)

Data response question

'The place is St George's House in the shadow of Windsor Castle; the occasion an Anglo–American seminar on bureaucracy; the time, the spring of 1984, well into Mrs Thatcher's second term; the speaker is a neat, precise, bespectacled Englishman in his forties, sporting a watch and chain.

"The British Civil Service," he declares, "is a great rock on the tideline. The political wave, Labour or Conservative, rolls in, washes over it and ebbs. The rock is exposed again to the air virtually unchanged." He pauses. "But Mrs Thatcher has been applying sticks of dynamite to that rock."

The speaker was Clive Priestly, a former Whitehall under secretary held in high esteem by the prime minister for the work he had done as a chief of staff to Lord Raynor of Marks and Spencer, her efficiency adviser. Mr Priestly's remarks were addressed to Mrs Thatcher as dynamiter of bureaucratic waste ... But there are observers in Parliament, the press and Whitehall itself who believe that more than one stick of dynamite has been applied by the demolition expert in No. 10, with damaging results to the constitutional masonry.'

Source: Peter Hennessy, *Contemporary Record*, Philip Allan, 1988

1 What 'sticks of dynamite', other than the one referred to in the passage have been applied to the British civil service by the 'demolition expert in No. 10'?
2 Discuss whether these sticks of dynamite' have produced 'damaging results to the constitutional masonry'.
3 What kind of work had Clive Priestly done as chief of staff to Lord Rayner?
4 How does this concern with civil service efficiency relate to the general context of the Conservative government's policies?

(ULEAC, June 1990)

8 The monarchy

Questions to be answered in this chapter
- What is the role of the monarch in contemporary society?
- What are the arguments for and against keeping the monarchy?

Terms to know

Authority
Civil List
Constitutional conventions
Constitutional monarchy
Divine right of kings

Head of state
'Reserve' powers
Royal assent
Unrepresentative

The development of the constitutional monarchy

The institution of the monarchy in Britain dates back to the ninth century. It has continued with only one interruption since. Theoretically, the throne is handed down on an hereditary principle to the eldest son or to the eldest daughter if there are no male children. However, at times, there have been departures from this principle, as kings and queens have been brought in from abroad to fill vacancies.

Originally, the monarch was extremely powerful, holding legislative and executive power. However, the monarch's power was always exercised in consultation with the barons. The Magna Carta, signed by King John in 1215, was intended to be a confirmation of the monarch's relationship with the barons rather than a new departure. It was signed by the king in order to prevent a civil war with barons from the north and east.

Magna Carta

During the thirteenth century the barons continued to be uneasy about the power of the king. In 1258 there were demands for the monarch to hold a *Great Council*. In fact it did meet in 1264 and is widely considered to be the origin of the English Parliament. The Council met more regularly at the end of the century as Edward I requested funds to finance his campaigns to pacify the Scots and Welsh. By this time it was beginning to be called Parliament.

Great Council

The reasons for the extension of Parliament's power was the king's need for money. The monarch's normal sources of revenue were insufficient to fight extended wars and so additional taxation was required. In view of this, the composition of Parliament had to be broadened in order to include the rich merchants whose support the monarch needed. Increasingly, merchants and knights met separately from the lords and clergy and Parliament began to develop two houses – the Commons and the Lords.

Finance

It is from the end of the thirteenth century that Parliament's function of controlling finance originates and from this function many significant battles between king and Parliament would unfold.

Tudors and Stuarts

Tudor monarchs consulted Parliament regarding finance and, increasingly, with regard to making law. As they did so, they gave Parliament legitimacy and helped to establish its **authority**. The power and legitimacy of Parliament became an important issue under the Stuart monarchs. James I dissolved Parliament over a dispute concerning finance. When he recalled it ten years later, he rapidly dismissed the members again, believing that they were exceeding their power.

The idea that Parliament was becoming too powerful and encroaching on the power of the monarch came to a head during the rule of Charles I. Charles believed in the **divine right of kings**. According to this theory, the king was given his authority by God and so all institutions were subordinate to the monarch and their powers derived from him.

Civil war

Once again, under Charles, king and Parliament could not agree about finance and the king viewed its members' intransigence as a challenge to his authority. Parliament was dissolved for eleven years until 1640, but then recalled. The new Parliament, known as the Long Parliament, ordered the arrest and execution of Strafford, one of the king's ministers, passed laws that limited the power of the monarch and attempted to insist that the king's ministers should be approved by Parliament. This was too much for the king and the war between royalists and parliamentarians broke out in 1642. Charles I was beheaded in 1649.

Glorious Revolution

After a short period of republican government, the monarchy was restored in 1660 when Charles II assumed the throne. Nevertheless, conflict between the monarch and Parliament broke out again under James II who believed in the divine right of kings and was also a Catholic. The religious issue caused considerable division and in 1688 James was forced to flee to France. He was replaced on the English throne jointly by William of Orange and Mary.

The accession of William and Mary was a crucial turning point in the relationship between monarch and Parliament. In 1689 both monarchs signed the Bill of Rights which confirmed the supremacy of Parliament. As a result, **constitutional monarchy** was born and since 1689 the power of Parliament has never been in doubt.

Walpole

At the beginning of the eighteenth century, George, Elector of Hanover, became king when Anne died without an heir. George I's command of English was poor and he seemed to care little for England. Therefore, he left much of the day-to-day running of his government to Sir Robert Walpole, his chief minister – later to be known as the prime minister.

For a short time, George III attempted to bypass the prime minister and cabinet by attempting to manipulate voting in Parliament. However, this was short lived and with the 1832 Reform Act the dawn of democratic government had arrived. By this time, the power of the monarch to dissolve Parliament and to choose the prime minister had largely passed to the prime minister, the Commons and the electorate.

The power of the monarch

The 'reserve' powers

Traditionally, the monarch had the power to summon and dissolve Parliament, to appoint the prime minister and to grant the **royal assent** to acts of Parliament.

Although the monarch retains these powers, in practice they have passed to the prime minister or the Commons as a whole or, to some extent, the people.

A monarch who refused to give the royal assent to a bill would be likely to face the threat of abolition from Parliament. The first-past-the-post electoral system (see page 18) engineers such majorities in the House of Commons that it is usually quite clear who should become prime minister and that prime minister is normally given a general election when it is requested.

Realities of power

However, it is perhaps too easy to discount the powers of the monarch. As the extract from *The Economist* on pages 119–20 shows, there are circumstances in which the power of the monarch would be extremely important. In addition, there are no rules about how these powers should be used. However, if the powers were used, the monarch would be put into a political situation.

The fact that the monarch could still, in a constitutional democracy, become involved in a political situation disputes the common belief that the monarch is now above politics. It is true that, since Queen Victoria, monarchs have been required to be non-partisan, but they can become embroiled in political controversy.

Non-partisan

'The right to be consulted . . .'

The constitutionalist Walter Bagehot believed that the monarch had 'the right to be consulted, the right to encourage and the right to warn'. These rights are based on the non-partisan nature of the monarch. The prime minister meets the monarch every week to give a brief on the affairs of state and can take advantage of any advice the monarch wishes to give. In this way, the monarch can act as a check on politicians.

Bagehot

By early 1995 Elizabeth II had seen nine prime ministers come, and eight go, and so had a great deal of experience of government. The historian Peter Hennessy quotes the queen as saying: 'They know that one can be impartial. I think it's rather nice to feel that one's a sort of sponge and everybody can come and tell one things. And some things stay there and some things go out of the other ear and some things never come out at all.'

The authority of the monarch

Although, under most circumstances, the powers of the monarch are exercised on the advice of ministers, monarchs derive authority from their position in the British political system.

Head of state

As **head of state** the monarch performs many ceremonial functions both at home and abroad. While the political head of government is the prime minister, the monarch can take advantage of their non-partisan position to unite the country and to build relationships with foreign leaders independently of the political process. This has been particularly important in the Commonwealth. While Margaret Thatcher was prime minister, there were often divisions between Commonwealth leaders over, for example, the American invasion of Grenada in the West Indies and the issue of sanctions against South Africa.

Ambassador

As head of state the monarch also has a symbolic role to perform. Many officials of the state see themselves as loyal to the state rather than to the government of the day.

Symbolic role

This might be true of civil servants or members of the armed forces. The monarch provides a focus for such loyalty.

Tradition

As the longest surviving political institution in Britain, the monarchy is a symbol of the history and tradition of the British political system. In this role the monarchy also becomes a symbol for continuity and stability. Critics argue that this even extends to the class system, which the monarch heads. As long as the monarchy survives, they argue, so will the British class system.

Arguments for and against the monarchy

Class system

The monarch, as head of the class system, represents the feudal system of medieval England and not the classless society that modernizers would like to see. This criticism does not only come from the left of British politics. Liberals believe in equality of opportunity and upward mobility in society. They believe in a meritocratic system in which people are appointed and promoted according to talent rather than birthright. The monarch is not identified with these ideals.

Unifying force

The fact that the monarch is not elected and stands apart from partisan politics allows the monarch to act as a unifying force in British politics and society. The military take an oath of allegiance to the monarch and many civil servants see the monarch, the symbol of the state, as the focus of their loyalty. Also, as we have seen, the non-partisan position of monarchs allows them to give independent advice to the prime minister.

Undemocratic

Not only are monarchs **unrepresentative** as head of the class system, they are also unelected. If the queen's role were purely ceremonial, say critics, this might be tolerable. However, we saw above that she does have the power to become involved in politically sensitive issues, such as the appointment of a prime minister or the dissolution of Parliament. Critics also question whether an unelected individual should have the power to become involved in politics since they consider it to be out of step with the rest of Britain's political system.

Constitutional check

The vagueness that surrounds the monarch's **'reserve' powers** is typical of the vagueness of many of Britain's **constitutional conventions**. However, ideas such as the monarch's ability to act as a check on the power of politicians in order to safeguard constitutional propriety or to prevent the abuse of power is a misleading fiction. In reality, the monarch does not have the power to check the politicians. If a monarch attempted to do so, they would run the risk of being ignored or the monarchy abolished. Therefore, to suggest that the monarch could act as a check is to give the British Constitution an additional safeguard that does not really exist.

Expense

Finally, critics point to the high cost of keeping the monarchy. The money to finance members of the royal family is provided from the **Civil List** and in the 1990s amounts to almost £8 million per year. Some suggest that this is far too expensive, especially the amount of money that is given to peripheral members of the family who, according to the argument, perform no useful function. It is argued that a president would be much cheaper and adhere more closely to the principles of democratic government.

Tourist attraction

The alternative view is that the pomp and ceremony surrounding the monarchy is a tourist attraction and as such earns a large amount of revenue for the British economy.

Ultimately, as the Duke of Edinburgh pointed out in an interview with the *Daily Telegraph* in 1994, the monarchy should survive only so long as the British people wish to see it survive. In a Guardian–ICM poll of 1,000 people conducted in January 1995, 28 per cent stated they would like to see the monarchy abolished and 34 per cent stated that they were 'not especially keen' on the monarchy, but supported it because it is 'better than the alternatives'. Only 36 per cent of respondents described themselves as strong supporters of the monarchy which compares to 90 per cent ten years ago. Perhaps recent changes in public opinion are partly attributable to the scandal that has surrounded individuals within the royal family over recent years. However, perhaps the British people are becoming less tolerant of the monarchy and as *The Economist* has said, it is 'an idea whose time has passed' (22 October 1994).

Exercises

Short questions

1 Distinguish between the power and authority of the monarch.
2 Outline a case for and against the retention of the monarchy in Britain.

Essay questions

1 Does the monarchy still have a significant role to play in the British political system?
  (Cambridge, June 1994)
2 Is it any longer possible to justify an hereditary monarch and an unelected House of Lords within a modern democratic system of government?
  (Oxford and Cambridge, June 1993)

Data response question

The powers of the monarch
'... from overt and covert sources, through discreet conversations over lunch, in the interstices of chats about entirely different matter, as is the British way, I have distilled the following details of the monarch's "reserve powers" as they are thought to exist by those in a position both to know and, if circumstances require it, to advise on the basis of that knowledge:

- *Only the monarch can dissolve Parliament, causing a general election to be held;*
- *Only the monarch can appoint a prime minister;*
- *After an indecisive election, the monarch is required to act only if the incumbent prime minister resigns before a queen's speech is presented to Parliament, or after failing to win a majority for that legislative programme in the House of Commons;*
- *The overarching principle at such delicate times is that the queen's government must be carried on and that the monarch is not drawn into political controversy by those politicians competing to receive her commission to form a government;*
- *Normally, an outgoing prime minister is asked to advise the monarch on the succession, but it is for the monarch to ask for that advice, and, if given, it is proffered as informal advice that can be rejected, not formal advice that must be acted upon;*
- *After an inconclusive election result, if the prime minister resigns, the monarch will normally offer the first chance to form an administration to the party leader commanding the largest block of seats in the Commons;*
- *A prime minister can "request" but not "demand" a dissolution of Parliament, and the monarch can refuse. Circumstances in which this might happen are, in the words of a*

former cabinet secretary, Lord Armstrong, "improbable", but the power to withhold consent is a check on any "irresponsible exercise" of a prime minister's right to make such a request.

The circumstances in which a royal refusal could be forthcoming are, in the words of the late Sir Alan Lascelles, former private secretary to George VI and Elizabeth II, if "the existing Parliament was still vital, viable and capable of doing its job" or if the monarch "could rely on finding another prime minister who could [govern] for a reasonable period, with a working majority in the House of Commons".'

Source: Peter Hennessy, 'The Throne Behind the Power', *The Economist*, 24 December 1994

1 What effect might reform of the electoral system have on the role of the monarch?
2 How far do Peter Hennessy's arguments suggest that Britain is in need of a written constitution?

9 The judiciary

Questions to be answered in this chapter
- How is the judiciary organized in Britain?
- To what extent are judges independent of politics?
- What is the role of the judiciary in the UK?
- Should the power of the judiciary be increased?
- How adequately are civil liberties protected in Britain?

Terms to know

Bill of rights	Lord chancellor
Freedom of movement	Non-partisan
Freedom of speech	Politicization
Judicial creativity	Rule of law
Judicial independence	Separation of powers
Judicial inquiries	Treaty of Rome
Judicial restraint	*Ultra vires*
Judicial review	Unelected
Law lords	Unrepresentative

Judges and the constitution

Traditional liberal constitutional theory states that the three main branches of government should be separate. Each should have their own functions and their own personnel. This idea is known as the **separation of powers** and is usually traced back to the eighteenth-century French philosopher Montesquieu. Heavily influenced by John Locke, he believed that liberty could only be preserved and tyranny avoided if the doctrine of the separation of powers was adhered to. Without it there 'could be no liberty' and there would be 'an end to everything'.

In line with this doctrine, each branch of government has its own functions. The legislature makes the law, the executive implements the law and the judiciary applies the law.

The process of applying the law involves interpreting the laws made by Parliament and applying them to particular cases. As they carry out their functions judges should not be subjected to political interference. If politicians were to be involved in the judicial process, they might be tempted to influence the way that judges apply the law. In doing so, the impartiality of the law would be impaired and individuals might not be treated equally and fairly. Political opponents, hostile groups, different classes or races might not receive equal treatment at the hands of a politically motivated judiciary. The opportunities for political influence are, as John Locke said, 'too great a temptation to human frailty'.

Separation of powers

Political independence

Maintaining judicial independence

The British Constitution contains a number of provisions to ensure that judges remain independent of politicians.

Appointment

1 Judges should be selected in a **non-partisan** manner. Those to lower courts are appointed by the **lord chancellor**, who also advises the monarch on appointments to the High Court. Appointments to the Court of Appeal are made by the monarch on the advice of the prime minister. However, political matters should not be considered when these appointments are being made.

Tenure

2 Judges should have security of tenure; in other words, they are permanent. They cannot be changed when there is a new government and do not have to shape their decisions in order to hold on to their jobs.

Once appointed judges of the High Court hold office 'during good behaviour' and can only be removed by the monarch following a vote in both houses of Parliament. Only one judge has been removed in this way since 1701. Sir Jonah Barrington, a judge in the High Court of Admiralty in Ireland, lost his position in 1830 for taking money paid to the court.

Judges in lower courts can be removed by the lord chancellor on the grounds of incapacity or misbehaviour. In 1983 Judge Campbell was dismissed after being caught smuggling cigarettes and alcohol into Britain.

Salaries

3 Judges' salaries are relatively high in order to prevent corruption and to reflect the responsibility of their positions. In addition, their salaries are paid from the Consolidated Fund. This means that Parliament does not vote on the appropriation of money for judges' salaries and so they do not become subject to party political debate.

Debate

4 Judicial decisions or matters awaiting a judicial judgement are not discussed in Parliament. This is a parliamentary convention to prevent the work of the judiciary becoming part of political debate.

Judges' salaries

Judges' salaries are traditionally paid from the Consolidated Fund, although in recent years the system has changed.

In 1973 it was decided that the Top Salaries Review Body (TSRB) would recommend pay rises which the government would then implement. This was the case until 1992 when the TSRB recommended an increase of 20–30 per cent. The government decided not to accept the recommendations, instead offering an increase of 4 per cent.

It is possible that such government interference might jeopardize a traditional element of **judicial independence**.

Salaries in 1992 were:

Lord chief justice	£112,082
Law lord	£103,790
Lord justice of appeal	£99,510
High Court judge	£90,147
Circuit judge	£65,912

Preserving judicial independence does not only mean that judges should be protected from interference by politicians. It also means that judges should be prevented from entering political debate.

5 Judges do not take part in partisan political activity. They are not allowed to join political parties although they are allowed to vote.

Non-partisan

6 Traditionally, judges do not make any public comments on matters of party political debate. This convention was clearly stated in 1955 by the lord chancellor Lord Kilmuir in a letter to the director-general of the BBC in which he stated that it was 'undesirable for members of the judiciary to broadcast on the wireless or to appear on television . . . [because] . . . every utterance which he makes in public, except in the course of the actual performance of his judicial duties, must necessarily bring him within the focus of criticism' (see page 128).

Kilmuir rules

Political and judicial decisions

As part of the drive for judicial independence, political thinkers have attempted to make a distinction between political and judicial decisions. Political decisions are policy-making decisions involving choices between alternative courses of action. They should be made by elected politicians and so, to an extent, are biased according to the political outlook of the governments of the day.

Political decisions

Judicial decisions are procedural or mechanistic decisions based on the laws already laid down by Parliament. Therefore, they are merely concerned with applying the law, not with making the law. They are limited in scope and should be politically unbiased.

Judicial decisions

The rule of law

The need for judicial independence is reinforced by the doctrine of the **rule of law**. This is usually associated with A V Dicey and has become a central pillar of the British Constitution.

Rule of law

According to Dicey the concept can be divided into a number of parts:

- All citizens should be limited by the law.
- The government should be limited by the law.
- Everyone should be treated fairly by the normal courts of law.

> ### The doctrine of the rule of law
> In 1885 A V Dicey wrote *Introduction to the Study of the Law of the Constitution*. He divided the doctrine of the rule of law into three components:
>
> - 'The absolute supremacy of regular law as opposed to the influence of arbitrary power and excluded the existence of arbitrariness, of prerogative or even wide discretionary authority on the part of the government . . . a man may be punished for a breach of the law, but for nothing else.'
>
> - 'Equality before the law, or the equal subjection of all classes to the ordinary law of the land administered by the ordinary law courts.'
>
> - 'The constitution is the result of the ordinary law of the land.'

Government of 'laws not men'

The aim of the rule of law is to create 'a government of laws not men'. This means that laws will be applied in a predictable manner by neutral judges and all citizens can rely on equal treatment from the courts. If a person is arrested they should know which law they are accused of breaking and should expect to receive specified treatment at the hands of the law. The treatment will include access to a lawyer, trial by jury and the right to be considered innocent until proven guilty.

The rule of law is designed to avoid a situation in which politicians might try to apply laws according to their mood, particularly against their political opponents. Furthermore, the government itself is subject to the law and cannot act outside the law.

The judiciary and politics

Although judges should not be involved in politics, to a greater or lesser extent they are. Constitutionally, judges are expected to make mechanistic decisions with little or no room for their own opinions, but this is impossible. The nature of their political involvement is partly attributable to the nature of their position, but to some extent they have been brought further and further into politics over recent years both by their own actions and by those of the government.

The lord chancellor

Separation of powers

The lord chancellor is an institutionalized infringement of the separation of powers. Although head of the judicial branch of the government, the lord chancellor is also a member of the executive and the legislature and so crosses the dividing lines laid down by Montesquieu.

Legislature

In his role as a member of the legislature, the lord chancellor presides over the House of Lords. He acts as speaker of the Lords but, unlike his counterpart in the Commons, he is not a neutral referee – he is a government spokesperson in the chamber.

Executive

As a member of the executive, the lord chancellor is appointed by the prime minister and is a member of the cabinet. He presides over a department of approximately 12,000 staff with an annual budget of around £2,500 million. His responsibility is to supervise the running of the English legal system and therefore, he would be responsible for judicial reform. It is not the lord chancellor's role to offer legal advice to the government, that is the province of the attorney-general.

Judiciary

In his judicial capacity the lord chancellor heads the judiciary and regularly liaises with other senior members of the judiciary. He is also able to sit as one of the law lords to hear appeal cases.

'Constitutional buffer'

Although his roles are obviously an infringement of the doctrine of the separation of powers many holders of the office have attempted to justify the lord chancellor's ability to straddle all three branches of government by viewing the position as a 'constitutional buffer'. This has been most clearly expressed by the former lord chancellor, Lord Hailsham:

'In the absence of a paper constitution, the separation of powers is the primary function of the lord chancellor, a task which he can only fulfil if he sits somewhere near the apex of the constitutional pyramid armed with a long barge pole to keep off marauding craft from any quarter.' – Lecture to the Holdsworth Club, quoted in Joshua Rozenberg, *The Search for Justice*, Hodder & Stoughton, 1994

The law lords

As well as being part of the legislature, the House of Lords is the highest court in the land. As such, it functions as a court of appeal and cases are heard by a panel of senior judges appointed to the Lords for this purpose. They are known as the **law lords**.

In 1994 these were the law lords, shown in order of precedence, with their ages in brackets:

Lord Keith of Kinkel (71)
Lord Templeman (73)
Lord Goff of Chieveley (67)
Lord Jauncey of Tullichettle (68)
Lord Brown-Wilkinson (63)
Lord Mustill (62)
Lord Slynn of Hadley (63)
Lord Woolf (60)
Lord Lloyd of Berwick (64)
Lord Nolan (65)

Precedence in the Lords is based on the order of appointment.

Over half of the law lords have been appointed since 1991. Lords Brown-Wilkinson, Mustill, Slynn and Woolf are all considered quite liberal, while Lords Lloyd and Nolan are believed to be less obviously liberal, but nonetheless committed to overturning miscarriages of justice. It was Lord Lloyd who presided over the final appeal of the 'Birmingham Six' in 1991, when he overturned the conviction of six men for the bombing of a pub in Birmingham in 1974. Lord Nolan presided over Judith Ward's appeal in 1992. Judith Ward had been convicted of the murder of twelve people who died when a bomb exploded on a coach. Her conviction was overturned due to the unreliability of the evidence given by the police forensic scientist, Dr Frank Skuse, who had also been involved in the Birmingham Six case.

In Lord Hailsham's view, the lord chancellor is acting to *preserve* the separation of powers, rather than undermining it. However the appointment of judges is one area where there is a danger of such a breach.

Appointments

As we have seen, judges should be independent of politics and should be unbiased. The fact that a member of the government is responsible for making judicial appointments potentially puts judicial neutrality at risk.

Politicization

In 1992 the lord chancellor Lord Mackay made, or recommended, 1,300 appointments and so had ample opportunity to make political appointments had he so wished. However, evidence of **politicization** is hard to find. It is widely believed that the Labour government of 1974–9 stood in the way of Lord Donaldson's promotion to master of the rolls because he had held office as president of the National Industrial Relations Board, a body set up under the Conservative government of Edward Heath (1970–4). Lord Donaldson was only promoted when a Conservative government came to power in 1979.

Secrecy

The secrecy surrounding judicial appointments does not help to reduce the fear of politics playing a part in the judicial arena. There are no job descriptions; the higher appointments are not advertised and there is no interview process. As David Pannick has written: 'Judges are appointed by a process that resembles a pre-1965 Conservative Party leadership contest or a Papal Conclave rather than the choice of law-makers in a modern democracy' (David Pannick, *Judges*, Oxford University Press, 1987).

In 1986 Lord Hailsham published a guide to appointment policies and procedures in order to 'dispel any lingering sense of mystery or obscurity'. His successor, Lord Mackay, published his own version in 1990, but the terms of reference continue to be vague.

Judicial law making

Mechanistic decision making

The main function of a judge is to apply law. According to constitutional theory, law is made by Parliament and judges decide how the law should be applied to a particular case. The implication of this is that a judge's decisions are mechanical and straightforward – the judge picks up a law and applies it to a case almost like completing a multiple-choice question paper. However, this could not be further from the truth. No law is so straightforward that it can be interpreted in such a mechanical way.

Judicial decision making interpreted

Lord Templeman describes the law lords at work:

'One of the five will say: "Looks to me as though the Court of Appeal got it quite right." . . . And somebody else will say: "Oh, I'm not at all happy about the way they argued this point." . . . And at that we'll go up and listen to the argument. And in the course of the argument, we'll argue amongst ourselves: when a law lord makes a point to a counsel, he's asking for the answer from the counsel, but he's also pointing out to his colleagues the way his mind is working. And then another law lord, who at that stage takes a slightly different view, comes in. Well then, of course, we have lunch. And at lunch, as we're going down, we'll have a sort of mild discussion and at the end of the day we'll have a mild discussion, and then the first serious discussion comes when counsel have finished. We throw everybody out, the doors are shut and the five of us sit in our horseshoe – five of us rather like the forward line of Manchester United. And the outside left who's the junior, he gives his opinion; he says he would dismiss this appeal for the following reasons, and we each do the same in turn. If we're agreed, then the presiding judge asks one of us, usually an expert in the particular field, to write the first judgement. If we're not agreed, we have a further discussion and then we all write separate judgements.

The next thing that happens is that whoever drafts a judgement circulates it to all the others. And even if we're agreed on it, each goes through and criticizes it, each asks for amendments. And so even if there's one judgement, it's a concerted team effort.

If we're not agreed, we might have lots of discussions. Although people don't believe this, it is a fact that one changes one's mind in the course of a case, if it's one of those knife-edge cases, in deference to the views of the other law lords. Sometimes I have said: "Well, I'm not convinced you're right, but I think it would make for unease and uncertainty if I dissented on this particular point, and therefore, I'm not going to dissent, although I have my doubts."'

Source: Hugo Young, *The Judges*, BBC Radio 4, 13 April 1988

As H L A Hart said: 'All rules have a penumbra of uncertainty where the judge must choose between alternatives' (*The Concept of Law*, Clarendon Press, 1961). In effect, the judge must decide what the law actually means in order to apply it to a case. It is at this stage that there is room for *judicial discretion* or **judicial creativity**. The judges must choose between different interpretations of the law and in doing so they are creating law – this is known as *common law*. Judicial interpretation of statute law is unavoidable, but nevertheless, it puts judges in a political position because they are, in effect, making law.

Judicial creativity

How far judges are willing to make use of opportunities to use their judicial creativity varies between courts and between individual judges. To a large extent, judges tend to follow judgements made in previous cases, i.e. precedent.

Precedent

Traditionally, judges' attitudes have been conservative and they have often been unwilling to depart from precedent, preferring to leave law making to the politicians. It was not until 1966 that the House of Lords changed its procedures to allow the law lords to depart from precedent. Since then the law lords have been prepared to move away from precedent in civil cases, but have been much more reluctant to do so in criminal cases.

Nevertheless, there are a number of well-known examples of judges interpreting law and in so doing, they have become involved in controversial policy areas. In *Gillick v. West Norfolk and Wisbech Area Health Authority* (1987), Victoria Gillick sought assurances from her area health authority that contraceptives would never be prescribed for her children, below the age of 16, without her consent. This case embroiled the law lords in a controversial area of social policy concerning the degree of control parents may exercise over their children. The Lords ruled that, if a doctor believed that the prescription of contraceptives was in the interests of the child, parental consent was not required.

Gillick case

A similar area of controversy was marital rape. Traditional common-law interpretation of the 1976 Sexual Offences (Amendment) Act was that unlawful sex meant sex outside marriage, and that a husband could not be convicted of raping his wife because the woman was said to have given her consent during the marriage ceremony. A series of decisions in the lower courts that eroded this exception to the crime of rape finally culminated in *R. v. R.* (1991) before the House of Lords. In this case, the law lords ruled that the exception of marital rape should be overruled and in doing so were making policy in a controversial area.

Marital rape

When judges decide to reinterpret the wording of statute law, they tend to follow the wording of the parliamentary statute quite closely. As Lord Diplock said in *Duport Steels Ltd v. Sirs* (1980):

'*Parliament makes the laws, the judiciary interpret them . . . The role of the judiciary is confined to ascertaining from the words that Parliament has approved as expressing its intention, what that intention was, and giving effect to it. Where the meaning of the statutory words is plain and unambiguous it is not for the judges to invent fancied ambiguities as an excuse for failing to give effect to its plain meaning because they themselves consider that the consequences of doing so would be expedient, or even unjust or immoral.*'

Such an interpretation of the role of judges can be considered conservative or one of **judicial restraint**. Judges following such a line are reluctant to have the judiciary become politically involved to a greater extent than is necessary.

Judicial restraint

Some judges, notably the former master of the rolls Lord Denning, have argued that judges should be free to be much more active, in that they should be able to

Lord Denning

examine not only the words of a statute but also the motives of the law makers lying behind the statute. This would involve examining the records of parliamentary debate in *Hansard* as well as any law Commission reports that may have preceded the law. Lord Denning, in *Davis v. Johnson* (1979), commented:

'Some may say – and indeed have said – that judges should not pay any attention to what is said in Parliament. They should grope about in the dark for the meaning of an Act without switching on the light. I do not accede to this view . . . And it is obvious that there is nothing to prevent a judge looking at these debates himself privately and getting some guidance from them.'

The danger of this attitude is that judges could be accused of 'usurping the role of the legislature'.

Judges and the media

Kilmuir rules

Traditionally, judges have been encouraged to keep their opinions and attitudes to themselves. The Kilmuir rules, laid down in 1955, were designed to prevent judges speaking their minds on radio and television (see above). In 1987 Lord Mackay abolished these rules as one of his first acts on taking office. Since then, judges at all levels have spoken for and against government policies. Lord chief justice Taylor, for example, has spoken out against government policy on legal aid, in favour of the incorporation of the European Convention on Human Rights into British law and against the Government's Criminal Justice Act of 1994.

Judge Pickles

Lower down the judicial hierarchy, Judge Pickles achieved notoriety by appearing regularly on television and radio and in newspaper articles, even before the abolition of the Kilmuir rules. His comments included the suggestion that young women might become pregnant in the interval between arrest and sentencing, in an attempt to avoid prison.

While it is possible to argue that judges have a right to give their opinions on legal matters and even matters of opinion, such pronouncements do little to reinforce the separation of the political and judicial branches of government.

Judicial attitudes and background

The fact that judges make law through their interpretations and that some have become outspoken in their comments regarding government policies means that judges' attitudes are a cause for concern.

John Griffith

In 1977 Professor John Griffith of the London School of Economics first argued that British judges could be viewed as an homogeneous group who share a set of views and attitudes. He described them as having 'a unifying attitude of mind, a political position, which is primarily concerned to protect and conserve values and institutions' (*The Politics of the Judiciary*, Fontana, 1977). In fact, John Griffith went further and argued that 'the judicial conception of the public interest . . . is threefold. It concerns, first, the interest of the state (including its moral welfare); secondly, the preservation of law and order, broadly interpreted; and, thirdly, the promotion of certain political views normally associated with the Conservative Party.'

Issues

He identified a number of areas which illustrate these shared attitudes. They include race relations, industrial relations and public order issues. Of the three, industrial relations has probably been the most controversial area for judges. The industrial relations measures introduced by the Conservative governments of 1970–4 and 1979 until now have forced judges to become involved in a highly political area.

It can be argued that judges' perceptions of the national interest are a result of their backgrounds. From a Marxist point of view, the background of judges can be considered to be indicative of their likely attitudes. Hugh Collins, the legal academic, stated: 'From [a] materialist perspective, ideas, knowledge and motivation were neither arbitrary flights of the imagination nor the product of research into the recesses of the mind, but were constructed in response to practical experiences' (*Marxism and Law*, Oxford University Press, 1982).

Judges are generally male and white. They are usually from the middle/upper-middle classes, with a public-school background and are graduates of either Oxford or Cambridge University. Of the law lords listed on page 125, eight attended Oxford or Cambridge.

As John Griffith has said: 'Judges have by their education and training and the pursuit of their profession as barristers, acquired a strikingly homogeneous collection of attitudes, beliefs and principles, which to them represent the public interest.'

At the beginning of 1994 there were no black or Asian judges among the 122 judges of the Appeal or High Court, while only four of the 487 judges on the Circuit bench were from ethnic minorities. There was only one woman, Lord justice Butler-Sloss, in the Court of Appeal and 28 on the Circuit bench.

However, John Griffith's argument is not completely watertight. The fact that the majority of judges come from a particular background does not necessarily indicate their belief systems and the ways in which they behave. Almost half of Labour cabinet ministers between 1964 and 1979 were Oxbridge educated and almost a third had attended public school; nevertheless they were committed to socialist policies.

Griffith is also concerned that judges 'do not regard their role as radical or even reformist'. However, it is by no means clear that judges should see themselves as reformers. Given that they are **unelected**, perhaps they should confine their activities to applying the laws made by the legislators. From this position it is difficult to behave in a radical way.

This argument may be taken one step further. Marxists argue that every state has a dominant ideology. The function of the ideology is to lay down the belief system of a society. It shapes the formation of political institutions, the relationships between institutions and individuals and the relationships between individuals. The laws of the state are designed to preserve the ideology. The dominant ideology in Britain is liberal and capitalist. Therefore, the laws are designed to preserve the system. Judges, as an arm of the British state, are required to uphold these laws and in turn to uphold the ideology. According to this view, it is unrealistic to expect judges to act in a way that is contrary to the dominant ideology of the society.

Controversial law

Judges should apply the laws made by legislators and as they do so, they may be drawn into the middle of heated political debate. If the government, via Parliament, is passing laws that concern controversial areas of policy, it is only to be expected that judges will be called upon to apply these laws.

The Conservative governments of 1979–90 illustrate very well the effect on the judiciary of controversial laws and the manner in which government chose to enforce them. Although the Official Secrets Act dates from 1911, the prime minister

Social background

Education

Race and gender

Conservatism

Marxism

Margaret Thatcher's governments

Margaret Thatcher used the Act to hunt civil servants leaking information. The Ponting case (1985) (see page 102) and the Spycatcher case (1986) (see page 136) are examples of this. Although it was the government that chose to pursue the civil servants, it was the judges who were perceived to be in favour of the Official Secrets Act. Similarly, it was the Conservative government of 1979–90 which initiated legislation to limit the power of trade unions, but it was the judiciary that was called upon to apply the law and so became labelled anti-trade union.

Judicial inquiries

Governments have also drawn the judiciary into the political debate by taking judges out of the courtroom and asking them to head **judicial inquiries** into a variety of incidents and issues. In 1994 lord justice Scott chaired the 'arms to Iraq' hearing in which government ministers were accused of breaking their own code of conduct by exporting weapons to Iraq. Lord justice Taylor investigated the Hillsborough disaster of 1989 in which 93 people were killed and 200 injured in the crush inside a football stadium. Lord Nolan reported in May 1995 on his inquiry into the standards of ethics expected of MPs.

All of these areas are controversial and potentially political. The judges' reports are always eagerly awaited and often form a basis for future government policy. Obviously, the reason for asking judges to chair such inquiries is their experience in dealing with a wide range of evidence and opinion. Nevertheless, from a constitutional point of view they may threaten judicial impartiality because judges are asked to draw conclusions on debatable matters.

Lord Scarman and the Brixton riots

Perhaps the most outstanding example of a government placing a judge at the head of a politically controversial inquiry occurred in 1981 when Lord Scarman was asked to look into the causes of the Brixton riots. During one weekend in April riots broke out in the Brixton area of London. At the height of the disturbances 279 police officers and many members of the public were injured and 28 buildings were damaged or destroyed. Margaret Thatcher's government was heavily criticized for the unemployment and social deprivation that many believed had been the cause of the riots while the prime minister herself believed that social deprivation could never justify criminal behaviour. Lord Scarman, a moderate judge, was asked by the home secretary William Whitelaw to produce a report. To take on such a politically explosive task put Lord Scarman in a very delicate position and, as Hugo Young said: 'Almost all that Scarman had to say about strengthening the police, and almost nothing he had to say about social reform, was put in train with Whitelaw's blessing' (Hugo Young, *One of Us*, Macmillan, 1989).

Judicial review

Judicial review concerns the ability of courts to review the action of other branches of government in order to determine their legality and constitutionality. It is an important element of the separation of powers as it offers a means to prevent the abuse of government power. It is most clearly illustrated in the USA where the Supreme Court, at the head of the judicial branch of government, has the power to check the other branches of government. It can do this by declaring acts of Congress and action by the president unconstitutional. Such decisions take the courts into controversial areas of governmental power and often require the judges to make political decisions.

In Britain the power of judicial review is limited by the fact that there is no codified constitution and by the doctrine of parliamentary sovereignty. Traditionally, in Britain any act of Parliament is, by definition, constitutional and is not subject to review by the courts. However the judiciary does have the right to review the actions of the executive branch and local government.

Parliamentary sovereignty

Ultra vires

The basis for the review of the executive and local government is administrative law. Every action by central or local government must be based on law. If it is not, that branch of government is said to be acting beyond its powers or **ultra vires**.

The courts can declare an action *ultra vires* if it is contrary to the 'express terms' or the 'implied terms' of a statute. The former relates to terms specifically outlined in the statute, while the latter is concerned with the spirit of the statute. Both principles are illustrated by *Bromley LBC v. Greater London Council* (1983), also known as the 'Fares Fair' case.

'Fares Fair' case

In this case the Greater London Council (GLC) was taken to court over its policy towards fares on London Transport facilities and their impact on ratepayers. The GLC proposed to reduce the fares on public transport, in line with election promises, even though this would cause an increase in the bill facing ratepayers. The House of Lords ruled that in doing so the council was acting *ultra vires*. By not trying to run public transport along traditional business lines it was acting contrary to the express terms of the Transport (London) Act 1969. The Lords also ruled that the GLC was acting outside the implied terms of the GLC's remit in that the council had a duty to ratepayers not to spend their money recklessly. The increases in rates were said to be contrary to this commitment.

More recent examples of the executive branch being checked by the judiciary include the Pergau Dam affair of 1994. The courts ruled that the foreign secretary, Douglas Hurd, had acted *ultra vires* by linking the distribution of foreign aid to orders for British products. In this particular case, the Foreign Office granted aid to the Malaysian government to build the Pergau Dam in return for which the Malaysian government placed an order for British arms which was worth millions of pounds.

Pergau Dam

Judicial review and the EU

Since Britain became a member of the European Community, now known as the European Union (EU), the powers of judicial review available to British courts have increased.

According to the **Treaty of Rome** (see page 154), which Britain signed to become a full member of the Community, EU law is supreme and therefore, takes precedence over the legislatures and laws of individual states. Although the treaty itself had no validity in British law, an act of Parliament – the European Communities Act (1972) – brought it into domestic effect.

Treaty of Rome

As a result of this act, European law is now supreme in Britain and British law must adhere to its provisions. For the first time since the establishment of parliamentary sovereignty there is now a body of law against which British statute law can be judged. If a parliamentary statute contravenes EU law it must be repealed or amended by Parliament. If Parliament decided not to do so, it would, in effect, be tantamount to leaving the European Union.

Factortame case

The best-known case illustrating the supremacy of European law is *R. v. Secretary of State for Transport, ex parte Factortame Ltd (No. 2)*(1991), which is also known as the Factortame case. The House of Lords judged the 1988 Merchant Shipping Act to be unlawful because it contravened EU law and suspended it. The attitude of the judiciary to the EU was summed up by Justice Hoffman in *Stoke-on-Trent County Council v B & Q Plc* (1991):

> '*The EEC Treaty is the supreme law of this country taking precedence over Acts of Parliament. Our entry into the EEC meant (subject to our undoubted but probably theoretical right to withdraw from the Community all together) Parliament surrendered its sovereign right to legislate contrary to the provisions of the Treaty on matters of social and economic policy.*'

By giving up much of its sovereignty as a result of the European Communities Act, Parliament has allowed the courts greater power of judicial review, so bringing them further into the political arena.

Judicial power

Despite the fact that membership of the EU has extended the powers of judicial review many observers believe that the UK judiciary should be given still greater powers by increasing judicial review.

In order to give the courts wider powers of judicial review, Britain's unwritten constitution would have to be replaced by a codified constitution together with a **bill of rights**. Such a document would give the courts an authority, higher than parliamentary law, against which to scrutinize the actions of all branches of government.

Limit Parliament

This would have a considerable impact on the other branches of government. Parliamentary sovereignty would be restrained and the executive would be kept in check. However, the body responsible for such regulation would be the unelected and **unrepresentative** judiciary. As a result, several observers have argued against giving such enhanced powers to the courts. Some of these issues are discussed more fully in chapter 1, but the political implications for the judiciary are examined here.

Judicial review and policy making

US Supreme Court

We saw above that the power of the judiciary to interpret law gives the courts considerable opportunity to make law. This would be much greater if the power of judicial review was extended. The implications of such a change in Britain can best be seen in the USA where the Supreme Court has the power to interpret not only law but also the Constitution. Naturally, this is a broad, and in some cases vague, document so the court has considerable scope in its interpretations.

Abortion

The policy-making power of the Supreme Court is well illustrated by the issue of abortion. Until 1973 individual state governments were free to determine their own policies regarding the legality and availability of abortions in their state. 'Jane Roe', a resident of Texas, wanted an abortion in order to avoid the social stigma of single parenthood and the economic hardship it would involve. However, abortion was outlawed in her state. She took the case to the Supreme Court. The justices ruled that it is a woman's right to make her own decision about whether to have an abortion. Therefore, the court overruled the laws of many states and set up a constitutional right to have an abortion.

This case, known as *Roe v. Wade*, shows the extent of the Supreme Court's ability to interpret the constitution and to make policy without reference to elected politicians. If the power of judicial review was extended in Britain, with the adoption of a written constitution, British judges would have similar power to make policy.

Politicization

The American experience also suggests that the more power the courts possess, the more interested politicians become in the appointment of judges. If judges have considerable policy-making power, there is obviously an incentive for politicians to harness that power. In the USA the nine justices of the Supreme Court are appointed for life by the president, with Senate ratification. Many presidents have appointed judges who share their political beliefs and attitudes in order to shape the composition of the court and so influence its decision making. Presidents Reagan and Bush were in office for twelve years and during that period appointed five justices. As a result the court moved to the right as its decisions reflected the views of its new members.

We have already seen that it is desirable for the judiciary to be independent of politics. Political interference in the appointment of judges brings it to the very centre of the political world and puts judicial independence at risk.

Appointments

Civil liberties

Liberties, or rights, are entitlements and freedoms. *Natural rights*, sometimes called *human rights*, are considered to be liberties to which we are entitled solely because we are human beings. There is often wide disagreement about which rights may be considered human rights. The European Convention on Human Rights (1951) includes rights as wide as the right to life (Article 2), the right to peaceful enjoyment of possessions (Protocol No 1, Article 1), the right to marry and build a family (Article 12) and freedom from torture or inhuman or degrading punishment.

Natural rights

Human rights are often termed *inalienable* because they can never be removed or given up. Of course, this does not mean that every individual in every state is benefiting fully from their human rights.

Inalienable rights

In each state citizens are granted certain rights, known as *civil rights*. They vary widely from one state to another. In 1973 General Augusto Pinochet came to power in Chile, ending 40 years of democracy and civil rights. All democratic institutions were closed; the security forces murdered, imprisoned and tortured thousands of citizens; and freedoms of association, speech and the press were withdrawn. In the USA, on the other hand, citizens' rights are outlined in the Bill of Rights and are preserved, at least theoretically, by the courts and politicians who respect the citizens.

Civil rights

Even within democratic states, such as Britain or the USA, there is disagreement about which civil rights should be guaranteed to citizens. Those on the right of the political spectrum tend to emphasize *individual rights* and *political rights*, e.g. the right to a fair trial, the right to take part in elections and the right to own property. Those on the left tend to stress *collective rights*, or the rights of the group, along with *economic rights*, e.g. freedom of association, including membership of a trade union; the right to education and the right to work (see chapter 4).

Disputes over rights

A further distinction can be made between *negative* and *positive* rights. The former involve freedom from government restriction, while the latter involve the freedom to reach one's full potential, perhaps with the assistance of the state. Liberals or

Conservatives tend to emphasize an individual's freedom from government interference and regulation, while socialists tends to favour government intervention to enable individuals and groups to achieve their full potential.

Civil rights in Britain

Bill of Rights

As Britain has an unwritten constitution, there is no codified document to list the rights and liberties of citizens. The Bill of Rights of 1689 was written in the wake of the Glorious Revolution and was designed to limit the power of the monarch in relation to Parliament rather than to outline the rights of citizens. Therefore, all of the rights available to British citizens rest in statute or common law. In other words, our rights are derived from Parliament or from the decisions of judges. Often our liberties are not explicitly spelt out, rather they need to be extracted from the tangle of restrictions. Those things not restricted are our rights. As Geoffrey Robertson said: 'Liberty in Britain is a state of mind rather than a set of legal rules' (Geoffrey Robertson, *Freedom, the Individual and the Law*, Penguin, 1993).

Parliament and rights

Given the sources of our rights, it follows that it falls mainly to Parliament and to the courts to protect civil liberties in Britain. In Parliament it is the responsibility of MPs and peers to scrutinize proposed legislation carefully and to decide if it unduly threatens civil rights. Similarly, in the courts judges should ensure that individuals are treated equitably by the law. However, as both Parliament and judges take into consideration civil liberties in Britain, they are also required to balance the preservation of one person's liberties against the rights of others because frequently liberties conflict. Decision makers search for the greater good either of individuals or of the country as a whole. The conflict between different civil liberties is illustrated very simply by the issue of **freedom of speech**. Although this freedom is desirable and necessary in a democracy, for it to be unrestrained would damage the right of others to be free from slanderous, blasphemous or discriminating remarks.

Civil rights since 1979

Some commentators have argued that the balance between individual liberty and the rights of the wider society has been upset by Conservative governments since 1979.

Freedom of speech

We have already seen that there are a number of restrictions on absolute freedom of speech, including laws. However, since 1979 the government has acted to reinforce restrictions on a number of occasions.

The Official Secrets Act

Throughout Margaret Thatcher's period of office the Official Secrets Act (1911 and a new act in 1989) was enforced with vigour. Civil servants, past and present, were taken to court on a number of occasions to prevent them making their views public or to punish them for doing so. For example, Sarah Tisdall (1984) (see page 110) and Clive Ponting (1985) (see page 102) were two of 29 prosecutions under the Official Secrets Act in Margaret Thatcher's first seven years in office. Both civil servants believed they were acting in the best interests of the state by making information public, but the government through the courts showed its displeasure. Sarah Tisdall received a prison sentence, while Clive Ponting was found not guilty.

Table 9.1

Rights	Explanation
Freedom of speech	The freedom of speech can be interpreted widely to include the rights to speak, publish and broadcast without government interference. There is no right to freedom of speech in Britain. The law places restrictions on the freedom of expression, anything outside these restrictions is lawful. Legal restrictions cover obscenities, racial taunts, libel, slander and official secrets.
Freedom of the person	These rights concern the rights of the individual vis à vis the police, e.g. freedom from unlawful arrest, the right to a lawyer, habeas corpus and the right to silence. These rights rest largely on statute law, e.g. Police and Criminal Evidence Act 1984.
Freedom of association and assembly	Freedom of association refers to citizens' entitlement to form groups, e.g. political parties and trade unions. Freedom of assembly concerns the people's right to gather together, e.g. to demonstrate or to organize a procession. British law does not give a citizen any absolute right of association or assembly. It places restrictions on these rights, e.g. to prevent a breakdown of public order or to prevent incitement of racial hatred.
Freedom of movement	This freedom concerns the citizen's right to move freely around the country without restriction. Although British citizens have no legally enforceable right to freedom of movement, there are relatively few restrictions. The police are able to restrict travel to demonstrations and the Prevention of Terrorism Act allows the authorities to prevent those suspected of sympathizing with terrorism from entering the mainland from Northern Ireland.
Freedom of religion and thought	Although Britain has an established religion, the Church of England, there is freedom of worship in Britain. Religious meetings are protected by law from disturbance. Since 1677 Britain has had a law against blasphemy which prevents remarks or the publication of material that is insulting to the Christian religion. The law only applies to Christianity, hence the author Salman Rushdie could not be prosecuted by Muslim groups for writing *The Satanic Verses*.
Property rights	This includes the right to possess property and to use it as one sees fit. A great deal of British statute and common law is designed to preserve property rights. However, the government has restricted this right through nationalization and compulsory purchase orders.
Right to privacy	This concerns citizens' rights to respect for their private life. Telephones should not be 'bugged', correspondence should not be opened and individuals should not be harassed by the media. There is no right to privacy in Britain although the law does protect citizens from trespass, nuisance and breach of confidence.
Right to equal treatment	Citizens have a right to expect equal treatment before the law, in their employment and in terms of political rights. The law upholds the right to vote, equality before the law and should prevent race or gender discrimination.

Spycatcher

Former MI5 agent Peter Wright (1986–8) was taken to court in order to prevent the publication of the memoirs of his life in MI5 (*Spycatcher*). Despite the fact that much of the information was dated, the government was determined to use the law to gag Wright.

The Sinn Fein broadcasting ban

In 1988 the government ordered that no interviews with representatives of Sinn Fein (see page 196), the political wing of the IRA, or any other Irish organizations that supported the use of violence, should be broadcast on the television or radio. The justification for the ban was that many viewers would be outraged by such interviews and that their access to the broadcast media might also give the groups a degree of respectability.

This was an example of political censorship that would appear to be contrary to the freedom of speech provision of the European Convention on Human Rights. As such, it removed the opportunities for the public to judge the acceptability of politicians, and their beliefs, for themselves.

Freedom of association

GCHQ

There is no absolute freedom of association in Britain and the government is able to ban organizations if it can justify its actions. In 1984 the government decided to ban trade unions at the Government Communications Headquarters (GCHQ) for reasons of national security.

The ban was initially overturned in the High Court on the basis that the trade unions had not been adequately consulted before the action was taken. However, in the Court of Appeal the government convinced the court that national security was of paramount importance because the centre had been affected by a strike two years earlier.

Freedom of movement

Miners' strike

The British police have the power to restrain people who are likely to create public disorder that will lead to a 'breach of the peace' – damage to property or persons. These powers were used controversially in 1984 during the miners' strike when the police intercepted miners travelling across the country to picket other pits. The miners were turned back several hundred miles from their destination.

A great deal of violence had occurred during the miners' strike and there was some sympathy with their desire to prevent further incidents. The courts agreed with this attitude. However, the line between crime prevention and infringement of civil liberties is narrow.

The right to silence

Traditionally, the police have been required to caution an arrested person before beginning an interview: 'You do not have to say anything unless you wish to do so, but what you say may be given in evidence.' The caution was the embodiment of the 'right to silence' which means that no one should be required to incriminate themselves. A person is innocent until proven guilty and it is the responsibility of the prosecution to prove guilt, if necessary without the assistance of the accused.

Some observers objected to the right to silence on the grounds that if the accused is unwilling to answer questions they are obstructing justice and so may have something to hide.

In 1988 the government abolished the right to silence in Northern Ireland where failure to answer police questions can be given an adverse connotation by the court. This was followed by the Criminal Justice Act in 1994 which removed the right to silence in the remainder of the UK.

Abolition

The courts and civil liberties

The judiciary in Britain has only limited ability to preserve civil liberties. It does not have the power to review the actions of Parliament and so any statute law that might be considered to include infringements of civil liberties, such as the Criminal Justice Act, is beyond the reach of the courts.

However, the courts do have the power to review the actions of the executive branch of government and so here the judiciary has more discretion in preventing the infringement of civil liberties.

As a result of their limited power, judges often appear to be inadequate guardians of civil liberties. Furthermore, as we have seen, in recent years judges have found in favour of the government as a series of civil liberties has been eroded, giving the impression that they share the government's conception of the national interest. However it would be unfair to accuse all judges of failing to protect civil rights.

The Matrix Churchill case (1992) clearly illustrates a judge's willingness to protect civil liberties. In 1991 Paul Henderson, managing director of Matrix Churchill, a Coventry-based engineering company, was arrested by customs officials. He, and two colleagues, were accused of illegally exporting £70 million of arms to Iraq between 1987 and 1990. It was alleged that they had deceived the Department of Trade and Industry (DTI) by claiming that the exports comprised engineering equipment.

Matrix Churchill case

Prior to the case coming to court defence lawyers requested certain documents from a number of civil service departments. In September 1992 four government ministers, Kenneth Clarke, Tristan Garel-Jones, Malcolm Rifkind and Michael Heseltine, all signed 'public interest security certificates'. The purpose of these was to prevent the release of the documents for reasons of national security.

Under these circumstances, the presiding judge was required to decide if some or all of the material should be released. Judge Smedley released some of the papers. They showed that the Matrix Churchill executives had informed the DTI of the nature of the exports and that a government minister, Alan Clarke, had encouraged the executives to avoid the restrictions on military exports to Iraq by hiding their true purpose. As a result of these revelations, the trial collapsed and the government set up the Scott Inquiry into Britain's export of arms to Iraq.

The European Convention on Human Rights

The European Convention on Human Rights was designed to improve the observance of human rights by governments throughout Europe. Britain ratified the Convention in 1951 but did not incorporate it into domestic law. Therefore, British citizens who feel that their human rights have been infringed cannot appeal on the

European Court of Human Rights

basis of the Convention to British courts. They can, on the other hand, take their case to the European Court of Human Rights (ECHR) in Strasbourg.

ECHR decisions against the government have included the treatment of suspected terrorists in Northern Ireland; the banning of newspapers publishing extracts of Peter Wright's memoirs; and the use of corporal punishment in schools. In fact, the British government has been taken to the ECHR more than any other signatory of the treaty.

A bill of rights

Supporters of a bill of rights in Britain include lord chief justice Taylor, the pressure groups Charter 88 and Liberty, and many members of the major political parties.

The basis of their argument is that nowhere are the rights and liberties of British citizens clearly outlined in a single document. Therefore, it is unclear what rights citizens can expect. Governments, MPs, judges and citizens themselves would all benefit from the clarity that such a document would bring.

Contents

Opponents of a bill of rights believe that even the initial stage of drawing up the document would involve political conflict. As we have seen, there is some disagreement between parties of the left and right about the type of rights to which citizens should be entitled. Therefore, far from clarifying the situation a bill would become the object of political dispute.

Judicial power

If a bill of rights were created, it would be enforceable by the judiciary. This would lead to an increase in the power of the courts at the expense of Parliament. The principle of parliamentary sovereignty would be ended to ensure that statute law could no longer infringe on civil liberties. Therefore, the courts would be better equipped to protect freedoms and rights.

Judicial bias

The difficulty of abandoning parliamentary sovereignty and increasing the power of the judiciary is that a democratically elected assembly would be subordinated to a panel of unelected and unrepresentative judges. This is of particular concern given John Griffith's view that judges hold a particular set of attitudes which reflect their backgrounds (see page 128).

USA

The operation of a bill of rights in the USA illustrates both the advantages and the dangers of such a document. The Supreme Court has used the Bill of Rights to preserve the rights of citizens. In *Brown v. The Board of Education, Topeka, Kansas* (1954) the court ruled racial segregation unconstitutional. In *Miranda v. Arizona* (1966) the court established the procedure of the accused being read their rights as they are arrested. Judgements such as these are particularly important for minority groups which might not receive full protection from the legislature as they have a limited impact on election results.

Cases such as Miranda's and Brown's are well known. However, less well-known are cases such as *Plessy v. Ferguson* (1896) and the Hirabayashi case (1943). The former ruled racial segregation constitutional and the latter allowed Japanese Americans to be held in internment camps for the duration of World War II. Therefore, despite its powers the Supreme Court has not always acted to preserve the liberties of citizens, as we perceive them today.

Limits on courts

The assumption that a bill of rights and courts with greater powers would automatically preserve civil liberties is simplistic. Courts cannot initiate cases; they must wait for cases to be brought before them. They cannot enforce their decisions, for this they rely on the other branches of government and ultimately, courts are only effective if politicians are willing to abide by their decisions. Therefore, the effectiveness of courts depends on the constitutionalism of the politicians.

Exercises

Short questions

1 What justifications might there be for limiting freedom of expression?
   (ULEAC, June 1992)
2 Outline, with examples, judges' attitudes towards the issue of official secrecy.
   (ULEAC, January 1993)

Essay questions

1 Discuss the problems involved in drawing up a written constitution for Britain. (ULEAC, June 1994)
2 How adequately do judges protect civil liberties? (ULEAC, June 1993)
3 Discuss the view that demands for a bill of rights are a result of Parliament's failure to protect civil liberties. (Oxford and Cambridge, June 1992).

Data response question

'In short, it is suggested that judges are too stuffy and remote; that they are out of touch with society today, with its lifestyle and its standards; that they are all in the same mould – white, male, public school, Oxbridge...

It is true, until recently, barristers and therefore judges tended to be drawn from the middle class upwards ... But the idea that judges should be more representative would be taken too far if judges were not drawn from those trained in the law, experienced in the courts and best suited for the job...

The suggestion that judges are biased towards the Establishment does not stand up to examination. For example, in a recent case a judge ordered disclosure of government documents and thereby enabled three defendants to be cleared of criminal charges.'

Source: adapted from: Lord Taylor, *The Judiciary in the Nineties*, BBC Education, 1992

a According to the passage, why might judges be regarded as unrepresentative of society?
b Is it important that judges should be representative?
c State an argument supporting the view that judges are not biased towards the Establishment.

(ULEAC, January 1995)

10 Local government

Questions to be answered in this chapter
- What is the function of local government?
- What are the functions of local councillors?
- How is local government structured?
- How is local government financed?
- What is the relationship between central and local government?

Terms to know

Capping	Politicization
Corporatism	Poll tax
Council tax	Privatization
Councillors	Providers
Enablers	Rate support grant
Grant Related Expenditure Assessment (GREA)	Thatcherism
	Two-tier structure
Internal market	Uniform Business Rate (UBR)
Marketization	*Ultra vires*
Metropolitan authorities	Unitary
Municipal socialism	Wards
Ombudsmen	

Why local government?

Functions

Local government fulfils two major functions: democratic and administrative. The former allows members of the local community to participate in local affairs both by standing as **councillors** and by voting in local elections. Although the turnout in local elections is significantly lower than in general elections (40 per cent compared to 70 per cent) and the quality of councillors has often been criticized, the system does allow local people to have a voice in local affairs.

Non-partisan competition

Traditionally, individuals have been able to take part in local politics independent of political parties. A great deal of local competition was non-partisan. The advantage of this was to allow individuals to put forward their point of view for the benefit of the community without having to follow a party line. In the 1970s, however, local politics became more partisan and political parties now dominate local elections as they do at national level.

Politicization

Many observers have mourned the passing of the independent councillor, but wherever there are elections, political parties will follow. Their rise in the 1970s can probably be attributed to the polarization of national politics. The breakdown of the postwar political consensus and the emergence of adversarial politics made electoral competition at all levels of great importance to the parties. Local politics became particularly important as Margaret Thatcher's governments pushed the national political agenda to the right. The Labour and Liberal Parties saw local government as a means to oppose the advance of Thatcherism and when the Conservative governments began to reassess the role of local government, the other parties saw the need to defend local democracy. Events such as the abolition of the **metropolitan authorities** in 1986 were seen as overtly political, as they were all Labour controlled, and this gave further impetus to the **politicization** of local democracy.

The results of politicization have been changes in the nature of representation at local level, along the lines of those that have already occurred at national level. Councillors, like MPs, no longer represent only their constituents; they must consider the party line as well.

Administratively, local government allows policies to be given a local flavour. Although laws are made at Westminster and many policies are determined by central government, local authorities have the freedom to shape policies to suit local conditions. In addition, local government allows services to be delivered to the community in a sensitive and responsive manner, which means that people receiving important services, such as policing or housing, are able to take up any difficulties or complaints with local bodies rather than with a vast bureaucracy in London.

Local conditions

The role of local councillors

Councillors are elected locally from constituencies known as **wards** which they represent on the council. In order to stand for election, an individual must be 21 years old. However, almost half of councillors are aged 55–74, a group which accounts for only 30 per cent of the national population, and only 17 per cent of councillors are women. This has led to charges that councillors are unrepresentative of the population. In fact, local councils are no more unrepresentative than the House of Commons, where, for example, only 9 per cent of MPs are women.

Election

The role of local councillors differs significantly from those of MPs (see chapter 5). Local authorities are not local legislatures: they cannot make law, other than local bylaws. Councils fulfil an executive role, not a legislative role, in that they implement policies that have been made by central government, perhaps putting a local perspective on the delivery of these policies. Therefore, their responsibilities are purely local. Since local councils perform an executive function, they are under the supervision of Parliament and so councillors are subordinate to MPs.

Role

Within the authorities most business is carried out via committees that specialize in policy areas and have authority that has been delegated to them by the full council. The chairpersons of council committees are powerful. They determine the agenda, make many of the decisions regarding policy and finance and liaise with the chief officer of the council.

Committees

The chief officer or chief executive of the council heads the local authority's permanent staff who fulfil a similar role to civil servants at central government level. They are expected to implement local authority policy and provide information for relevant committees.

The structure of local government

The structure of local government in Britain was set up by the Local Government Act of 1972 which was based, to some extent, on the Redcliffe-Maud Report of 1968. This report had found that Britain had too many local authorities, the majority

Redcliffe-Maud Report

of which were inappropriate for dealing with the problems faced in their areas. Some were too small to provide the required services economically; others were based on electoral boundaries that no longer reflected demographic realities; and the **two-tier structure** was confusing for the population.

Recommendations

Maud recommended that the two-tier structure be replaced by a **unitary**, or one-tier system which would provide all of the services for a given area. The population of these areas should be between 250,000 and one million people and boundaries should be redrawn to reflect movements in the population. Finally, it was recommended that metropolitan counties should be created to co-ordinate the services and cope with the special problems of the large conurbations such as Birmingham, Liverpool and Greater Manchester – London already had the Greater London Council (GLC).

Local Government Act 1972

The 1972 Local Government Act adopted some of Maud's proposals. It distinguished between the conurbations and areas that combined urban and rural areas by setting up metropolitan counties in Greater Manchester, Merseyside, Tyne and Wear, the West Midlands, West Yorkshire and South Yorkshire. However, it retained the two-tier structure for the non-metropolitan areas. In fact, if parish councils are included, the non-metropolitan counties have a three-tier structure.

Two-tier structure

The adoption of the tier system reflects the difficulties faced by central government in creating a workable structure for local authorities. On the one hand, many services can only be provided on a large scale. Economically and logistically, services such as the fire service and the police force need to be delivered by a body that is sufficiently large to give an overview to the service. However, the large-scale local government that this requires, conflicts with the need for local democracy. The larger the units of local government, the more bureaucratic and less accessible they are likely to be and the less responsive to the needs of the local community. The two-tier structure was an attempt to solve this conflict. Table 10.1 shows the tiers of local government in England and the services for which they are responsible.

County councils

The top tier of the non-metropolitan structure includes the shire counties or county councils. They are responsible for the 'big-budget' services that require co-ordination on a large scale and are expensive to provide. Their responsibilities include major roads, policing and education.

District councils

The second tier, shire districts or district councils, is responsible for delivering the services that are less expensive and need to be attuned to the needs of local people. Its responsibilities include housing, planning and refuse collection.

Banham Committee

The confusing nature of the two-tier system remains a problem. In 1992, Michael Heseltine, during his second term at the Department of the Environment, initiated a review of local government organization, under the leadership of John Banham, former director-general of the CBI. Its early proposals in 1993 included a unitary council for the Isle of Wight; the division of Cleveland into four unitary counties and the replacement of Avon, Gloucestershire and Somerset with eight unitary councils. It is believed that the intention is to abandon the two-tier system in favour of a unitary system.

Metropolitan counties

In fact, a unitary system is already in place in the metropolitan districts. In 1986 the metropolitan counties were abolished and replaced by metropolitan districts and the functions of the GLC were incorporated into the London boroughs. Margaret Thatcher's government believed that the metropolitan counties were bureaucratic, wasteful and were abusing their positions by using taxpayers' money for political

Table 10.1 Local government in England

Area	Tiers of local government	Functions
Metropolitan areas	*Unitary* 36 metropolitan districts and 33 London boroughs created when the metropolitan counties were abolished in 1986. They cover large urban areas and provide most services in that area.	Education Social services Housing Roads Refuse Leisure
Non-metropolitan areas	*Top tier* Shire counties or county councils: 39 in England covering large areas and providing 'big-budget' services.	Police Fire Major roads Refuse disposal Social services
	Second tier Shire districts or district councils: 296 in England. They are sub-divisions of the shire counties.	Housing Planning Refuse collection Local roads Leisure
	Third tier Town and parish councils: 11,000 in England. They cover a very small area.	Footpaths Lighting Local amenities

ends. These were alleged to include anti-government propaganda and the promotion of left-wing ideas, such as 'nuclear-free zones' and police monitoring units.

Even in the metropolitan districts, the need for an overview of some services is recognized. For example, police and fire services are provided by specialist authorities which are made up of representatives from the districts or boroughs of the area.

The central–local relationship

The constitutional position

Constitutionally, local government is in a very weak position compared to its central counterpart. Britain is a unitary state and at the centre of the system is a parliament with sovereign power. This means that there is no countervailing power to that of Parliament. Statute law is supreme and local authorities derive their powers entirely from Parliament. It follows that what Parliament gives, it can also take away.

Unitary state

One aspect of the sovereignty of Parliament, and, therefore, of central government, is that the courts have the power to review the actions of local government. If a local authority exceeds the authority given to it by Parliament, the courts can declare it to be acting *ultra vires*, or beyond its powers. Famous cases of local authorities exceeding their powers have included the 'Fares Fair' case (1983), in which the courts ruled the GLC's public transport fare cuts were illegal (see page 131), and *Hazell v. Hammersmith and Fulham London Borough Council* (1991) in which the House of Lords

Ultra vires

143

declared that the council's speculation on option swaps on the London money market was illegal. (Option swaps involve swapping a loan with a fixed rate of interest for a loan at a variable rate of interest. Under certain conditions, the market rate of interest will fall and the speculator will be better off.)

Tameside decision

The courts do not always find against local authorities. In 1976 Tameside Metropolitan Borough Council decided to abandon comprehensive education, despite government policy to the contrary. The minister of education, Shirley Williams, issued a directive to the council in an effort to force it to comply with government policy. The council refused. The courts found in favour of the local authority, explaining that the government had acted beyond the powers given to it by the Education Act of 1944. Like local authorities, the central executive is subject to judicial review in the light of parliamentary statutes. However, the government was quickly able to pass a new Education Act which gave it the power to prevent other local authorities following Tameside's example.

Other controls

In addition to statute law and judicial review, the central government has a wide range of methods to control local authorities. Apart from financial intervention (see pages 145–6), central government can launch an inquiry into local authority affairs, for example the Widdicombe inquiry into the conduct of local authority business, which recommended the banning, among other things, of political advertising by local authorities and the employment of political advisers. In 1972 central government set up **ombudsmen** – commissioners for local administration – to investigate complaints against local authority actions. Central government can also organize systems of inspection over local authority services, for example, schools and the police force.

Changes in centre–local relations

Given the constitutional weakness of local government, the stimulus for the nature of the centre–local relationship tends to come from the dominant partner, central government. It has three options:
- It can treat the local authorities as partners in a single governmental system, both levels of which have common aims for delivery of services to the public.
- Central and local government can see themselves as independent units bargaining with each other for power.
- Central government can view the local authorities as merely agents through which to carry out its own policies.

Consultation

The political scientist R A W Rhodes ('Local Government', in B Jones and L Robbins (eds), *Two Decades in British Politics*, Manchester University Press, 1992) incorporated the above options into his analysis of changes in the nature of centre–local relations since 1970. Between 1970 and 1974 the tone of centre–local relations was one of partnership. According to Rhodes, 'Consultation was the "normal" style of central–local relations throughout the postwar period until the mid-1970s. For most of this time, local service spending was buoyant, and the numbers of local government employees grew fairly regularly.' Such an approach recognizes the democratic credentials of local government and attempts to build an effective relationship through consensus rather than confrontation.

Corporatism

During the Labour government of 1974–9 local authorities were caught up in the **corporatism** of government at the time. Like trade unions, local authorities were co-opted into government decision making. The government set up the

Consultative Council on Local Government Finance which allowed the local authorities and the Treasury to negotiate over the financing of local government.

Since 1979 the relationship between central and local government has changed, some might say, beyond recognition. The era of consensus and co-operation came to an end with the Conservative governments which tended to adopt a confrontational approach to local government. Margaret Thatcher did not accept the democratic qualifications of local government, because the turnout in local elections is so low (see page 140), whereas she believed her governments had a national mandate to carry out their economic and social policies. Therefore, the period since 1979 has seen the ever-greater centralization of policy making and the rise of the view that local authorities are agencies for the delivery of those policies.

Confrontation

Centralization under Margaret Thatcher

The Conservative government of 1979 came to power with an agenda and a leader with sufficient conviction to see those policies implemented. Margaret Thatcher was not a supporter of consensus and would countenance no opposition.

The main aims of what became known as **Thatcherism** were the control of inflation and the limiting of the role of the state in an effort to free the market place for private competition. For Margaret Thatcher, these basic aims would lead to efficiency, consumer choice, economic prosperity and a healthier democracy. To achieve these aims, the Conservative government needed to reduce government spending, both to bring down inflation (according to monetarist theory – see page 179) and to reduce the size of the state to leave more room for private industry.

Thatcherism

Margaret Thatcher believed that local authorities, at least some of them, stood in the way of reducing public expenditure. At the time, local authorities were spending almost 13 per cent of Britain's Gross National Product (GNP), accounting for 28 per cent of all government spending. From the point of view of local authorities, such expenditure was necessary given the extent of their responsibilities, the rise in wage costs and the increases in the population. However, Margaret Thatcher was determined to *reduce* local authority expenditure.

Spending controls

The Conservative government's first attempt to control local authority spending was the Local Government, Planning and Land Act (1980). This sought to exert tighter control over local authority spending as a whole and particularly on capital expenditure.

Until 1980 central government had given financial assistance to local government via the **rate support grant** which was, at least partially, calculated according to how much local authorities intended to spend. The government could vary the rate support grant only as a total figure; it could not alter the amount received by individual authorities. This scheme was replaced by a system of block grants which was intended to give central government greater control of the overspending of specific authorities. Under the new system, central government calculated what it believed each authority should be spending – the **Grant Related Expenditure Assessment** (GREA) – and compared this figure to the local council's estimated spending for the year. The greater the excess of the local authority's estimates, the more the block grant to that authority was reduced.

Rate support grant

The government took the provisions of the 1980 act a step further in 1981 by introducing targets and penalties for council spending. The targets were separate from the GREAs. For example, in 1980 local authorities were told to cut 5.6 per cent from their 1979 expenditure figure for the new year or to face reductions in their block grant as a penalty.

Rate rises

The government's intention was to discourage high spending by forcing local councils to make up any shortfall in their budget from local taxation – the rates. It anticipated that the local electorate would be disgruntled by the spiralling rates bill and would vote against the sitting council at the next election. Therefore, not only would local spending come under control, but local accountability would also be improved. Not all observers believed the government's motives to be so high-minded – most of the high-spending authorities were under Labour control.

Capital controls

The 1980 act also introduced controls on local authorities' capital expenditure. Councils undertook a great deal of expensive projects, such as the maintenance of school premises and housing construction. By introducing the need to seek central government permission for such spending, between 1979 and 1983 local authority capital expenditure fell by 60 per cent.

Rate capping

Although central government's contribution to local government financing had fallen from 60 per cent in 1979 to 48 per cent in 1983, local government spending had not decreased significantly and rates had risen dramatically. Therefore, in 1982 the Local Government Finances No. 2 Act removed the councils' right to levy an extra rate in the middle of the financial year. This was followed in 1984 by the Rates Act which enabled the government to cap the level of rates to be charged by an authority. The decision to cap was to be taken by the secretary of state on the basis of their assessment of whether spending in that authority had been excessive.

As a result of these spending restrictions, many local councils ran into serious financial difficulties. For example, Liverpool City Council set a budget that would see them through only nine months of the year. Many other councils turned to 'creative accounting' and imaginative financial deals. These included selling council properties in order to raise money and then renting the property back from its new owner. We saw above how the London Borough of Hammersmith and Fulham engaged in illegal trading on the London financial markets in order to raise money.

Abolition of the metropolitan authorities

GLC

Considerable opposition to Margaret Thatcher's attempts to control local authority spending came from the metropolitan authorities that were responsible for the large conurbations. The GLC in particular had been determined, under the leadership of Ken Livingstone, to confront the government.

Municipal socialism

The metropolitan authorities were controlled by the Labour Party. Their control of key local authorities was seen as an opportunity to present alternative policies to Thatcherism. This is often referred to as **municipal socialism**. The councils believed that they had a local mandate for their policies and were committed to protecting their vision of local democracy.

Margaret Thatcher believed that the metropolitan authorities were irresponsible, out of touch with the public, bureaucratic and wasteful. The Local Government Act of 1985 abolished the metropolitan authorities, including the GLC, and replaced them with metropolitan districts and London borough councils.

Local authorities and the free market

Perhaps the main element of Thatcherism was the nurturing of the free market economy in Britain. Margaret Thatcher wanted to create a democracy in which consumers could own shares, own their homes, have choice regarding education and could expect local authorities to deliver services of a high standard at the right price. She intended to do this through the **marketization** of the public sector.

Marketization

Privatization and housing policy

Privatization first came to local councils in the Housing Act of 1980. They were forced to make local authority housing available for purchase to tenants of three years standing or more. This was extended in 1984 by the Housing and Building Control Act and again in 1992 by the Housing, Land and Urban Development Act. In addition the 1988 Housing Act enabled tenants of derelict council housing to vote to replace the local authority as landlord by a landlord of their own choice. The Act also created Housing Action Trusts (HATs) (see page 191) that could take over dilapidated estates, improve and sell them into private ownership. The aim of all of these policies was to remove the stock of public housing from local authority control and put it in private-sector hands.

Privatization

Consumer sovereignty and education

Since the 1944 Education Act local authorities had been given a virtually free hand in the deciding the school curriculum. This came to an end in 1988 with the Education Reform Act. For the first time, central government had the power to lay down a national curriculum. In addition, the act weakened, and even ended, local authority control over schools, colleges of further education and polytechnics. Parents were given the opportunity to vote on whether their child's school should opt out of local authority control. If they did so, the responsibility for staffing and budgets was to be transferred to the head teacher and the board of governors with finance coming directly from the central government.

National curriculum

The introduction of mandatory testing at a range of ages and league tables of school examination results were further steps towards the marketization of education. The government's intention was to increase the power of parents as consumers. If a school's examination results were poor, parents would be able to move their child elsewhere. As a result, all schools would be encouraged to maintain standards. Critics of the system argued that the emphasis on examination success was too great and that it, in effect it recreated a two-tier education system with the academically talented students being accepted at high-calibre schools and the less-gifted being relegated to poorer-quality schools (see page 189).

League tables

The marketization of services

The 1988 Local Government Act forced local authorities to accept the practice of competitive tendering. This entailed a fundamental revision of the role of local authorities. No longer would they necessarily be the **providers** of the service; they might only be the **enablers**, i.e. local authorities would ask private firms to bid for the opportunity to provide services. For example, many leisure facilities and sports halls are no longer managed by the local authority, but by a private firm employed to do so by the council.

Competitive tendering

The government believed that this would encourage a higher standard of service at a more competitive price. Local authority departments were allowed to bid for the contracts against private competitors and the government hoped that this would provide sufficient incentive to keep costs down and standards high. If the delivery of service was unsatisfactory the firm, local authority or private company could be replaced.

Internal market

There was also a drive to create an **internal market** within local authorities. This means that departments within the authority had to charge each other for the services they provided. This was an attempt to make authorities more efficient and cost conscious, but also to create fair competition for private firms. Before the internal market many authority departments were able to win contracts because their costs could be kept artificially low – many of the services they received, for example, accountancy and legal advice, were provided free of charge by other council departments.

Quangos and the avoidance of local authorities

In its desire to inject more private enterprise into the local economy the government occasionally ignored the local authorities, turning instead to quasi-governmental bodies ('quangos'), such as Training and Enterprise Councils (TECs).

TECs

There are 82 TECs in England and Wales designed to build up the level of skills within the British workforce. They are private limited companies run by businesspeople from the private sector with funding from central government. Local authorities were bypassed because the government felt that businesspeople would shape the curriculum to suit the needs of the local business community in a way that the local authorities would not.

Education

In education, while local authorities lost control of grant-maintained schools, sixth form colleges, further education colleges and the former polytechnics, central government reinforced its dominance through the Funding Agency for Schools, the Further Education Funding Council, the Higher Education Funding Council and the School Curriculum and Assessment Authority.

Numbers

The Conservative government's extensive use of quangos came after their pledge to wage war against quangos in 1979. According to the Cabinet Office, the number of quangos has indeed fallen from 2,167 in 1979 to 1,389 in 1993. However, these figures do not include executive agencies (see page 111), TECs or NHS trusts (see page 186). At the other extreme, Charter 88, a pressure group seeking constitutional reform, claims that there are 5,521 quangos, including grant-maintained schools, further education colleges and HATs.

Accountability

Considerable controversy surrounds quangos because, critics argue, they are not accountable to any elected authority. Many of the functions carried out by quangos were once the responsibility of elected local authorities which allowed citizens opportunities to influence the policies adopted and the services provided by quangos. Other functions were carried out by civil service departments in Whitehall and so ministers were accountable to Parliament for the performance of these functions. Therefore, in both cases elected bodies played a role in maintaining accountability.

Ministerial responsibility

All quangos are directly responsible to central government, so ultimately ministers are responsible for their performance, despite the fact that the quangos are so far removed from the central government system. John Stewart, professor of local government at Birmingham University, argues (*The Economist*, 6 August 1994) that, since ministers cannot realistically be held accountable for the whole range of matters under their direct control, let alone for quangos, the doctrine of ministerial responsibility (see page 99) is under increasing strain.

Not only might the public accountability of quangos be rather difficult to maintain, the technical checks on their performance and financial affairs are also less stringent than those on local government. The Audit Commission checks the works of local authorities and NHS trusts, but it is not responsible for TECs, urban development corporations or the governing bodies of the grant-maintained schools. In addition, quangos do not have to keep a register of members' outside interests (in case a conflict of interest should arise) and their members are not personally liable to be financially charged for misuse of public funds. Of all the quangos, only the NHS trusts are required to make their meetings open to the public. Local authorities are subject to all of these controls.

Checks on quangos

Controversy also surrounds the appointment of personnel for quangos. In 1993 the Cabinet Office stated that ministers were responsible for 42,600 appointments to public bodies, with approximately 10,000 coming up for renewal each year. *The Economist* reported that 'in written answers to parliamentary questions, the government has admitted that it advertised only 24 of these appointments in 1992' (6 August 1994). The bulk of quango positions are often appointed on the recommendation of ministers or by the Public Appointments Unit of the Cabinet Office. There is some concern that the government has used this extensive power of patronage to reward its friends, for example. the wives of 34 Conservative MPs are members of quangos. Sir Derek Barber, former chairman of the Countryside Commission (CC) wrote in the CC's newsletter in 1991: 'I became chairman . . . as a consequence of sharing a cab with a stranger. Another chairman was appointed following a pheasant shoot at which the secretary of state was a fellow gun; the subsequent chairman of a water authority bumped into a cabinet minister while birding on a Greek island. It is a splendidly capricious and British way of doing things.'

Personnel

Financial reform

The poll tax

The rating system had long been considered unfair and inadequate as a system of local taxation. It was a property tax which could fall on families or individuals, old or young, regardless of income, i.e. it was a *regressive* tax.

Rates

In view of its regressive nature, many were exempted from payment and only about one-third of the electorate paid the full amount. Businesses accounted for a great part of the revenue from the rates, but had no vote in elections. These two factors undermined the accountability of local authorities and enabled them to continue increasing rates in view of the central government's spending controls (see page 145).

Accountability

In 1985 the rateable value of properties in Scotland was reassessed resulting in a 50 per cent increase in some cases. A review of rateable values in England was due and it had been postponed since 1973. The outcry that resulted from the increase in rates in Scotland persuaded the government to look seriously at an alternative local tax.

Alternatives considered included a local income tax and a local sales tax, but in 1988 the Local Government Finance Act introduced the government's solution – the community charge. There was a great deal of hostility to the charge resulting in a

Community charge

backbench revolt of 38 Conservative MPs, and the bill only passed through the Lords when the government called up its 'backwoodsmen' (see page 58).

Poll tax

The community charge was a flat-rate tax to be paid by every adult, i.e. a **poll tax**. Some people were exempted from full payment of the tax, including 18-year-olds at school, those in nursing homes and those in prison (unless imprisoned for non-payment of the charge). The level of the tax was to be set by district councils.

Uniform Business Rate

Businesses could not pay a poll tax and so were subject to the **Uniform Business Rate** (UBR), which was based on property values but set and collected nationally and redistributed to councils through government grants. The system of grants was simplified into one payment, the level of which was set by central government according to its assessment of the finance needed to provide a standard level of service (Standard Spending Assessment – SSA).

Capping

The government retained the right to cap the poll tax by setting an upper limit to the level of tax. In order to be capped, an authority originally needed a budget of over £15 million, but this qualification was soon dropped. In addition, its spending estimates had to exceed the SSA by 12.5 per cent and £75 per resident. In 1990, 20 local councils were capped. However, the secretary of state's use of his **capping** power seemed to be biased against Labour-held councils. For example, the London Borough of Brent, a Labour-controlled council, where spending rose by 1.4 per cent was capped, while Berkshire Country Council which was Conservative controlled and where spending rose by 20.6 per cent, was not. The courts ruled that capping was legal, but that the secretary of state should make clear the circumstances under which a council could be capped.

Dissatisfaction

The government had announced that the average poll tax bill was expected to be £276. It soon became clear that this would not be the case. Businesses in the south were unhappy at the level of the UBR and many people demonstrated against the unfairness of the poll tax.

Objections were mainly based on its regressive nature. Once more, the local tax took no account of the ability to pay. It was also an expensive and difficult tax to collect – twice as expensive as the rates. The register of taxpayers was difficult to keep up to date and easy to avoid. As a result, councils lost revenue.

Local authorities also complained that the new system concentrated power and control in the hands of central government. According to many, this had been Margaret Thatcher's aim since 1979.

The council tax

Amid fears that the Conservative Party would lose the next election, Margaret Thatcher was replaced as the party's leader in November 1990. During the campaign to choose her successor the poll tax became an issue and all candidates committed themselves to a review of the tax.

Reform

On his election John Major appointed Michael Heseltine, a long-time critic of the poll tax, as secretary of state for the environment. In March 1991 the government announced an across-the-board reduction in poll tax bills of £140 in order to defuse the poll tax crisis. By September 1991 the poll tax had been abolished to be replaced by the **council tax**.

The council tax combined a personal tax with a property tax. Local authorities set a council tax (which was still subject to capping), a proportion of which would be paid by each household, how much depended on the valuation of their property. Properties were graded into bands related to the capital value of the property. The higher the grade, the higher the proportion of council tax to be paid. It was hoped that linking the council tax to property values would remove the most regressive elements of the tax.

The status of local government today

Local government has probably never been at such a low ebb as it is today. The Conservative governments since 1979 showed considerable hostility to local government and sought to remove power from local authorities and transfer it to central government.

However, as important for local authorities is their changing role in the governmental system. It seems clear that the Conservative governments moved local authorities away from their traditional function as provider of local services to a new function as purchaser of those services. Therefore, local government has become an agent of central government rather than a policy maker and service provider in its own right.

Exercises

Short questions

1 a What was the community charge (poll tax)?
   b Why was it introduced?
   c Outline a case against it. (ULEAC, June 1990)
2 Can local government be considered democratic given that participation at local level is often extremely limited?
3 a What are the main functions of district councils?
   b How has the manner in which these functions are performed been affected by changes since 1987? (ULEAC, January 1992)
4 a What are the functions of the metropolitan district councils?
   b Is the distribution of functions to such authorities administratively rational? (ULEAC, June 1990)

Essay questions

1 To what extent can local government act independently of central government? (ULEAC, June 1993)
2 How far, and by what means, has the role and power of local government been changed in recent years? (Cambridge, June 1994)
3 How and why does central government attempt to control local government expenditure? (Oxford, June 1992)
4 How true is it that central–local government relations in recent years have been characterized by increasing central control and a consequent enfeeblement of local democracy? (Oxford and Cambridge, June 1992)

Data response question

Councils 'put party interests above the public's'

'Councillors throughout Britain are increasingly putting party loyalty above the interests of their constituents, according to a new survey of 407 local authorities in England, Wales and Scotland, which found that most important decisions were taken in private political group sessions at which councillors were told how they should vote at public council and committee meetings.

So formalized had the position become that in half of all councils the chief executive officer now attended meetings of the ruling party group to advise on policy. The result was that meetings attended by the public were rendered virtually meaningless because the outcome of every debate had already been decided behind closed doors.

The report by Professor Ken Young of London University and Mary Davies of the Institute of Local Government Studies at Birmingham University found that councillors were also taking a bigger part in appointing middle-ranking council officers, especially in the big cities. "Partisan conduct is rapidly becoming commonplace with members of both major parties increasingly bound by group decisions and with more consistently partisan voting in both council and committee meetings," the report said. While Labour councils remained more politically partisan than those under Tory control, figures showed that Conservatives are rapidly catching up.'

Source: adapted from *Local Government Since Widdicombe*, Joseph Rowntree Foundation, November 1990

Consider the view that the problem of local government is the dominance of party political control exercised not at central government level but rather within each locality.

(AEB, June 1992)

11 The European Union

Questions to be answered in this chapter

- What is the history of the European Union (EU)?
- What are the relationships between the institutions of the EU?
- What effect has membership of the EU had on British sovereignty?
- What are British political attitudes to the EU?

Terms to know

Common Agricultural Policy (CAP)
Committee of Permanent Representatives (COREPER)
Delors plan
Exchange Rate Mechanism (ERM)
Federalism
Factortame case
European Free Trade Area (EFTA)

Luxembourg compromise
Maastricht Treaty
Single internal market
Social chapter
Sovereignty
Supranational
Treaty of Rome

The history of the European Union

Between 1800 and 1945 major European nations had taken part in four major wars, two largely confined to Europe (the Napoleonic Wars and the Franco-Prussian War) and two taking on a more international character (World Wars I and II). It was in the light of this intra-European conflict that the idea of a European 'community' was born. The French, in particular, felt that Germany was a naturally aggressive nation that would go to war once more if not controlled. This was understandable since France had been attacked by Prussia or Germany three times in less than 100 years.

Origins

In 1946 Winston Churchill called for a United States of Europe in order to entwine the political and economic future of the European nations so closely that Germany would be unable and unwilling to turn on its neighbours again. However, he did not believe that Britain should play a role in such a body.

Two French politicians, Jean Monnet and Robert Schuman, were the moving forces behind the early stages of European co-operation. In 1950 they suggested that France and Germany should combine their coal and steel industries under a **supranational** authority. In 1951 France, Germany, Italy, Belgium, the Netherlands and Luxembourg signed the Treaty of Paris which set up the European Coal and Steel Community (ECSC).

European Coal and Steel Community

Soon after the formation of the ECSC two more European communities were proposed: the European Atomic Community (Euratom) and the European Economic Community (EEC). The former was concerned with the development of nuclear energy; the latter was intended to further economic integration.

Euratom and EEC

153

Treaty of Rome

The **Treaty of Rome**, setting up the EEC, was signed by the six members of the ECSC in 1957. The treaty set up a customs union in which the six member countries would trade freely with each other, without any tariffs. They also set a common tariff (Common External Tariff – CET) against non-member countries to enable them to trade as a bloc with the rest of the world. In addition to the trade provisions the treaty also committed the members to the creation of a common regional policy and agricultural policy (**Common Agriculture Policy** – CAP). The ultimate aim was to co-ordinate the economic and monetary policies of the membership to such an extent that the EEC could be managed as a single economy.

The EEC was designed not only to increase economic co-operation and integration but also to bring greater political union, and in the late 1960s the institutions of Euratom, the ECSC and the EEC were merged to create the institutions of the European Community (EC).

Britain and the EEC

Britain did not become involved in the early stages of European co-operation. Its links with the empire and the United States persuaded Britain's leaders that greater union with Europe would undermine Britain's position in the world. Of all the European nations Britain was in a unique international position and considered itself to be a world power with a global, rather than European, perspective on events. The difference in attitude was clearly illustrated by the issue of tariffs. Britain was in favour of global free trade and viewed the creation of a European customs union as bad for the world economy.

Furthermore, the internal upheaval created by the post-war Labour government's nationalization of key industries and the creation of the National Health Service meant that the prime minister Clement Attlee decided to shun what he perceived to be 'European experiments'.

Sovereignty

A conclusive reason for Britain's reluctance to welcome the EEC was the threat to Britain's **sovereignty**. British politicians believed that European co-operation, the creation of supranational institutions and the aim of greater European union would undoubtedly limit Britain's national sovereignty.

European Free Trade Area

In the late 1950s, under the leadership of Harold Macmillan and a Conservative government, Britain's attitude towards Europe began to change. The disintegration of the empire, the uncertainty of the special relationship with the United States and the fear of being excluded from the European markets led Britain to look more seriously at European co-operation. As a result, Britain was instrumental in creating the European Free Trade Area (EFTA), consisting of Britain, Denmark, Austria, Sweden, Switzerland and Portugal, which was a much looser organization than its EEC counterpart.

Application for membership

By 1961 there had been a further revision of Britain's European policy as it was decided that Britain's future lay inside the EEC rather than with a number of minor European countries, outside the group of six. Therefore, in 1961 Harold Macmillan announced that Britain would seek EEC membership. A year later the French president Charles de Gaulle vetoed the British application.

The Labour government of 1964 did not continue the overtures towards Europe until 1967 when Charles de Gaulle again used the French veto to exclude Britain, and it became clear that Britain would not be admitted until he had left office. The French president resigned in 1969 and Britain was encouraged to reapply.

The Conservative Party came to power in 1970 led by Edward Heath who had been Harold Macmillan's envoy to negotiate EEC membership. As prime minister, Edward Heath enthusiastically pursued membership of the EC. The European Community Act was finally signed in 1972 and Britain became a member of the EC in 1973.

Edward Heath and EEC membership

However, the issue of EC membership continued to be a thorny one when Labour was returned to power in 1974. While Harold Wilson was committed to Europe, many of his party were not. Faced with a divided cabinet and unable to enforce collective cabinet responsibility (see page 80), he declared that such an important constitutional issue as continued EC membership should be put to the British electorate through a referendum in 1975. At that time, a unique event in British politics, the referendum campaign created unusual partnerships as Labour left-wingers, such as Michael Foot, spoke on the same platform as Conservative right-wingers, like Enoch Powell. The electorate voted 65:35 in favour of continued membership.

Referendum on Europe

Developments in Europe

In the 1980s the EC moved towards a new stage of European integration. First, the net of integration was widened as the number of states involved in the EC increased. The Republic of Ireland and Denmark had entered the EC with Britain in 1973. They were joined by Greece in 1981 and Spain and Portugal in 1986.

Second, the level of integration was intensified under the presidency of Jacques Delors. Members initiated the creation of a **single internal market**, the European Monetary System (EMS) and changes to the methods of voting in the Council of Ministers.

The objective of a single internal market was adopted by all members of the EC in 1985. The aim was to ensure the free movement of goods, capital and labour within the EC by 1992. Remaining internal barriers to free movement were abolished and members moved to adapt their laws and regulations to a common European standard. Parliament confirmed British commitment to Europe by passing the Single European Act in 1986.

Single internal market

The 1986 Act also amended the Treaty of Rome to allow the Council of Ministers to make decisions on the basis of support of a majority of members rather than on the unanimous voting that had effectively given each member a veto over EC policies. This was considered necessary due to the expansion of the EC to twelve members. The **Luxembourg compromise** of 1966 is still in force, which gives individual states the power to veto if they feel that their national interest is threatened by a policy and the EC remains committed to avoiding a vote and seeking consensus on the major issues concerning EC development, such as extension of membership, the powers of the community, tax and treaties.

Majority voting

Pressure for greater economic integration has included greater co-ordination of European monetary policies. The first stage of this process was the creation of the European **Exchange Rate Mechanism** (ERM) within which the currencies of EC countries were partially fixed relative to each other. The ultimate aim is to create a single European currency controlled by a European central bank that would also control a Europe-wide monetary policy. The result of all of these policies would automatically be a greater correlation of economic policy.

Exchange Rate Mechanism

Alongside the drive for greater economic integration has been a move to co-ordinate the social policies of the member countries. The **social chapter** – the brainchild of Jacques Delors – is an attempt to develop common policies on areas such as

Social chapter

employment law, trade union representation on companies' boards of directors and hours of work.

Maastricht Treaty

The moves towards greater integration were formalized at the Maastricht summit in 1991. Here the members of the EC adopted the **Delors plan** for greater integration. Divided into three stages, the plan envisages an independent European bank and the ECU (European Currency Unit) becoming the currency of the community by 1999.

As the EC, now known as the European Union, moves towards greater integration, its route seems likely to be complicated by the addition of new members – Austria, Sweden and Finland joined on 1 January 1995 – and by the uncertain commitment of some of its current members, including Britain.

Margaret Thatcher, John Major and Jacques Delors

EEC budget

Like Charles de Gaulle before her, Margaret Thatcher was highly suspicious of supranational institutions. At the beginning of her term of office she made the reduction of Britain's contributions to the EEC budget a main priority. In fact, in 1980 and 1981 she gained rebates worth £1.4 billion, with a further instalment in 1982.

Margaret Thatcher's scepticism

Following this move, she set about resisting, in her opinion, the continual interference in British affairs by Brussels' bureaucrats. She did not approve of the social chapter and often referred to it as the socialist chapter because she saw it as 'socialism through the back door'. Nor was Margaret Thatcher happy with the idea of the ERM. She, and her economics adviser, Alan Walters, believed that sterling should be able to float freely. This issue led to the resignation of the chancellor of the exchequer, Nigel Lawson, in 1989, although Britain subsequently joined the ERM in 1990.

Ultimately, Europe was a major factor in Margaret Thatcher's downfall. Her deputy prime minister, Geoffrey Howe, resigned in 1990 and later cited the prime minister's unconstructive attitude towards Europe as a major reason for his decision.

John Major

John Major came to power with a more positive attitude to Europe, being a supporter of the ERM and a believer in negotiation rather than confrontation. However, his premiership was beset with difficulties rooted in the European question: how far should Britain go down the road of European integration?

British opt-out clause

At the Maastricht summit in 1991 John Major negotiated an 'opt-out' clause for Britain with regard to the third stage of the Delors plan, leading to a single European currency. He also persuaded the other member nations not to include the social chapter in the **Maastricht Treaty**. The social chapter is a separate protocol of the treaty to which Britain has not given its support. The 'opt-out' clause has led to concern over an inner and outer circle of the European Union.

ERM problems

John Major's European difficulties were heightened in 1992 when Britain was forced to withdraw from the ERM. The prime minister had committed Britain to continued membership at the high rate of DM2.95 fixed by Margaret Thatcher. However, the financial markets felt that this was too high and after a period of heavy selling of sterling, the chancellor, Norman Lamont was forced to announce Britain's withdrawal from the ERM.

Euro-rebels

Ratification of the Maastricht Treaty, the prospect of rejoining the ERM and, more recently, increases in Britain's contribution to the EU budget have provoked serious divisions in the Conservative Party. With barely a working majority after the 1992 election, John Major by early 1995 had been able to hold the parliamentary party together only with threats of a dissolution if defeated. Indeed, in November 1994 the party whip was withdrawn from nine Conservative MPs who abstained in the Commons vote on Britain's contribution to the EU budget.

The institutions of the EU

The institutions of the European Union were established in the late 1960s when Euratom, ECSC and the EEC were merged. The range of institutions, including the Council of Ministers, the European Council, the European Commission, the European Parliament and the European Court, all reflect the dual concerns of the supranational organizations – the national interests of the members and the general interest of the community.

The Council of Ministers

Voting in the Council of Ministers

Votes in the Council of Ministers are distributed as follows: Germany (10), France (10), Britain (10), Italy (10), Spain (8), Belgium (5), Greece (5), Netherlands (5), Portugal (5), Austria (4), Sweden (4), Finland (3), Denmark (3), Ireland (3), Luxembourg (2).

A *simple majority* is required on procedural matters.

A *qualified majority* (61:86 majority) is necessary for issues like the completion of the internal market, discrimination and the free movement of capital.

A *unanimous vote* is required to enlarge the community, extend the EU's powers, make changes to laws regarding training, changes in treaties and harmonization of taxation systems.

The Council of Ministers is the main policy-making body of the EU. In fact, there is not one single council but a series, all operating at different levels. The senior council is known as the General Council and is made up of the foreign ministers of the member countries. Below it are the Technical Councils which deal with specific areas of policy and are composed of the relevant ministers from each state.

Councils

There is also a **Committee of Permanent Representatives** of each state – the ambassadors to the EU. This is known by the French acronym COREPER.

COREPER

All of these levels are supported by a series of working groups made up of civil servants. It is in these groups that proposals from the European Commission are first discussed and passed on to COREPER for agreement. If agreed at COREPER level, the Technical Councils are likely to concur.

Working groups

Traditionally, the Council of Ministers has endeavoured to avoid taking a vote on issues, in order to determine policy via a consensus. However, as the membership has increased and the emphasis has begun to move away from national interests towards the well being of the community, voting has become more common.

The European Council

Since 1974 the heads of government of the member states have met twice a year at a summit meeting. The purpose is to discuss and decide on the main strategic issues facing the EU. Matters for discussion have included the creation of the ERM, the expansion of membership and budget issues.

The European Commission

The Commission was created by the Treaty of Rome and was intended to be the most 'European' of all the institutions. It is composed of bureaucrats from each of the member nations, all of whom are required to be loyal to the Commission rather than to their parent states.

Jacques Delors

The Commission is headed by the president, until 1994 Jacques Delors, who co-ordinates the work of the Commission and has the opportunity to give direction to the Commission. Hence, the plans for development of the EU to the end of the century are known as the Delors plan. In January 1995 the new president, Jacques Santer, succeeded Jacques Delors.

Commissioners

Below the president are seventeen commissioners with specific areas of responsibility. Each is nominated by a member state, two from the larger states; one from each of the smaller states. The commissioners are usually former politicians of considerable stature – in 1995 Britain's commissioners were Leon Brittan and Neil Kinnock. The commissioners serve a four-year term of office that can be renewable.

The Commission is responsible for initiating the legislative proposals of the EU which are put before the Council of Ministers for approval. In addition, it administers those policies once they have been approved.

Bureaucracy

Over recent years, the Commission has been the focus of much British criticism of the EU. It is an unelected body with a great deal of power to 'interfere' in the affairs of the member states. In addition, it has often seemed to be beset by the problems of a bureaucracy: red tape, lack of common sense and high costs.

The European Parliament

Powers

The European Parliament is not the legislature of the EU. Treaties, laws and policies are all drawn up by the Commission and approved by the Council of Ministers. The Parliament merely has the right to be consulted on most, but not all issues. It has the power to suggest amendments to Commission proposals, but not to impose them on the Commission. It does have the power to reject the annual budget of the EU, but in a direct confrontation with the Council of Ministers is likely to lose. A final power, which has never been used, is the right to dismiss the Commission.

Composition

The Parliament is made up of 518 directly elected Members of the European Parliament (MEPs). Each of the large states, Britain, Germany, France and Italy, elect 81 MEPs each, with the smaller states sending a proportionate number.

Within the Parliament, the party representatives from each member state have tended to join supranational party groupings. The Labour Party participates in the socialist grouping, which is the biggest in the Parliament; while the Conservatives are part of the most nationalist grouping, the European Democratic Group.

The European Court of Justice

European Union law

The European Court is made up of thirteen judges appointed by the member states for fixed terms of office. Their role is to apply Community law and decisions, regulations and directives of the Commission. Community law is derived from the treaties on which the EU is based, while all the decisions of the Commission and the Council of Ministers also have the force of law. The Court hears cases against the member states and against the Commission itself.

The role of the European Court has serious implications for all of the member states because community law takes precedence over domestic law. Domestic law , therefore, has to be in line with European law or face being struck down by the court. This occurred for the first time in the UK when the **Factortame case** (1991) declared the Merchant Shipping Act (1988) to be contrary to European law (see page 132). As with all courts, the greater their power the more likely they are to become law makers rather than simply law enforcers. The European Court is no exception and its power to interpret the treaties of the EU gives it the opportunity for judicial creativity.

However, it is important for the European Court, as for all courts, to keep in touch with public opinion. If it fails to do so, it is in danger of losing the respect of the member states. For example, when France refused to allow Britain to export lamb freely, the court ruled in Britain's favour, but France refused to accept the decision and only complied after considerable negotiation.

Supremacy of EU law

The European debate

Since 1945 the 'European question' has caused divisions in British society. Initially, the conflict was based on whether Britain would be better off throwing in its lot with the Europeans or with the empire and with the Americans. As the empire changed into the Commonwealth and the United States turned its attention away from Europe towards Asia, many felt that Europe was the only option if Britain wanted to maintain its position as a trading nation with full access to European markets. However, as the trading argument seemed to have been won and Harold Macmillan's government sought membership of the EEC, the argument shifted away from trade towards sovereignty.

The attitudes of British politicians can perhaps be divided into three groups:
- those favouring withdrawal
- those favouring caution
- those urging progress with integration.

The anti-Europeans

During the referendum campaign in 1975 the most vociferous anti-European groups were from the left of the Labour Party. Michael Foot, Tony Benn and Peter Shore all feared the loss of British sovereignty to a supranational government in Brussels. More recently, the anti-European focus has shifted to the right of the Conservative Party – Bill Cash, Teddy Taylor and even Margaret Thatcher herself have been strident in their criticism of the EU. The power of the unelected Commission, the bureaucracy and inefficiency of rule from Brussels, interference in 'the British way of life' and the dominance of the Franco–German alliance within the Community have all provoked harsh criticism of the EU.

Conservative critics

The organization of the EU and many of the aims of its former president, Jacques Delors, have been fundamentally contrary to those of the Thatcherite right of the Conservative Party. Margaret Thatcher believed that she had worked hard to decentralize decision making, to reduce the regulation of British markets and to pull

Centralization

159

down the structures of socialism, as she saw them, in the UK. She did not wish to have those 'evils' reimposed by Brussels.

Sovereignty

Thatcherite objections have focused attention on the loss of sovereignty involved in membership of the EU. We have already seen that European laws and regulations are superior to domestic law and can be enforced by British courts as well as by the European Court of Justice. No longer can the British Parliament be considered sovereign because it is constrained by European laws. As a result, British governments might be forced to follow policies that are contrary to those on which they were elected. Therefore, legal and political sovereignty has been lost.

Their concern over Britain's loss of sovereignty has led some to label the Thatcherites as 'little Englanders', with a narrow, nationalistic perspective on policy making. In fact, this is an exaggeration. Few members of the Conservative right have actually called for Britain's withdrawal from the EU. At the 1994 Conservative Party conference the former chancellor of the exchequer, Norman Lamont, raised eyebrows by calling for discussion of withdrawal from the EU, but few have taken up his theme.

In fact, elements of the philosophy of the EU are very appealing to the right. The creation of a single European market and free competition between nations is equivalent to deregulation in the Thatcherite mould. While prime minister, Margaret Thatcher was not so much anti-European as in favour of a different conception of Europe. She was strongly in favour of the expansion of membership of the EU to include the newly independent states of eastern Europe and even Russia. She was equally strongly opposed to the idea of a United States of Europe, set up along federal lines, preferring instead a *confederal* Europe with all of the member states joined in a loose organization.

Federalism

Federalism involves a group of independent states giving up some of their power to a central government.

Many Euro-critics fear that further European integration will lead to a United States of Europe. Under these circumstances many, but not all, policies would be determined by a central government in Brussels.

The cautious Europeans

The 'anti-Europeans' are probably more accurately described as extremely cautious Europeans. The more moderate version includes the majority of the Conservative Party and perhaps the left of the Labour Party.

Labour Party

In recent years the Labour Party seems to have overcome the divisions of the 1970s and has been united in its support for the EU. However, some commentators argue that while in opposition the party has been happy to unite against the Conservative Party which is deeply divided over the future of the EU.

John Major

John Major's approach to Europe has been generally enthusiastic, while keeping one eye firmly on Britain's national interests. He has sought to prevent interference from Brussels in the social policy of the UK by persuading the other member states to sign the social chapter as a separate protocol rather than as a part of the Maastricht Treaty.

He has also attempted to provide a voice and a point of focus for those members of the Community who were less enthusiastic about the idea of a federal Europe. Many of his critics have claimed that John Major is seeking a 'two-tier' Europe with a hard core of federal European states subscribing to *all* elements of EU policy, while the outsiders, including Britain, would only join up for *selected* elements of EU policies.

Pro-Europeans

Many of the pro-Europeans are found at the centre of British politics. The left of the Conservative Party, the right of the Labour Party and the Liberal Democrats all support a strong EU with Britain at its core. They argue that Britain's economic future lies inside Europe and that arguments about the loss of sovereignty are merely 'red herrings'.

Illusion of sovereignty

They suggest that true national sovereignty is an illusion in the contemporary world. Multinational companies, advances in telecommunications and the interdependence of financial markets mean that, metaphorically at least, Britain is no longer an island. Therefore, whether inside or outside the EU, Britain is not in control of its own destiny and so would be better served by being at the centre of the decision-making process rather than sitting on the sidelines.

Ultimately, however, legal sovereignty resides with the British Parliament. Although the Treaty of Rome does not include any detail about how countries can withdraw from the EU, the British Parliament could repeal the 1972 European Communities Act and so resign its membership at any time, although this would involve a breach of the country's treaty obligations.

Exercises

Short questions

1 a Define sovereignty.
  b Outline the effect of membership of the European Community on the sovereignty of Parliament. (ULEAC, June 1993)
2 Give two arguments for and two arguments against further integration of nation states within the European Union?
3 a What is meant by a two-tier or two-track Union?
  b Give arguments for and against such a proposal.

Essay questions

1 In what ways might Britain's membership of the European Community undermine the sovereignty of Parliament? (ULEAC, January 1992)
2 Assess the impact upon domestic government and politics of Britain's membership of the European Community. (Oxford, June 1992)

Data response question

'What is Europe for? That simple question is a vital one for an entity so liable to disunity among the nation-states that compose it, to becoming mired in the technical details of the Union's bureaucratic, commersial and legal affairs, and to dreaming up structures before sorting out foundations. Should Europe have a single currency, admit new but poorer members, narrow its democratic deficit, increase its fiscal transfers, or forge a common

security policy? Answers to such questions can be found, and agreed upon, only once the prior question is answered. And it is on that question that there is the most disagreement and disillusion.

The broadest – and best – answer came from the Community's founding fathers in the 1950s. To such as Jean Monnet and Robert Schuman, Europe's primary aim was to end the continent's ancient rivalries by replacing them with a sense of mutual interest. It followed that the motive for ceding sovereignty to European institutions was the same that leads individuals in a nation-state to agree to give powers to their own governments: the idea that some things can be done better together than separately. Only when that is thought to be the case should powers be transferred.'

Source: *The Economist,* 21 May 1994

1 To what extent has membership of the European Union undermined the sovereingty of the British parliament?
2 Do you believe that the European Union has brought an 'end to the continent's ancient rivalries'?
3 What effect has membership of the European Union had on the rivalries within the Conservative Party in Britain?

12 Pressure groups

Questions to be answered in this chapter
- What are pressure groups?
- Why are some groups more powerful than others?
- What factors determine the power of groups in society?
- Are pressure groups a good or bad influence in society?

Terms to know

Access points	Low profile groups
Corporatism	Oligarchy
Direct methods	Outsider groups
Elites	Pluralism
High profile groups	Pressure group
Indirect methods	Prisoner groups
Insider groups	Promotional groups
Interest groups	Sectional groups

What are pressure groups?

A pressure group can be defined as a group of like-minded people who are organized with a view to influencing the formulation of government policy. Unlike political parties, they do not put forward candidates for election to government office and so they do not seek to become government, only to influence the outcome of government decisions. The aims of pressure groups are usually relatively narrow as they tend to concentrate on a limited range of issues. Unlike political parties, they do not put together a manifesto covering a broad spectrum of policies.

Definition

Despite the differences between pressure groups and political parties, the distinction between them can often become blurred. Some parties are so small that they can never hope to form the government. Instead, they must attempt to influence the government. The Ulster Unionists, Plaid Cymru (the Welsh Nationalists) and the Scottish Nationalists are all small parties at Westminster and so can only hope to influence policy in Northern Ireland, Wales or Scotland by influencing the government or the opposition.

Influence of small parties

Pressure groups, like the trade union movement, have such close links with political parties that they are virtually indistinguishable. The trade unions account for more than 50 per cent of Labour Party finance, 70 per cent of the votes at the annual conference and 33 per cent of the vote for the leader of the party. In addition, they sponsored 173 candidates in the 1992 election.

Ties with parties

Large pressure groups, such as the Confederation of British Industry (CBI) and the trade unions, are concerned with a wide variety of issues. The CBI speaks on behalf

Range of issues

> ## The Confederation of British Industry
>
> The Confederation of British Industry (CBI) was created in 1965 to represent the interests of a wide range of firms. In fact, the broad spectrum of firms under its banner has *undermined* its influence for it has been difficult to unite them behind a single line.
>
> Its influence has waxed and waned since the 1960s. Its high point was probably in the 1970s when it was consulted regularly by the Edward Heath and Harold Wilson governments.
>
> Since 1979 it has largely been excluded from government deliberations, although after 1990 it regained a little influence.

of much of British industry and therefore, is interested in all the policy areas that affect industry from employment to the environment and from education to exports.

The classification of groups

The traditional means of classifying pressure groups is to distinguish between groups according to their aims and the issues they represent. The most common distinction is between promotional and sectional groups.

Sectional groups

Sectional groups act on behalf of a particular part of society. They are also known as protectional groups and interest groups because they protect the interests of a section of society. Therefore, they are sometimes referred to as self-interested groups. Examples of interest groups include the British Medical Association (BMA), the CBI and the Trades Union Congress (TUC).

Promotional groups

Promotional groups endeavour to promote a particular cause and for this reason, are sometimes called cause groups. They are not self-interested in that they promote an idea or cause to further the general good. Examples include the Campaign for Nuclear Disarmament (CND), Greenpeace UK, Shelter and Amnesty International.

Short and long term

Pressure groups can also be classified according to their potential lifespan. Interest groups are likely to be long-term groups, unless the section of society that they represent disappears, whereas promotional groups may be short lived because their aims are finite. A promotional group knows when its goals have been achieved because, for example, the fifth runway at Heathrow Airport has or has not been built or nuclear weapons have or have not been destroyed. Of course, this is not true of every cause. Some may be ongoing issues, for example, it may never be clear whether whales or the rainforest are actually safe.

Insider and outsider

A political scientist, Wyn Grant (*Pressure Groups, Politics and Democracy in Britain*, (Philip Allen, 1989), has established a classification of pressure groups based on their status and methods rather than their aims – insider and outsider groups.

Direct methods

Insider groups have strong links with decision makers and are regularly consulted. This may be because these groups are acceptable to the government or helpful for the consultation process. The fact that insider groups are part of the consultation process enables them to use direct methods in order to exert influence. This means that they can gain direct access to decision makers and put forward their case face to face. An example of an insider group under Margaret Thatcher was the Institute of Directors. Insider groups tend to be very powerful and long term. It is more

164

common for interest rather than promotional groups to be insiders, although this is by no means always the case.

Outsider groups do not participate in the consultation process, either by choice or because they are excluded by government. In the 1980s CND was excluded from any consultation process with the government because its aim was unacceptable to the Conservative government. An extreme example of an outsider group is the Irish Republican Army (IRA) which seeks a united Ireland but, until recently, has been considered an illegitimate organization by the British government. It was considered anti-constitutional because its violent indirect method – terrorism – is unacceptable in a democratic country (for a full discussion on Northern Ireland, see Chapter 15).

Indirect methods

Wyn Grant takes the division between insider and outsider groups a step further by distinguishing between different types of insider and outsider group. He divides insiders into high profile, low profile and prisoner groups. **High profile** groups have good contacts with decision makers, but also choose to build a high public profile. They may do this by gaining exposure through the media. A **low profile** group has good contacts with decision makers and chooses to concentrate on these as a means of gaining influence. The CBI was traditionally seen as a low profile group, working quietly behind the scenes. However, in the 1980s, perhaps as its influence with government declined, it turned to a more high profile strategy.

Types of insider

Prisoner groups have insider status not by choice but by necessity. Public-sector groups, for example, the Consultative Council on Local Government Finance, are part of the governmental process and so must consult regularly with government. To fail to approach such consultation in a constructive manner might result in the loss of finance or the cancellation of a favoured project.

Outsider groups can be divided into *potential insiders, outsiders by necessity* and *ideological outsiders*. Potential insiders seek insider status. In order to achieve this, they use discreet, acceptable methods in the hope that they will be seen as sufficiently legitimate to gain insider status in the future. Their ability to reach insider status depends on the political skills possessed by the group. Groups that do not possess the necessary abilities to become insiders are doomed to remain 'outsiders out of necessity'.

Types of outsider

Ideological outsider groups remain outside the consultative process because their beliefs are beyond the realms of normal political acceptability. The Animal Liberation Movement has used violent techniques and so its presence in negotiations has generally been seen as unacceptable.

The Trades Union Congress

The Trades Union Congress (TUC) is the umbrella organization of the trade union movement. It consists of over 70 unions with a combined membership of almost 8 million.

In the 1970s it spoke for labour in trilateral meetings with the government and the CBI, but since 1979 has lost influence. Recently, it attempted to revive its fortunes through a process of modernization and to some extent, shed the ideological paraphernalia that hindered its progress in the 1980s.

All of the unions retain their independence within the TUC and there are serious divisions, similar to those that beset the Labour Party – between the traditionalists and the modernizers.

Groups can easily move between insider and outsider status. Between 1974 and 1979 the TUC was very much an insider group, representing trade unions as a whole in negotiations with government regarding economic, industrial and employment policy. Meetings at 10 Downing Street were regular events. However, in 1979 when Margaret Thatcher came to power, the trade unions were excluded from all discussions and became an outsider group. As a result, they turned to indirect methods – marches, demonstrations and rallies – in an effort to influence public opinion.

Determinants of the power of individual groups

Pressure groups attempt to influence decision makers in the hope that their favoured policies will be adopted. In order to do so, they must be able to attract the attention of the decision makers and be able to compete against other pressure groups. The resources, whether economic or political, of any government are limited. However, there is almost an infinite number of groups which seek to benefit from those resources. Therefore, competition between groups can be fierce. How powerful an individual group becomes depends partly on the nature of the group itself and also on the nature of the government it seeks to influence.

The nature of the group

The power of an individual group depends on a variety of characteristics of the group. They include membership, wealth, knowledge and importance in society.

Membership

Size

Although often the most obvious characteristic of a pressure group, the size of its membership is by no means the most important. Mass membership is extremely useful if a group wishes to make an impact in the media. Large-scale demonstrations, marches or even strikes are newsworthy and may catch the public imagination, but they do not necessarily lead to influence. In fact, the use of indirect methods, such as demonstrations, can be interpreted as a sign of weakness rather than strength. If such a group had the ear of the government, these types of action would be unnecessary.

Social background

Other characteristics of a group's membership can be at least as important as size. The social background of members could be extremely important. A membership with middle class, public school, university backgrounds could be very important in building contacts with members of the civil service or the government. This is perhaps one of the reasons for groups like the BMA and the Bar Association maintaining insider status over a long period of time. Similarly, 87 per cent of the members of the Friends of the Earth have senior managerial, administrative, professional, educational, technical or scientific occupations.

Wealth

Lobbyists

Obviously the wealth of a pressure group will be partly determined by the nature of its membership. The trade union movement's members are not particularly wealthy. However, their numbers make the movement relatively rich. The wealth of a group can be used to finance indirect campaigning, contributions to political parties and the employment of professional lobbyists. The Royal Society for the Protection of Birds (RSPB) hired approximately 50 lobbyists in order to have a significant voice in the Wildlife and Countryside Act of 1981.

Knowledge

Pressure groups must have a knowledge of the issues and the political system because a great deal of their influence depends on the credibility they can build with the decision makers.

Credibility

MPs, ministers and civil servants turn to pressure groups for information. To build a steady relationship this information must be reliable. If it is, a pressure group may be able to achieve insider status.

Information

Not only must a pressure group be a source of reliable information, it should also have a sound grasp of the British political system. A well-informed group will be aware, for example, of the limited power of MPs and will use them to ask questions of ministers, propose amendments to legislation and perhaps introduce private members' bills. It will also be conscious of the fact that ministers rely on civil servants for their advice and therefore, a civil servant is an excellent target for pressure group activity.

Importance in society

The more important a group in society, the more likely is the government to hear its opinions. Its importance might be in terms of its professional credibility and standing in society or in the negative power it might wield.

The BMA is well respected in society and so has the ear of government. However, even this group has, at times, turned to public campaigns to make its point, particularly over the Conservative government's reforms of the National Health Service.

Respect

Trade unions have often commanded the government's attention because of the threat of strike action if their demands are not heard. Chief among these groups was the National Union of Mineworkers (NUM). However, the strike weapon, certainly for the NUM, lost some of its potency during the 1980s with new anti-trade union laws and high levels of unemployment.

The nature of the government

The influence of an individual group does not solely depend on the nature of the group itself but also on the government it attempts to influence. The government is not a neutral force in pressure group activity and some governments will be more responsive to this type of activity than others.

Margaret Thatcher's governments were generally unresponsive to pressure group overtures, believing that the government had been elected to govern in the national

CLEARing the air

'Few pressure groups have succeeded in routing the combined forces of the government and industry as decisively as the Campaign for Lead-Free Air (CLEAR), which began its fight in January 1982. Tom King, then the environment secretary, had announced the previous year that oil companies would have to cut the lead in petrol from 0.4 grams per litre to 0.15 grams by 1985. Mr King had compromised between environmental campaigners, who wanted a complete ban, and the petroleum industry, which wanted no change.

CLEAR's media campaign highlighted mounting evidence that even small quantities of lead in the air could harm children. The oil companies countered that the dangers were exaggerated and that the cost of phasing out lead would be exorbitant. Godfrey Bradman, a property developer, gave CLEAR a boost by donating £100,000 ($154,000) and by then persuading Des Wilson, a ubiquitous pressure-group activist, to direct it. The decisions of America, Japan and Australia to phase out leaded petrol helped. But the coup de grace came when CLEAR, two months after its launch, leaked a letter by Sir Henry Yellowlees, the government's chief medical officer, warning that the lead in petrol was "permanently reducing the IQ of many of our children".

In April 1983, when the Royal Commission on Environmental Pollution published a report that confirmed the dangers to children and called for the banning of lead in petrol, Mr King gave in. He announced that the government would support the elimination of lead, that oil companies would have to provide lead-free petrol and that car manufacturers would have to make engines that could use it.

By 1990 lead emissions from car exhausts were 70 per cent lower than a decade earlier. In 1993 a European directive, requiring new cars to be equipped for lead-free petrol, came into force. Yet despite differential taxation that makes lead-free petrol cheaper, many older cars have not been converted to use it. Nearly half the petrol sold in Britain is still leaded. The oil industry does not expect all the British to stop buying the leaded sort until 2005. "You shouldn't get involved in group politics unless you realise that [success] may not happen in your lifetime," says Mr Wilson.'

Source: *The Economist*, 13 August 1994

Project

Choose an issue in which you have an interest and monitor the work of pressure groups in that area over the course of a year.

interest, not in the interests of pressure groups. Those governments that are responsive to pressure group activity are more likely to be amenable to approaches from groups that share their ideological perspectives than those that do not. Had the Labour Party won the 1983 election, for example, it is likely that CND would have been more influential.

Targets of pressure group activity

Access points

The influence of pressure groups as a whole within a political system largely depends on the range and usefulness of targets for pressure group activity. These targets are known as **access points** and they are, in effect, holes in the political system through which pressure groups can gain access.

The availability of access points is determined by the structure of government, the power of political parties and the openness of government. The United States with its strong federal and state governments as well as strict separation of powers (see pages 6 and 7) between the institutions of central government is riddled with access points. Britain, on the other hand, with its unitary state and limited separation of powers, is a much more closed political system and it is difficult for pressure groups to gain access.

Local government

Local government in Britain is in a weak constitutional position. Britain is a unitary state which means that all power flows from the central government and so local government is constitutionally dependent on the centre.

Unitary state

Since 1979 central government has taken advantage of its superior position to weaken still further the role of local government in practice. The privatization of council housing, the marketization of local authority services and tighter central government control of local government financing have diminished the position of local government.

Weakened local government

Nevertheless, local authorities do retain responsibility for the delivery of local services and for such important functions as local planning. Therefore, pressure groups concerned with issues such as local transport, land development or the provision of leisure facilities often turn their attention to local government.

In metropolitan areas pressure groups face a simple unitary system, with a metropolitan district responsible for the delivery of services. However, in the shires groups must focus their activities on either the county councils or the district councils, depending on the issue concerned. (For a fuller discussion of the role of local government, see Chapter 10.)

Central government

As we have seen, in a unitary state, power lies at the centre. Therefore, many pressure groups concentrate their activity on this level of government. Within central government the institutions do not share equal power, with Parliament being sovereign. However, the executive branch with a majority in the House of Commons and backed by strong party discipline is, in reality, in a very powerful position.

Parliament

Constitutionally, Parliament is sovereign, which means that it has the power to make any law and it controls finance (see pages 65–6). Therefore, it might be imagined that pressure groups would spend a good deal of time and money lobbying the legislature. However, in reality, the number and usefulness of access points in Parliament are limited.

Parliamentary sovereignty

Although Parliament is bicameral, the upper house, the Lords, has lost much of its power during the twentieth century. It no longer has the power to veto legislation and it plays no role at all in financial matters. Therefore, the usefulness of the House of Lords, from a pressure group's point of view, may be minimal. However, the Lords does retain the ability to amend or delay legislation and, by so doing, can provoke important changes to a bill or at least gain some publicity for a cause. The

House of Lords

Pressure groups and Parliament

'The House of Commons has a reputation as the best club in London. One can see why. Not only does it have a wonderful clubhouse, but many of its members are paid by eager lobbyists to pursue their clients' interests . . .

Following the lobbying industry's explosive growth in the 1980s, some MPs now seem to see their job more as peddling influence than pursuing the interests of their constituents. More than 200 MPs (out of 651) are employed as parliamentary consultants to lobbying companies and other commercial organizations. Their duties can range from mere advice on parliamentary procedure to supportive speeches, questions and lobbying of government ministers. The fees for such work can be considerable. A single parliamentary consultancy can pay £10,000 or more a year, a third of an MP's salary . . .

The Public Relations Consultants Association and the Institute of Public Relations, which between them represent more than 150 companies and 5,000 individual members, are jointly to set up a register of political lobbyists and establish a code of practice. This will require registered lobbyists to name MPs who work for them, and to give details of the clients to whom the service is provided, which goes a little further than the Commons' existing rule. But the lobbyists' new code will not require disclosure of what voters are entitled to know – how much is being paid and for what. The Association of Professional Political Lobbyists, a smaller group of lobbyists, has gone much further, in a bid to attract clients who want to look spotlessly clean. This group has ruled that none of its members may pay fees of any kind to MPs or employ them in any capacity . . .

The [Commons'] laissez-faire attitude has allowed a host of dubious practices to flourish. The most blatant is the way in which MPs with direct commercial interests are allowed to serve on committees that draft legislation that might affect those interests . . .

Abuse is also encouraged by the fact that MPs are not required to disclose any private interest when asking written or oral questions of ministers . . . A survey by the Study in Parliament group, an academic research team, found that 62 per cent of MPs said they had sometimes submitted written questions drafted by parliamentary lobbyists.

Source: The Economist, 24 September 1994

huge size of government majorities in the 1980s prompted some observers to suggest that the only real opposition to government policies came from the Lords. Therefore, pressure groups *may* choose to lobby the upper house in certain situations, especially if issues concerning the countryside, the constitution or the elderly are involved.

House of Commons party discipline

Within Parliament, sovereignty has passed to the House of Commons and it presents an attractive target for pressure groups. However, the first-past-the-post electoral system (see page 18) usually gives the governing party a working majority and as this is backed by strong party discipline, the government is often in a dominant position. In the 1950s and 1960s the government's position was almost absolute, with party discipline only rarely breaking down. In the 1970s and 1980s backbench revolts became more common. This gave pressure groups the opportunity to work on a group of government backbenchers in the hope of threatening government defeat.

Pressure groups also make use of MPs to ask oral and written questions of ministers, to suggest amendments to legislation and even to put forward private members' bills. Questions can be helpful to gain information or to bring an issue to the attention of Parliament, the media and the public.

Questions

Private members' bills (see page 65) can be very effective in promoting the aims of pressure groups. The most common method of introducing a bill is through the ballot by which half a dozen backbenchers are selected to put forward a bill of their choosing. The successful backbenchers are usually besieged by lobbyists immediately after the results of the ballot are known.

Private members' bills

Private members' bills are most likely to succeed when the government gives its tacit support to a piece of legislation. This is most common with matters of social morality which the government does not wish to make a partisan issue. Normally, under these circumstances MPs are allowed a free vote (see page 70) and so the stranglehold of political parties is relieved. An example of successful pressure group activity behind a private members' bill includes that carried out by the Abortion Law Reform Association which campaigned for the liberalization of abortion law in 1967 and has successfully prevented any retreat from this position.

Free votes

Pressure groups can also take advantage of the select committee system in the Commons (see page 75). These committees are permanent and shadow the work of most government departments. This allows pressure groups to build links with the members of the committees and to give evidence before the committee.

Committees

The executive

The government is responsible for initiating and implementing policy. Therefore, the greater part of policy making takes place in the executive branch rather than in the legislature. The responsibility for this decision making rests with ministers on the advice of civil servants.

It is not easy for pressure groups to gain access to ministers. They are at the apex of the governmental system and their time is precious. Groups such as the CBI and the TUC have been able to gain regular access to ministers at times, but most will attempt to build relationships with the civil service.

Civil servants are often willing to consult with pressure groups because they can be a source of information and co-operation. The former helps to give administrators a sound understanding of important issues. The latter is necessary to implement government policy effectively. Peter Middleton, a former permanent secretary to the Treasury, summed up the position of civil servants: 'If you want information, you've got to allow people to give you opinions too' (quoted in *The Economist*, 13 August 1994).

Civil servants

From a pressure group's point of view, civil servants can provide information and, most importantly, an indirect route to the minister. The two-way nature of these relationships is often referred to as *clientelism*. Insider groups that might claim to have such a relationship include the National Farmers Union with the Department of Agriculture and the Howard League for Penal Reform with the Home Office.

Clientelism

The judiciary

Although the power of the English courts is limited by the doctrine of parliamentary sovereignty, pressure groups can bring cases before the judiciary. Between 1989 and

Courts

1991 members of the Anti-Poll Tax movement adopted a policy of civil disobedience by refusing to pay the community charge. They were taken to court and imprisoned and, as a result, gained considerable publicity for their cause.

Political parties

Strong parties

We saw above how the strength of political parties in Britain reduces the opportunities for pressure group activity in the Commons. The reasons for their strength lie largely in their electoral role. They nominate candidates, organize and finance their campaigns, provide a manifesto and command voter loyalty. Therefore, MPs owe their positions in the Commons to their party rather than to their own personality or organizations. They are likely to pay more attention to the views of their party than to those of their constituents. This reduces the effectiveness of *grass-roots lobbying*.

Grass-roots lobbying

In the United States members of Congress are keenly aware of their constituency interests and so are very susceptible to pressure group activity that might influence their chances of re-election. Campaigns to influence public opinion and the provision of election finance give pressure groups the opportunity to influence the views of members of Congress.

Perspectives on pressure group activity

Although pressure groups are now a well-established part of the political scene in democratic countries, there remains considerable disagreement over the desirability of pressure group activity. Broadly speaking, opinions can be divided into three perspectives:
- pluralism
- sectionalism
- corporatism.

Pluralism

Made popular in the 1950s and 1960s in Britain and the USA by political scientists such as Anthony Downs (*An Economic Theory of Democracy*) and David Truman (*The American Governmental Process*) **pluralism** identifies pressure groups as the main means of participating within a political system and argues that, as such, they improve democracy.

Participation

There are three methods of participating in a political system:
- voting
- joining a political party
- joining a pressure group.

Postwar consensus

Pluralists consider voting to be of only irregular significance. General elections occur only periodically and individuals are asked to vote for packages of policies put together by political parties. Therefore, voters do not have an opportunity to wield influence on the specific issues that concern them. In addition, for much of postwar British political history, those packages of policies provided little choice for the electorate. The postwar political consensus meant that there was little difference between the Conservative and Labour Parties, so the electorate was trapped in the status quo agreed upon by politicians.

Oligarchical parties

Joining a political party is also an inadequate form of participation because parties tend to be dominated by a few leaders at the top of the party hierarchy – parties are oligarchical. Therefore, individuals joining a party would have little influence and, once again, would have to support a whole range of policies without the opportunity to specialize in their area of interest.

Pressure groups, on the other hand, can be formed around any political issue. They can be long or short term and they give the individual the opportunity to have influence over specific issues. Pluralist theorists believe that democracy could be redefined in terms of groups rather than individuals. Groups would be free to form around any issue and they would compete freely with each other, with the government acting as a neutral referee and arbiter of their claims. The result would be the best possible outcome for society.

Group competition

This vision of pressure group competition can be compared to the perfect competition of economic theory and the free market doctrines of the eighteenth-century economist Adam Smith. According to this view, if each pressure group pursued its own self-interest, it would collectively determine the national interest and the country as a whole would benefit.

A criticism of pluralist theory is that all pressure groups are not equal and therefore the competition between groups is not free. Critics dispute the argument that pressure groups can form around any issue. Some issues, for example, are considered socially unacceptable and so it is difficult for groups to form. The unemployed do not have a pressure group to speak on their behalf partly because they are difficult to organize and to contact.

Unequal competition

Critics also point to the fact that pressure groups, like political parties, are hierarchical. Robert Michels, a German sociologist, in what he termed the 'Iron Law of Oligarchy', argued that all organizations become more bureaucratic and oligarchical as they grow in size (Robert Michels, *Political Parties*, The Free Press, 1949).

Oligarchical groups

Some pressure groups are much more powerful than others. They will be able to dominate the decision-making system, often influencing the outcome in their favour. Several pluralists have accepted this criticism and have absorbed it into a new theory of *elite pluralism*. According to this perspective, the government, as neutral referee, will act on behalf of the weaker groups in society, thus compensating for their disadvantaged position.

Elite pluralism

A final criticism can be levelled at both pluralism and elite pluralism: the government and the state are not neutral. The attitude of the government changes as the personnel of government change, even within the same party. Moreover, Marxists would argue that the state is not neutral. All states are run along the lines of an ideology (see page 51). Britain is a liberal-capitalist state and is therefore dominated by a liberal ideology. Groups operating within this ideological framework will automatically be favoured by the system.

State bias

Sectionalism

The sectionalist perspective is largely an extension of the criticisms of pluralism. Sectionalism believes that the most powerful pressure groups are the interest groups. By definition, these groups are dedicated to furthering their self-interests. In so doing, they distort the national interest in their favour and can dominate the system to such an extent that they undermine democracy.

New right

In Britain this view is most closely associated with the right of the Conservative Party. The *new right* argues that in the 1970s the trade union movement became too powerful. The trade union legislation of Edward Heath's government (1970–4) led to strikes, a three-day week and, eventually, an election fought on the question of who governs the country – the government or the unions. The Conservative Party lost the election and the Labour Party came to power introducing an era of unprecedented consultation between trade unions and government. According to new-right analysis, the trade unions had exceeded the role of a pressure group and had been given too great a voice in the management of the country. They were not elected to take part in government decision making and they were undermining the authority of those who had been elected to govern the country.

As a result, Margaret Thatcher's governments were reluctant to involve pressure groups too closely in the consultation process and trade unions were excluded completely.

Corporatism

Corporatism involves bringing pressure groups totally inside the governmental process. The pressure groups sacrifice their independence in return for the protection and patronage of the government. Traditional corporatism is often found in dictatorships such as Nazi Germany and Mussolini's Italy.

Tripartism

The theory of corporatism has been amended to explain the involvement of the TUC and the CBI in government decision making in the 1970s. This is known as *neo-corporatism*. The *tripartism* of the social contract era (1974–9), in which the CBI and TUC were involved with the government in the determination of economic policy, was an attempt to use the experience and information of the two leading industrial groups in an effort to bring down the level of inflation and to improve Britain's economic performance.

Such incorporation of pressure groups is common in many European countries, including Sweden and Germany. The philosophy is that pressure groups can bring information and co-operation to the governmental process and therefore the quality of government decision making will be improved.

Critics of such a philosophy argue that the government has been elected to govern and it should do so in a responsible manner. It should not allow unelected and unrepresentative pressure groups to have undue influence in this process.

Exercises

Short questions

1 a Distinguish between political parties and pressure groups.
 b Why is it sometimes difficult to distinguish between the two? (ULEAC, January 1995)
2 a Distinguish between two types of pressure group.
 b Explain, with examples, how this distinction is blurred. (ULEAC, January 1991)

Essay questions

1 a Why is Parliament subjected to so much lobbying by pressure groups?
 b Should there be greater control over lobbying? (ULEAC, June 1992)

2 'We have elections and opinion polls, hence pressure groups are unnecessary.' Do you agree? (Cambridge, June 1993)
3 What distinguishes successful from unsuccessful pressure groups in Britain? (Oxford and Cambridge, June 1994)
4 To what extent do pressure groups pose a threat to democracy? (Oxford, June 1992)
5 How do environmentalist groups seek to influence policy making?

Data response question

Consider the fictitious press report printed below involving two pressure groups, Friends of the Earth (FoE) and the National Farmers Union (NFU), and suggest the tactics that would in your view probably be adopted by each group. Using your knowledge of pressure group behaviour and successes, suggest which group would be most likely to win, indicating any other factors that could be important influences on the final outcome. (AEB, June 1992)

Friends become foes for farmers!

'Plans to build a new reservoir at Applecombe Moor as part of a national water grid which were last week welcomed by the County NFU branch received a hefty "thumbs down" on Monday when leaders of the nationwide conservation body, Friends of the Earth, came out strongly against the proposal.

Both the MPs for the County have been heavily lobbied by members of both organizations during the past week and it seems that both Margaret Winter (Appleton North) and Larry Havant (Appleton South) are still undecided, even though Mrs Winter has long been known as a member of FoE and, as a farmer with 1,000 acres adjacent to the moor, Mr Havant is a member of the NFU.

The County Council has indicated informally that it will support the water authority if, as now seems likely, the Minister feels it necessary to order a public inquiry into the proposal.

However, the reservoir idea seems likely to become a major issue at the next election. Prospective Green candidate, Polly Shaw, said this week that she will be organizing a county-wide petition and a water rates boycott against the plan. "This whole matter is too important for the NFU steamroller to crush the opposition of all of us who really care."'

13 Economic policy

Questions to be answered in this chapter
- What is the government's role in the management of the economy?
- How has economic policy changed since 1945?
- What is privatization and why is it so controversial?

Terms to know

Cost-push inflation
Demand
Devaluation
Economic boom
Exchange Rate Mechanism (ERM)
Exchange rate policy
Free collective bargaining
Free market
Fiscal policy
Fixed exchange rates
Floating exchange rates
Keynesian economic theory
Marketization

Monetarism
Monetary policy
Nationalization
Prices and incomes policy
Privatization
Recession
Reflation
Social contract
Supply and demand
Sterling crisis
Stop-go economics
Winter of discontent

The government and economic policy

Prior to World War II government intervention in the economy was relatively limited. The dominant economic theories of the time saw the economy as an organism that the government could do little to change. Intervention had occurred during World War I, but not on the scale of the 1940s, and it had not been sustained in the interwar years. World War II was different in that 'total war' demanded total commitment from all sectors of the economy and absolute co-ordination of those elements. Thus the government intervened on a scale never before witnessed in Britain and seemed to do so effectively. As the historian Paul Addison wrote:

'. . . the command economy had an indirect influence. In a general sense, it was taken to prove the efficacy of state action. But the wartime economy prescribed the ends, rather than the means, of postwar reconstruction. Wartime Britain served as an example of full employment and maximum industrial output. It served as an example of social welfare. The problem of reconstruction planning was to discover methods by which a peacetime state could achieve the same objectives.' – Paul Addison, 'The road from 1945', in Hennessy and Seldon (eds), Ruling Performance: British Governments from Attlee to Thatcher, Blackwell, 1989

For those methods, the Labour government of 1945 looked to the economic theories of John Maynard Keynes. Keynes' *General Theory of Employment, Interest and Money* had been published in 1936, but it was not until the war years that his ideas began to be accepted. Keynes had argued that the level of employment in the economy could be controlled by government through its influence on the level of **demand** in the economy. If unemployment began to rise, the government could induce more demand for goods and services in the economy. This would stimulate industry and encourage firms to take on more workers, who, in turn, would have more money to spend, thus further stimulating industry.

In fact, Keynes' ideas dominated the whole of postwar economic policy making with government intervening to reduce unemployment or to bring down the level of inflation. It was not until the 1970s that governments began to rethink their Keynesian strategies and to turn to monetarism as a means of achieving economic stability.

Regardless of the economic doctrines being followed, every government became aware of the fact that the economy was the most important issue and that the success or failure of its economic policies would determine its political success in the polls.

Postwar economic management

Keynesian economic theory was based on the idea that the general level of economic activity could be influenced by adjusting the level of demand in the economy. The higher the level of demand, the more workers would be employed, but there would come a point when the level of demand would be too great for the economy to cope – production could not be expanded any further. Under these circumstances, the demand for goods and services would outweigh their supply, and the competition for the goods would lead to persistent price rises, or *inflation*. Therefore, unemployment and inflation were seen as opposite sides of the same coin. In fact, there was a trade-off between the two economic evils: when unemployment was high, inflation would be low and vice versa.

Broadly speaking, the government had three tools at its disposal to influence the level of demand:

● **Fiscal policy** concerns the government's budget, i.e. how much the government is spending and how much it expects to receive as tax revenue. If government spending rises, there will be greater demand in the economy and economic activity will expand. As a result, unemployment will fall and inflation will begin to rise. The same effect could be achieved by reducing the level of taxation because lower taxes would leave people with more money to spend. If these policies were reversed, with lower government spending and higher taxes, unemployment would rise and inflation would fall.

● **Monetary policy** concerns the quantity of money circulating in the economy. The more there is in the economy, the higher the level of demand will be and so economic activity will rise. The amount of money in the economy is largely determined by the level of lending and borrowing taking place. A great deal of the money that governments, firms and individuals spend is borrowed from banks. Therefore, if the government could restrict the banks' ability to lend money, the level of demand in the economy would fall. A government can do this by imposing restrictions on the banks and by manipulating the level of interest. Simply, the higher the level of interest payable on a loan, the fewer people will want to borrow money and so the level of demand falls.

Keynes

Demand management

Economic tools

Fiscal policy

Monetary policy

177

Exchange rate policy

● **Exchange rate policy** concerns the value of sterling on the foreign exchange markets. Most people only come across foreign exchange when they go abroad on holiday. For example, if the value of the pound is high, the number of French francs that it buys will rise. British holidaymakers going to France may buy more goods, so money is leaving the country and the level of demand at home will go down. On the other hand, if the value of the pound is low, the French have the favourable exchange rate and more are likely to come to Britain to buy British goods and services, so the demand in the British economy increases. More importantly, if the level of the pound is low, the prices of British goods will be lower abroad and companies will be able to sell more exports, and vice versa. Therefore, the level of the exchange rate affects Britain's trade with the rest of the world.

Fixed and floating rates

Until 1972 the level of the pound's exchange rate was fixed. This means that the pound was given a particular level against the US dollar and was expected to remain at that level. The aim of such a system was to bring stability to world trade. In practice, it meant that the British government had little room to manoeuvre.

Immediately after World War II, £1 = $4.03. The level of the pound was linked to the success of Britain's trade with the rest of the world. If Britain was importing more than it was exporting, there would be a flood of pounds on the market which would put downward pressure on the pound. The government would then have to purchase the excess pound or increase interest rates in an effort to increase the value of the pound. Such downward pressure became known as a **sterling crisis**. In 1949 the Labour government, under Clement Attlee, was forced to *devalue* the pound from $4.03 to $2.80. Harold Wilson's first Labour administration also faced a sterling crisis in 1967–8. Despite his determination to maintain the level of $2.80, the pound was once again devalued, this time to $2.40.

Devaluation

The 1967–8 sterling crisis illustrates very well the political aspects to a **devaluation**. Harold Wilson's efforts to prevent a devaluation were motivated by a desire to avoid a repetition of the crisis of 1949 following which Labour became known as the party of devaluation. In addition, many people believed that a devaluation was an indication of Britain's decline from its position as a world power and should therefore be avoided in order to maintain Britain's place at 'the top table'.

Only in 1972 did Britain abandon **fixed exchange rates**, allowing the pound to float freely (**floating exchange rates**). This meant that the value of the pound was free to rise and fall according to the **supply and demand** of pounds, and the government was not compelled to intervene to maintain a particular level. Not until Britain joined the European **Exchange Rate Mechanism** (ERM) in 1990 were exchange rates fixed again.

Stop-go economics

Given the apparent trade-off between unemployment and inflation, the course of Britain's postwar economic policy is not difficult to imagine. The postwar period until the late 1970s was dominated by **stop-go economics**.

Reflation

Very simply, the chain of events would run as follows. The economy would be stimulated (**reflation**) by increasing spending, reducing taxation or a reduction in interest rates. As a result, unemployment would fall, but inflation would begin to rise. In addition, with more money in their pockets, people would tend to spend more on foreign goods, i.e. imports. This would mean that imports would exceed exports and that there would be downward pressure on the pound leading to a sterling crisis.

In order to end a sterling crisis, the government would be forced to increase interest rates and reduce people's ability to spend on imported goods, by increasing taxes and generally deflating the economy. As a result the **economic boom** would come to an end and a **recession** would begin. Inflation would begin to fall and unemployment to rise.

After a time, the cycle would begin again, when unemployment was considered to have risen too far. However, the renewal of the cycle also had a political motivation. Governments tended to reflate the economy shortly before an election in order to create an economic boom in the hope that it would lead to, what is now called, the 'feel-good' factor and an election victory.

Deflation

The 1970s upheaval

For much of the postwar period, both the Conservative and Labour Parties had agreed on economic strategy and this was a major element of the postwar political consensus. However, this agreement began to break down in the 1970s as a new economic crisis loomed.

Postwar consensus

At the end of the 1960s the simple trade-off between unemployment and inflation broke down. As the economists Alan Griffiths and John Wall commented:

'In the 1950s, and for most of the 1960s, the evidence for the UK and other countries seemed to support . . . an apparent inverse relationship between inflation and unemployment . . . This "trade off" between unemployment and inflation could be roughly quantified, "for x % less unemployment we must accept y% extra inflation" . . . Since the late 1960s, however, the simple relationship has broken down . . . and at times both unemployment and the inflation rate have increased together, as in the periods 1967–71, 1974–5, 1979–80 and 1984–5.'
– Griffiths and Wall, *Applied Economics*, Prentice Hall, 1986

The Labour Party responded to the rise in inflation and unemployment by turning to a **prices and incomes policy** which became known as the **social contract**. This policy was designed to bring inflation under control by persuading trade unions to practise pay restraint by not seeking excessive wage rises. This was based on the theory of **cost-push inflation** which blames wage rises for increasing costs that are then passed on to the consumer as higher prices. The policy had seemed to be relatively successful until 1978 when the trade unions declined to participate in a further round of wage restraint and demanded a return to **free collective bargaining**, i.e. the determination of wage levels through negotiation between employer and employee. The result was the **winter of discontent** during which a spate of strikes caused havoc in both the private and public sectors.

Cost-push inflation

While the Labour government coped with the crises of the 1970s the Conservative Party elected a new leader, Margaret Thatcher, who brought with her a new approach to economic problems. The basis of her economic outlook was a belief in the **free market** (see below) and the identification of inflation as the primary economic problem. This approach was known as **monetarism**.

Monetarism

The doctrine of monetarism is associated with Professor Milton Friedman of Chicago University. The basis of the theory is that inflation is the primary economic evil. It makes firms uncompetitive in the world market, it leads to unemployment and it discourages investment in industry. It can be brought under control by limiting the amount of money in circulation, achieved by limiting bank lending.

When the Conservative Party came to power in 1979 Margaret Thatcher was determined to implement this policy. She was supported by the chancellor, Geoffrey Howe and the minister of Trade and Industry, Keith Joseph. In its first term of office the government doubled the level of value-added tax (VAT), reduced the level of income tax and maintained high interest rates in an effort to reduce inflation while giving individuals the incentive to work harder.

Recession

By 1983 inflation had begun to fall, but at the cost of spiralling unemployment and bankruptcies. Most of the firms and jobs lost were in the manufacturing industry. The monetarists argued that British industry was overstaffed, inefficient and uncompetitive, but would come out of the recession stronger, fitter and ready to do business with the rest of the world.

Economic boom

This seemed to be the case in 1985 when the economy began to boom. This was largely engineered by low taxes, low interest rates and increases in government spending, not untypical of the stop-go cycle that had dominated the early postwar years. As a result the chancellor, Nigel Lawson, was credited with the Conservative Party's 1987 election victory.

In line with the usual stop-go cycle, the election victory was followed by a renewed attack on inflation. The government's ability to control the money supply had proved limited in the 1980s, so the chancellor turned to exchange rates as a means of reducing inflation.

Nigel Lawson decided that the value of the pound should be kept in line with that of the Deutschmark. Germany had a low-inflation economy and as a result its currency was strong. He believed that to tie sterling to the Deutschmark would mean that British interest rates would need to remain high and so the money supply and the level of demand would be kept under control.

The economy and the ERM

Walters v. Lawson

Since sterling was already shadowing the Deutschmark, it seemed a small step to membership of the European Exchange Rate Mechanism by which sterling would be allowed to float only to a limited extent compared to other European currencies. However, Margaret Thatcher, on the advice of Alan Walters, her economics adviser, objected to Britain's membership, and Nigel Lawson resigned.

Entry into ERM

In 1990 his successor, John Major, persuaded the prime minister that membership of the ERM was a good idea and Britain joined with the pound at a high level against the Deutschmark (DM2.95). This rate was high enough to ensure that membership would be anti-inflationary; however, it was too high to be sustainable.

The penalizing level of the pound tightened Britain's anti-inflation policy which only served to exacerbate the recession that had begun after the 1987 election. The government argued that the recession was not peculiar to Britain and that all of the industrialized economies were suffering. Nevertheless, the combination of economic recession and a high exchange rate proved unworkable and Britain withdrew from the ERM in September 1992.

Inflation policy

Following this, the government repeated its commitment to the fight against inflation. Its aim (early 1995) is to keep it below 4 per cent. The anti-inflation policy largely rested on the government's interest-rate policy. The chancellor, Kenneth Clarke, moved to incremental increases in interest rates in the face of fears of inflationary pressure resurfacing again as the economy gradually moved out of recession.

Nationalization versus privatization

Public ownership

In 1945 the Attlee government came to power with the intention of taking over the 'commanding heights' of the economy. It launched a programme of **nationalization**, but the idea of the public ownership of commercial concerns was not new in 1945. The Post Office, for example, had been publicly owned for a very long time.

What was new after World War II was the scale of public ownership. In 1946 the Bank of England, civil aviation and the coal industry were all taken into public ownership. In the coming years they would be followed by, amongst others, railways (1948), gas (1949), electricity (1948) and iron and steel (1951).

Nationalization

The Labour government believed that control of key industries would give it better control over the economy. This would allow more planning and co-ordination of the economy. Also, industries such as coal were in need of considerable investment, which only seemed likely to come from the central government.

Planning

Of course, there was also an ideological component to the nationalization programme. According to socialist beliefs, public ownership could help temper the extremes of capitalism. Public ownership could reduce exploitation of consumers by ensuring that prices were equitable and that services were provided for all (see page 55).

Ideology

Even when the Labour government lost the 1951 election, the Conservative governments that followed only returned road haulage and steel to the private sector, despite the natural tendency of Conservatives to prefer private ownership to public (see pages 53–5). The attitude of the Conservative governments seems to have been based on their understanding of the practical problems faced by the postwar economy as reconstruction was undertaken. In fact, even as late as 1971 Edward Heath's government was prepared to take Rolls Royce into public ownership in order to rescue it from imminent collapse.

Conservative attitudes

Privatization

When Margaret Thatcher came to power in 1979 her attitude to public ownership was very different from that of her predecessors. She was more of a nineteenth-century liberal than a traditional Tory (see pages 51–2). She did not approach the nationalized industries in a pragmatic way but rather in the light of her belief in the free-market doctrines of the eighteenth-century economist Adam Smith.

Thatcherism

Margaret Thatcher was convinced that the role of government should be limited in order to give citizens freedom from regulation and government restraint. Therefore, she was committed to 'rolling back' the interventionist state that both Labour and Conservative governments had created. She did this through the policy of **privatization**. The policy of privatization, when interpreted narrowly, means the sale of publicly owned assets to the private sector. More widely, it can be used to mean the **marketization** (see below) of the public sector.

Rolling back the state

Since 1979 the Conservative governments have embarked on a programme of privatization that has been almost as radical as the nationalization programme of Clement Attlee's government 50 years ago. The government has sold its partial shareholdings in companies such as British Petroleum and has returned fully

Privatization

nationalized industries to private ownership. Some of Britain's leading private companies were once nationally owned and were only returned to private hands in the 1980s. They include British Aerospace (1981 and 1985); Jaguar (1984); British Telecom (1984); British Gas (1986); British Airways (1987); British Steel (1988); and the twelve electricity companies (1990).

Commercial principles

Margaret Thatcher's main argument in favour of privatization was that commercial concerns are best managed by those in the commercial world. Ministers and civil servants are accustomed to running government, not to running large companies. Also, by returning the nationalized industries to private hands, they would be in a competitive world which would encourage greater efficiency, further capital investment and a better service to the consumer. The nationalized industries had been monopolies with a guaranteed market and apparently unlimited funding from government and therefore they had no incentive to become efficient. This, Margaret Thatcher argued, would change in the private sector and all would benefit.

Competition

The right wing of the Conservative Party believed that competition was always healthy and would lead to efficiency, better use of resources and better services to customers; and therefore that it should not only be confined to firms in private ownership. Recent Conservative governments attempted to introduce marketization (see chapter 14) to many areas of the public sector. Local authorities were required to allow private companies to bid to provide services in their area; schools and hospitals were given the opportunity to opt out of local authority control; and even the civil service was split up into agencies which became responsible for the delivery of services in an efficient and cost-effective way.

Ideology

In line with the Labour government of 1945, Margaret Thatcher's actions had a strong ideological content. Like many Conservatives, she believed in private property as one of the greatest rights and freedoms in a democratic society. It gives people a reward for hard work and also encourages them to value stability. By creating a society of share owners, home owners and, she hoped, entrepreneurs, Conservative values would become entrenched in British society and an enterprise culture would be created.

An alternative interpretation is offered by critics of Margaret Thatcher's privatization campaign. The industries that were sold off were the most profitable and the less attractive industries have been made profitable, at the taxpayers expense, before being privatized. Therefore, the reason for the programme was not ideological because industry could be run efficiently in the public sector, but in order to finance borrowing and to allow the Conservative Party to present itself to the electorate as the party of tax cuts. The programme, the critics argue, was launched for the lowest political motives rather than for the high ideals of Thatcherite ideology.

Such critics also turn to the accusation that industries were sold off at bargain-basement prices in order to secure a sale. The National Audit Office has claimed that British Steel was underpriced by £100–£250 million and that British Aerospace was given a £44 million subsidy in order to persuade it to buy the car manufacturer, the Rover Group.

Despite these criticisms, and the departure of Margaret Thatcher from office, privatization has continued under John Major's government. Although plans to privatize the Post Office were shelved in the wake of backbench criticism in 1994, the coal industry was privatized that year and rail privatization is currently in progress.

Exercises

Short questions

Why did government economic policy become more interventionist after 1945?
(ULEAC, June 1992)
2 a What is the ERM?
b Why did Britain withdraw in 1992?
3 Distinguish between *privatization* and *marketization*.

Essay questions

How, and why, do the policies of the Conservative and Labour Parties differ on privatization? (Oxford and Cambridge, June 1993)
2 'I was all in favour of the redistribution of income until I realized it was my income they were going to redistribute.' (Voter quoted in *The Observer*, 22 March 1992.)
In what ways, and for what reasons, have political parties represented at Westminster disagreed over polices for inflation and unemployment, spending and taxation since 1979? (AEB, June 1994)

Data response question

'A privatization programme had been investigated while the Conservatives had been in opposition by a working party under Nicholas Ridley. However, the 1979 party manifesto had mentioned only the denationalization of the two industries nationalized under Labour (aerospace and shipbuilding) plus the National Freight Corporation. Now, under the influence of Sir Keith Joseph, a more ambitious approach was developed until in the end no nationalized industry was considered to be immune from eventual return to the private sector. The rationale was that this would make them more conducive to competition, enhance consumer choice, increase efficiency and reduce public-sector borrowing. In many cases, however, it was admitted that the industries concerned would either have to be made profitable before a return to the private sector could be envisaged or else only the profitable parts could be sold off.'

Source: Alan Sked and Chris Cook, *Post War Britain, A Political History*, Pelican, 1984

1 What were the arguments given in favour of the post-war nationalization programme.
2 Explain the justifications for privatization identified in the passage.
3 Assess the success of Conservative governments' privatization programmes, since 1979.

14 Social policy

Questions to be answered in this chapter
- What is the history of health, education, housing and social security policies in Britain?
- What is 'marketization'?
- How has marketization affected social policy?

Terms to know

Assisted places	Job seeker
Beveridge Report	Marketization
Butler Act	National curriculum
Dependency	Opt-out
Fundholding GPs	Parent governors
Grant maintained	Poverty trap
Hospital trusts	Public sector
Housing Action Trusts (HATs)	Rent controls

The development of social policy in Britain

Origins

Traditionally, the role of the state has been limited to the maintenance of law and order and the defence of the country. However, during the twentieth century governments have become more involved in the provision of an ever-wider range of services and benefits. In Britain this began with the Liberal government of 1906 which introduced old-age pensions and national insurance for the sick and unemployed. Since then government involvement in society has steadily increased to include the National Health Service, free education and a range of benefits such as unemployment, housing and family support.

Impetus behind such government intervention has come from two main sources. At the beginning of the twentieth century the development of socialist theories of equality encouraged members of all parties to take the provision of benefits seriously in order to take care of the less well-off in society. By the 1940s the advent of Keynesian economics (see page 177) encouraged governments to intervene in society, spending money in order to stimulate economic activity and create jobs. Welfare spending allowed the government to do this on a large scale.

Post–1945 consensus

In the immediate postwar period, as part of the political consensus of the time, both the Conservative and Labour Parties were agreed on the need for welfare provision. While there may have been some disagreement about the level of benefits, about spending on housing and about the universality of the health service, social policy was not a subject for bitter political debate.

Adversarial politics

In the 1970s the attitude towards social policy and the welfare state changed. Pressures on the welfare state were increasing with a growing, as well as ageing population and rising unemployment. At the same time, Britain experienced an economic crisis including rising inflation and cuts in public spending. For the first time, Britain's ability to afford the welfare state was called into question. Many also began to ask whether the service being received from the welfare state was sufficiently good enough to merit the level of spending.

Criticism of the welfare state came largely from the Conservative Party under the leadership of Margaret Thatcher. From the right of the party and under the influence of the followers of free-market economics (see page 179), such as Keith Joseph, Margaret Thatcher believed that 'big government' was bad. According to the 'new right', British government had taken on responsibility for the delivery of too many services; its delivery of those services was inefficient and ineffective; and the extent of government intervention in the economy was stifling the growth of the private sector. The solution, according to the right, was to prune and reform the welfare state.

The main thrust of the reform of all areas of social policy was **marketization**. This means that purchasers or consumers should be given more power to voice their dissatisfaction with the provision of services. In the world of education, this would allow parents to choose schools in the light of league tables showing attendance and examination results; in housing it would allow tenants to buy their local authority house; and in the National Health Service doctors would be allowed to purchase services for hospitals. In giving greater power to consumers, the intention was to encourage suppliers to be more efficient and so deliver a superior service which would, in turn, retain the loyalty of consumers.

Thatcherism

The National Health Service

The National Health Service (NHS) was created in 1948 by the Labour government led by Clement Attlee. The minister largely responsible for this was Aneurin Bevan who was committed to building a service that would provide universal health care. This meant that health would be available to everyone based on their need rather than on their income. The expense of such a service would be financed by a progressive tax system that forced the well-off in society to pay higher rates of tax than the poor. Therefore, the NHS was a means of redistributing income, as well as of providing health care.

Between 1948 and 1979 the popularity of the NHS was such that political parties felt unable to tackle the problems of rising costs and the apparently infinite demand for health care.

This situation changed when the Conservative Party came to power in 1979. From a practical point of view Margaret Thatcher had criticized the NHS as inefficient and, as a matter of principle, she was suspicious of the provision of any service, including health care, by the **public sector**. Nevertheless, for the greater part of her term of office Margaret Thatcher did little to reform the health service. The government encouraged the development and use of private health care, both as a means of relieving the pressure on the NHS and as a principle of free choice. However, aware of the popularity of the NHS, the government, rather than reform it, concentrated much of its energy on showing that its spending on the NHS had increased and that ever more patients were being treated by its hospitals.

Criticism of NHS

By 1987 many of the priority items on Margaret Thatcher's policy list had been tackled, but the health service remained untouched. After the general election the government turned its attention to NHS reform. Margaret Thatcher set up a 'prime ministerial review' of the NHS which she chaired herself. The results of the inquiry were made public one year later as a white paper, *Working for Patients*.

NHS reform

Trust hospitals

The aims of the Conservative governments of both Margaret Thatcher and John Major were to introduce elements of free-market economics into the health service. In order to do this, the reforms allowed hospitals to **opt out** of local health authority control by becoming self-governing **hospital trusts**. This meant that hospitals could operate as independent units providing services for those health authorities that were prepared to pay, while also staying within a limited budget.

Fundholding GPs

The government also introduced **fundholding GPs** who were allocated a budget on the basis of the number of patients receiving treatment. They were then expected to spend this budget on treatment for their patients by purchasing services from hospitals.

Providers and purchasers

The marketization process was brought into the structure of the NHS itself. The government believed that the NHS had become dominated by doctors and nurses and that the concerns of the 'producers' were dictating NHS policy. The government wanted the priorities of the NHS to be determined by the demands of patients. In other words, the government was drawing a distinction between 'provider' and 'purchaser'.

It therefore introduced the market principles of supply and demand to the health service. This meant that the government wanted the supply of health services to be dictated by the demands of the customers: the patients. Of course, these principles come easily to private health care services in which consumers pay directly for their treatment. However, within the NHS such market forces operate through intermediaries: GPs and district health authorities. We saw above that fundholding GPs became responsible for purchasing treatment for their patients. In addition, district health authorities were now to be responsible for purchasing services from the suppliers: the hospitals.

Efficiency

The aim behind the reforms was to make purchasers and providers more conscious of costs and quality. The resulting increase in efficiency, it was hoped, would reduce the waiting time for patients. Critics have argued that market forces should not be introduced to the NHS because they emphasize the economics of the service rather than patient need. For example, marketization might tempt hospitals to specialize in operations that are profitable rather than necessary. A two-tier NHS might also be created with the patients of fundholding GPs receiving treatment more rapidly than those of the non-fundholding GPs.

Education

Origins

Prior to 1870 the provision of free education for the mass of the British population was not the responsibility of the state; rather it was left to individuals and to religious bodies. The 1870 Elementary Education Act allowed local government to make a provision where none already existed. By 1876 attendance was made compulsory for children who lived within two miles of a school.

Development

The Education Act of 1902 allowed for the provision of secondary as well as elementary education. It was at this time that some important patterns in education became apparent. Grammar schools existed for children whose parents were prepared to pay for education and for the gifted children of the working class who could pass an entrance examination, whereas less-gifted children attended technical schools or remained at newly extended elementary schools.

The Butler Act 1944

In 1926 the Hadow Report recommended that there should be a break in education at the age of 11. This idea was developed by the Norwood Report in 1943 which identified three types of children: those who enjoyed learning for its own sake; those who enjoyed the practical application of ideas; and those who were more at home with tangible, physical matters rather than concepts and ideas. The newly developed IQ testing could be used to distinguish between these types of children and so schools could be set up to cater for each type of child: grammar schools for the first, technical schools for the second and secondary modern schools for the third.

The Education Act of 1944, also known as the **Butler Act**, laid the foundations for Britain's education policy for much of the postwar period. It set up a three-part system consisting of grammar, secondary and technical schools. Pupils underwent a selection process at the age of 11, with the brightest going to grammar schools.

Comprehensive education

The selective system of education, like the health service, remained at the centre of the postwar political consensus. However, this began to break down in the 1960s when the Labour Party criticized the grammar-school system as elitist and unfair, with only 20 per cent of children attending grammar schools. It was argued that at 11 years of age children were too young to be assessed and that many mistakes were made which undermined the value of the selection process. Critics pointed to the fact that the selection process was laying the basis for a divided society in the future. Children attending grammar schools often received a more academic education and were groomed to attend university. The results of the selection process also usually reflected the existing class system. The children of the middle classes often attended grammar schools while those of the working classes did not.

In the 1960s the Labour Party abandoned its support of the status quo in education and advocated the creation of a system of comprehensive education. According to this idea, selection would be ended and children of all abilities would attend the same schools. In this way, there would be no inequality in the standard of education received; there would be a tendency for divisions in society to be healed rather than intensified; and less able children would be encouraged to perform better, rather than feel abandoned to an inferior education system.

Since 1944 the management of schools had been the responsibility of local authorities and they had been left largely free of government interference. Therefore, the Labour government's approach to education reform in 1965 was to work with local authorities to create schemes of comprehensive education. However, the Conservative government ended that process in 1970.

Local authorities

When the Labour Party returned to office in 1974, it renewed its call for comprehensive education. This resulted in the Education Act of 1976 which required local education authorities to create a system of comprehensive education.

Conservative reforms

Margaret Thatcher's government came to power in 1979 seeking to improve educational standards and to control the commitment of resources to education. Like the NHS, it can be argued that the education system is a 'bottomless pit' with regard to finance. No matter how much money is allocated to education, it will never be enough because the demands for better facilities and for higher staff:pupil ratios are infinite.

Marketization

Therefore, Margaret Thatcher's governments embarked on a process of marketization. Their aim was the same as that in the NHS: to introduce market forces to the provision of education, with schools being viewed as providers and parents as consumers. It was hoped that reforms would give parents more power and more choice and so make schools more responsive to the needs of the customer.

Producer orientated

While the government believed the health service had become dominated by the needs of health authorities, hospitals, doctors and nurses, it believed the education system had become dominated by local education authorities and teachers. It thought that these groups were too concerned with financial resources and progressive teaching methods and not enough with delivering the high-quality, traditional service that the government required. The government focused considerable public attention on poor examination results and attendance; on the desire of some schools to remove elements of competition from the educational process; and on the desire of others to teach ideologically charged subjects such as peace studies.

Assisted places

The 1980 Education Act began the marketization process slowly by introducing the assisted place scheme by which children from the state, or maintained, school sector could apply for **assisted places** from schools in the independent sector. The government's intention was to increase parental choice by opening up more places in independent schools to families who could not afford fees. Critics of the plan argued that this was merely a method of channelling public money into the coffers of independent schools at the expense of the maintained sector.

Parental participation

The 1986 Education Act took the process one step further by increasing the voice of parents on school governing bodies. Since 1944 all state-sector schools have been required to have a board of governors who are responsible for policy decisions within the school. The 1986 Act increased the representation of parents on these boards – **parent governors** – at the expense of local authority representatives who were relegated to minority status. A system of secret-ballot elections was created to allow all parents to choose their representatives.

The 1988 Education Act

Local management of schools

The 1988 Education Act extended the responsibilities of school governors by removing the responsibility for running the school from the local education authority and putting it in the hands of the school's head teacher and governors. This is known as local management of schools (LMS) and was intended to make individual schools more responsive to the needs of parents and the local community.

Grant-maintained schools and the national curriculum

The act also enabled schools to opt out of local authority control completely. Those schools choosing to opt out become **grant maintained** and were then financed directly by central government. This tendency to bring more schools under the banner of central government was continued by the creation of a **national curriculum**. For the first time, central government laid down the subjects that children must be taught in maintained schools during the period of compulsory education. The curriculum consists of a core of English, mathematics and science with additional subjects of history, geography, technology, physical education, art, music, modern languages and, for pupils in Wales, Welsh.

The 1988 Act also introduced a system of open enrolment which allowed parents to choose the maintained school for their children rather than be allocated a school by the local education authority. The idea behind open enrolment was that parents would move their children from poor-quality schools to better schools. In the face of a falling student roll, schools considered to be of inferior quality would need to improve their standards in order to attract students. This type of competition between schools was further encouraged by the publication of school league tables covering examination results and records of absenteeism. The government intended these tables to help parents to make decisions about the standard of service at individual schools.

Critics of the government's education reforms feared that the marketization of education would result in a divided education system. Better-off parents would be able to take their children away from poorer-quality schools, either by moving house to a 'better' catchment area or by choosing private education. However, the less well-off would be unable to do this. As a result, 'ghetto schools' would be created and caught in a downward spiral of falling educational standards.

Some observers also argued that the information available to parents on which to base their decisions about choosing a school was misleading. Schools in poor and depressed areas might be achieving a great deal with weak students, but this would not be reflected in a string of A grades at GCSE or A level. Therefore, the achievements of the school, its teachers and its students were in danger of being undervalued.

Finally, while claiming to return power to the parents at the expense of the local education authorities, the government *increased* the power of central government against which, some suggested, parents would be in a much weaker position than they had been prior to the reforms. Grant-maintained schools, sixth-form colleges and further-education colleges are all funded directly by central government, which gives Whitehall a great deal of power without the need to be responsive to local conditions.

Housing policy

As was the case with other areas of social policy, the aftermath of World War II called for considerable government intervention. To some extent, government education and welfare policies were based on ideological ambitions for a postwar world that would make Britain a land fit for heroes. Housing policy, on the other hand, was determined largely by necessity. The war had destroyed or damaged 700,000 houses, which, combined with the demobilization of the armed forces and a rising birth rate, caused a housing crisis.

The Labour government of 1945 responded with a programme of house building in the public sector. While the funding for the programme came from central government, much of the control of the programme was put in the hands of local government. For example, the Town and Country Planning Act of 1947 gave local authorities the power to control the development of house building.

In 1951 the Conservative Party came to power having pledged to build 300,000

Side notes (margin):

Open enrolment and league tables

Divisive policies

Poor information

Post-1945

Public-sector housing

Private-sector growth

houses per year. However, during the following twelve years the role of the public sector was reduced to providing homes for the less well-off, while the bulk of building was undertaken by the private sector for private ownership rather than for renting. In 1952, 15 per cent of domestic property built was for owner occupation. By 1963 this proportion had reached 63 per cent. In addition, **rent controls** were eased in order to encourage private landlords to let property.

When the Labour Party returned to power in 1964, under Harold Wilson, there was, once more, a commitment to a programme of public-sector housing. The National Plan of 1965 pledged the government to the construction of 500,000 council houses per year. Rent rebates were also introduced along with rent controls in an attempt to prevent the exploitation of tenants by private landlords.

Partisanship

Therefore, unlike some other areas of social policy, housing was not a subject of agreement between the two main parties. The Labour Party, from the necessity of 1945, built an ideological commitment to public housing while the Conservative Party preferred solutions provided by the private sector.

Thatcherism and housing

We saw above that Margaret Thatcher was committed to 'rolling back the state' in as many areas of policy as possible, and housing was no exception. However, in housing policy two basic strands of Thatcherite ideology coincided:
● a limited role for the state
● the expansion of home ownership.

Home ownership

According to Conservative philosophy, home ownership encourages people to value stability. This idea is an extension of the broader principle of property ownership. If people work hard and use their money to help buy their own home, they have a tangible product of the capitalist system and so have an investment in the maintenance of that system. They value their freedom to own their own property, endeavour to increase the value of that property, and value the political and economic stability that makes this possible.

Privatization

Given the importance of private ownership of housing, Margaret Thatcher's government moved quickly to transfer the stock of public housing to the private sector. The Housing Act of 1980 gave tenants of council houses the right to buy their own homes. Furthermore, the homes were to be offered for sale at substantial discounts of up to 70 per cent depending on the length of tenancy and the type of property involved. Not only did the government encourage the sale of council houses, it restricted the local authorities from spending the income from sales on rebuilding the public-housing stock.

Private-sector role

The Housing and Planning Act of 1986 increased the incentives available to tenants of flats. However, the Housing Act of 1988 pushed the government's reforms much further. It encouraged the private rented sector by introducing deregulation of the rented sector and tax concessions for private landlords. It also allowed tenants of public-sector housing to vote to transfer control of the property from the local authority to a private-sector landlord or housing association. The private landlords could bid for ownership of public housing estates and tenants were given the power to prevent such a sale if more than 50 per cent of them voted against the move.

The prospect of private landlords taking over public housing estates acted as a spur to local authorities to sell more of their properties to tenants. As a result, there was a renewed surge of sales, with 140,127 properties being sold in 1988–9.

The 1988 Act also created **Housing Action Trusts** (HATs). These were agents of the central government and were intended to take over the management of some of the most difficult and dilapidated public estates in the country. After improving the standard of the estate, it would be handed back to the local authority or to a private landlord. However, tenants were often less than happy with a HAT taking over their estate. The installation of a new regime, sponsored by central government, to run the estate raised the spectre of a bureaucratic, unresponsive agency. Therefore, tenants were given the right to vote on whether their estate should be managed by the local authority or by a HAT. Due to their suspicions of central government interference, most tenants chose to remain under local control.

The Local Government and Housing Act of 1989 placed restrictions on local authorities' ability to subsidize the rents of council tenants. Following this, many experienced significant rent increases. However, the increases in council rents were outstripped by the increases in the private sector which further prevented the development of the private rented market and the move towards HATs. In view of the rent increases, the level of savings achieved by curtailing the role of government in housing was reduced because the level of housing benefit rose to help the less well-off pay their rents.

Social security

In 1942 the **Beveridge Report** proposed the idea that the British government should create a system of welfare that would protect people from 'Want, Disease, Ignorance, Squalor and Idleness'. Again, the Labour government of 1945 took the lead in the implementation of a social-security system. The Family Allowances Act (1945) set up the forerunner of child benefit; the National Insurance Act (1946) extended the benefits that covered the unemployed and the sick; the National Insurance Act (1948) created supplementary benefit to embrace those in need who were not covered by other legislation.

The system of benefits remained largely untouched for much of the postwar period. However, the breakdown of consensus politics in the 1970s brought with it criticisms of the benefits system. The ideological divide between Labour and Conservative saw the Labour Party committed to the preservation of a system of benefits, while the Thatcherite right, or the 'new right', advocated reform of the system.

Thatcherite critics argued that the British economy could not afford to maintain such an elaborate system of benefits. They argued that the socialist 'nanny' state had encouraged people to expect the state to provide for their needs, but in the 1970s economic growth slowed considerably and Britain could no longer afford such an elaborate system of benefits. The dependence on the state, that the system encouraged, was also undermining the entrepreneurial spirit and work ethic of the British worker. In the worst cases **dependency** led to the **poverty trap**. Individuals and families could, the critics of the system suggested, receive so much money from a portfolio of benefits that it outweighed any money they could earn in employment. Therefore, they would not actively seek work.

In response to these criticisms the Conservative government considered ways of reducing dependency on benefits. Reform was particularly apparent in the area of unemployment and supplementary benefits. In 1994 the government introduced the **job seeker** benefit to replace traditional unemployment benefit. Under the new scheme, unemployed people would be entitled to receive benefit for six months if

Housing Action Trusts

Origins

Adversarial politics

Thatcherism

'Job seekers'

they were prepared to sign a contract with the benefits agency to declare their willingness actively to seek work. Along with the contract there was to be a system of incentives and penalties to encourage the unemployed to find work as quickly as possible. This proposal will come into effect in 1996.

Exercises

Short questions

1 a Outline two measures which the Conservative government has taken since 1987 to change the scale and scope of welfare provision.
  b What criticisms have been made of these measures? (ULEAC, January 1991)
2 What have been the most significant changes in the NHS in recent years? (ULEAC, June 1994)
3 a How does the Conservative government justify its reform of the education system?
  b What criticisms have been levelled at these reforms? (ULEAC, January 1991)
4 a What are NHS trusts?
  b Why were they introduced? (ULEAC, January 1993)

Essay questions

1 Has the extent of reform in welfare provision since 1979 been exaggerated? (ULEAC, January 1992)
2 a Why did the Conservative governments favour changes in the scale and scope of welfare provision in the 1980s?
  b What criticisms have been made of such changes? (ULEAC, June 1990)

Data response question

'Britain, which pioneered "socialized medicine", the provision of health care to everyone mostly free at the point of use, is pioneering again. Thanks to an ageing population and new technology, demand for health care has ballooned ahead of supply. Hence the urgent need to introduce economic discipline, in the form of a so-called "internal market", into a monolithic, centrally directed NHS so as to deploy resources more efficiently. Starting from the opposite end of the spectrum, Britain's health-care reforms are aimed at the same goal as those in America and in other countries such as Holland and New Zealand – "managed competition", a combination of the efficiency that markets provide with the equitable distribution of benefits that they often fail to provide. The government's NHS reforms are sensible and should be pursued with more, not less, vigour . . .

First and foremost it must get across the case for separating purchasers (primarily health authorities) from providers (hospitals and doctors). Before this separation, decisions were made because of historical tradition or professional power. Big hospitals stayed in expensive inner cities, despite the fact that many patients had long since moved to the suburbs. The medical establishment, driven by scientific curiosity and professional hubris, channelled scarce resources into high-tech medical procedures such as by-pass surgery, rather than such unglamorous activities as geriatric care.'

Source: The Economist 19 February 1994

1 Explain the terms:
  a 'internal market'
  b 'purchasers' and 'providers'
  c 'socialized medicine'.

2 To what extent do the NHS reforms of the post-1979 Conservative governments conform to the patterns followed in other areas of social policy?

3 Outline the attitude of the Labour Party to the NHS reforms of the Conservative governments.

15 Northern Ireland

Questions to be answered in this chapter

- What is the history of the 'Irish problem'?
- How has the conflict developed since 1972?

Terms to know

Catholic	Official Unionist Party (OUP)
Colonization	Partition
Democratic Unionist Party (DUP)	Protestant
Direct rule	Sinn Fein
Downing Street declaration	Social and Democratic Labour Party (SDLP)
Hillsborough agreement	Stormont
Home rule	Sunningdale agreement
Irish Republican Army (IRA)	Unification

The historical background

To the popular imagination, the conflict in Northern Ireland means the IRA and the British army, Ian Paisley and Gerry Adams. However, the problem that we see today has its roots deep in Anglo–Irish history.

Colonization

Early history

Under the Normans the Irish kings became earls and were largely left to do as they pleased for many years. It was not until the reign of Elizabeth I that the English began to interfere significantly in Irish affairs. A rebellion was quashed in 1603 and land began to be confiscated. At the same time, and perhaps more significantly, Scottish Protestants were encouraged to settle in the north of Ireland with the offer of funds from the English government. It is from this time that the enclave of Irish Protestants in the north originates.

The Reformation

The remainder of Ireland remained almost wholly Catholic. The Reformation in England made little or no impact on Ireland and when civil war broke out in England in 1642, the Irish backed Charles I. Later when James II was forced to flee England over his Catholicism (1688) the Irish supported the Jacobite rebellions that followed.

As a result of the religious division between **Protestant** England and largely **Catholic** Ireland, much Irish land was confiscated. Prior to the civil war, the Irish owned 50 per cent of their own land. After confiscations by Cromwell (1649) and under the Treaty of Limerick (1691) the proportion of land owned by the Irish had fallen to only 20 per cent.

As well as the economic repercussions of the conflicts with England, there were political results. The Irish Parliament was made up solely of Protestants; Catholics were banned from taking public office and were also excluded from university education.

Unification

Following the **colonization** of Ireland, opposition to English rule gave rise to Irish nationalism. For a time the Society of United Irishmen, led by Wolf Tone, was able to unite Catholics and Protestants against English imperialism. However, such unity was short lived and conflict between the rival religious groups soon broke out. A bloody clash in Armagh saw victory for the Protestants and the formation of the Orange Society in 1795.

Irish nationalists

A further rebellion, backed by the French and led by Wolf Tone, was defeated in 1798. Wolf Tone was executed and the British government decided to end Ireland's status as a colony by unifying Britain and Ireland. The Protestant Irish Parliament, suspicious of the Catholic community, was prepared to accept **unification**, with the promise of greater economic prosperity. In 1800 the Act of Union was passed, the Irish Parliament was dissolved and unification was complete.

While the Protestant north reaped the economic benefits of unification, the south did not and the Act of Union became a new focus for Irish nationalism. In 1823 Daniel O'Connell formed the Catholic Association which sought to free Catholics from the restrictions on their ability to participate in public life. In 1828 he was elected to Parliament, but was unable to take up his seat because of the ban on Catholics holding public office. As a result, in 1829 an act was passed to emancipate Catholics.

Catholic emancipation

Irish nationalism

With Catholic emancipation achieved, a number of groups sprang up seeking varying degrees of independence from Britain. O'Connell turned his attention to repeal of the Act of Union through the Repeal Association, but his efforts had foundered by the middle of the nineteenth century.

The Young Ireland movement took up the fight, but was crushed by the Royal Irish Constabulary after an attempted rebellion in 1848. Many of the survivors of the rebellion fled Ireland but continued the campaign for independence by forming the Fenian Brotherhood in New York. Its counterpart in Dublin was the Irish Republican Brotherhood which was dedicated to the achievement of an Irish republic, by violent means if necessary.

Other groups had more limited objectives, including **home rule** within the British empire and land reform. The Land League, led by Charles Stewart Parnell, was the focus of loyalty for Irish MPs seeking land reform. Parnell's authority diminished in 1890 when he was disgraced by his involvement in an adultery case.

Parnell

On the mainland, the Irish issue had come to dominate the thoughts of William Gladstone. He was given one final attempt to solve the problem in 1893 when he returned to power with the support of the Irish MPs. He was able to push through the House of Commons a bill giving a measure of home rule, only to see it defeated in the Lords. No further effort to grant home rule was made until the Liberals returned to office in 1906 and passed the Home Rule Bill in 1912. By this time the House of Lords had lost its veto power and could do nothing to stop Irish home rule.

Easter rising

However, progress towards the reality of home rule was postponed by the outbreak of World War I. The Irish nationalists saw this as a betrayal by the British government, and the Irish Citizen Army and the Irish Republican Brotherhood launched an armed insurrection. This was put down at Easter 1916. Its leaders were shot and martial law was imposed in Ireland.

The brutality of the British reaction to the Easter rising served to reinforce the nationalists' commitment to independence. The Irish Republican Brotherhood, for example, gained more support. However, the focus of nationalism became Sinn Fein.

Sinn Fein

Set up in 1905 by Arthur Griffith, **Sinn Fein** had initially sought independence while recognizing the authority of the British monarch. In the wake of the Easter rising, however, its opposition to Britain hardened and it became committed to an Irish republic.

Sinn Fein

Provisional Sinn Fein was created in 1970 as a breakaway group from the Official Sinn Fein which it accused of being too weak in defending the nationalists in Northern Ireland.

Sinn Fein is often regarded as the political wing of the IRA. The two organizations are not identical, but they are closely linked and Sinn Fein does not make policy changes without IRA approval.

For much of its history Sinn Fein has been committed to a British withdrawal from Ireland and, ultimately, to a united Ireland.

Although Sinn Fein has never gained a majority of the nationalist vote in elections, it does represent a significant number of Irish Catholics. As such, it has become an important part of the move towards a negotiated settlement, under the leadership of Gerry Adams.

Eamon de Valera

Sinn Fein did not recognize the authority of the Westminster Parliament and set up an Irish Parliament in Dublin under the presidency of Eamon de Valera. At the same time, the **Irish Republican Army** (IRA) was formed and declared war on the British government. The IRA regularly came into conflict with the Royal Irish Constabulary and the British army's 'black and tans'.

The IRA

The Provisional IRA was created in 1970 after breaking away from the Official IRA.

Since then it has been responsible for a series of violent campaigns which were intended to put pressure on the British government in order to cause a withdrawal from Ireland.

The IRA's bombing and assassination campaigns were often concentrated on members of the police and armed forces in Northern Ireland. However, it also launched attacks on the British mainland, including the bombings in Birmingham, Guildford, Warrington, Brighton and the City of London and the assassinations of Lord Mountbatten, the MP Ian Gow and lord chief justice Gibson.

A ceasefire was declared on 31 August 1994.

In view of these 'troubles' Lloyd George began negotiations regarding Irish independence. The result was the **partition** of Ireland into the 26 independent counties of the south and the six counties of the north that remained part of the UK.

Some have argued that the impetus for the partition of Ireland came from the British who were reluctant to give up their Irish colony completely. However, a more likely explanation is that the Irish were unable to agree on independence given the religious divisions in the country. The Protestants of the north had shown their determination to avoid home rule as long ago as 1912 when they formed the Ulster Volunteers to fight the Home Rule Bill.

Independence

Partition

Post-partition in the north

After partition Northern Ireland was ruled by its own parliament at **Stormont**. This was dominated by Protestants, as was the police force in Ulster, the Royal Ulster Constabulary (RUC). Therefore, to Catholics, the government and the agents of law enforcement seemed to be biased in favour of the Protestant religion. Furthermore, they faced discrimination in employment and in elections.

Despite this state of affairs, the IRA, which continued to act on behalf of Catholics in the north, gained little support in the 1950s. This was largely due to the growing economic prosperity of the north compared to the new Republic of Eire in the south. It was felt that if both Catholics and Protestants could share in the prosperity, they would develop a common interest in peace in the north.

IRA

Nevertheless, there was pressure on the Northern Irish government to allow Catholics more civil rights. Terence O'Neill, the prime minister of the province, attempted to liberalize the Catholic position by allowing universal suffrage in all local elections. However, he faced opposition from the staunch unionists of the north who believed that to give Catholics more civil rights would be to give them more power and to threaten the unionist, and therefore the Protestant, position. Catholics also objected to O'Neill's efforts because they did not go far enough.

O'Neill

By 1969 violence in the province had begun to escalate. The British government sent in troops to keep the peace between the two groups. However, the two sides became more entrenched with both creating 'no-go' areas from which the RUC and the British army were excluded. The growing conflict between the two communities and the army finally erupted in the Bloody Sunday killings of 1972 in which British paratroops killed thirteen unarmed demonstrators in Derry. This saw the re-establishment of **direct rule** over the province from Westminster, via the Northern Ireland department.

Peace attempts since 1972

Talks between the British government and the constitutional parties of the province first took place in 1970 at Chequers, the country residence of the British prime minister. However, the first serious attempt to build peace came in 1973 with the **Sunningdale agreement**. This was an attempt to reconcile the demands of the Protestant and Catholic communities as well as the interests of the British and Irish governments. The republicans, including the Irish government, restated their commitment to a united Ireland, but accepted the principle of change through consent of the people, which was the fundamental principle governing the British position.

Sunningdale

> ## The Official Unionist Party
>
> The **Official Unionist Party** (OUP), known as the Ulster Unionist Party, ruled Northern Ireland from 1920 to 1972. It held the majority of the seats at Stormont and the majority of the seats at Westminster reserved for Northern Irish MPs.
>
> As a unionist party, it remains committed to the existence of the Northern Irish state as part of a union with Britain. However, there are serious divisions within the party regarding its attitude to civil rights for the Catholic minority and there is some degree of co-operation with the Social and Democratic Labour Party (SDLP).

The Sunningdale agreement created the Council of Ireland, made up of representatives of north and south, to consider the need for more civil rights in the province. The real decision-making body was the Council of Ministers. It consisted of seven representatives from both sides and unanimity was required for all decisions.

Unionist response

The agreement came into operation on 1 January 1974. However, the Protestant politicians of the province objected to power sharing because they believed it was the beginning of the road towards a united Ireland and the end of the dominance of Protestantism in Ireland. In May 1974 the strength of their objections was illustrated by the call for a strike. The Loyalist Ulster Workers Council called a power strike, the unionists resigned from all Sunningdale bodies and the agreement collapsed.

Since the Sunningdale agreement a number of attempts have been made to bring peace to Northern Ireland. Two of these centred on gaining agreement between the constitutional parties of Northern Ireland. In 1974–5 the Labour government set up the Constitutional Convention and in 1980 the Conservative government launched a Constitutional Conference. Both attempts collapsed because of the fundamental division between the Protestants and Catholics. For the unionists, power sharing was completely unacceptable because it threatened the security of a Protestant Northern Irish state, while for the nationalists power sharing was the minimum requirement to guarantee the rights of Catholics in the north.

Following the collapse of the Constitutional Conference, Margaret Thatcher's government turned to a new series of negotiations with the Irish government, under Charles Haughey. The change of direction reflected Margaret Thatcher's determination to tackle terrorism via cross-border co-operation and also the failure to reconcile the unionists to power sharing.

Anglo–Irish agreement

By 1985 the talks had led to the Anglo–Irish agreement, also known as the **Hillsborough agreement**. The agreement included recognition of no change to the position in Northern Ireland without the consent of the people; and the continuation of the Anglo–Irish Conference to stabilize north–south relations and to

> ## The Democratic Unionist Party
>
> The **Democratic Unionist Party** (DUP) was formed in 1971 as a breakaway from the Official Unionist Party. Its founders, Ian Paisley and Desmond Boal, represented the hardliners within the OUP who objected to Terence O'Neill's liberal attitude towards civil rights for Catholics.
>
> The DUP has tended to be the strongest critic of any attempts to find peace through power sharing with the involvement of the Irish Republic.

provide a framework inside Northern Ireland to allow all constitutional groups to participate in discussions. The functions of the conference concern civil rights, security policy and extradition policy.

Since 1985 the Anglo–Irish agreement has continued to operate and the suspicions of the unionists and the condemnation of Sinn Fein have largely proved unfounded. There is some evidence of improved cross-border relations, although Margaret Thatcher often expressed reservations about the Republic's apparent reluctance to extradite suspected terrorists.

John Major and Northern Ireland

In 1991 the Northern Ireland secretary, Peter Brook, began talks with the constitutional parties in Northern Ireland. These continued after the 1992 general election under the new minister, Patrick Mayhew. As a result, the British government returned to the earlier course pursued by Margaret Thatcher: negotiations with the Irish government while the Northern Irish parties were excluded.

However, far more significant was the British government's willingness to open secret talks with the IRA. Both the Edward Heath and Harold Wilson governments had held talks with the IRA, but in the 1980s no such links had been made. Throughout 1993 John Major denied that talks had taken place, but they are believed to have begun following an exchange of messages between the IRA and the government.

Talks with IRA

A number of factors came together to make the move towards peace possible. First, inside the British government there was a willingness to find a solution to the problem, given that the threat from the IRA had persisted for so many years. Second, the British government believed that there were signs that the IRA was ready to reach a negotiated settlement. Intelligence reports suggested that the IRA was suffering internal divisions over the way forward.

Conditions for peace

This seemed to be borne out by the talks between John Hume, leader of the **Social and Democratic Labour Party** (SDLP), and Gerry Adams, leader of Sinn Fein, that had begun in March 1993. The fact that Sinn Fein would participate in such talks seemed to indicate some willingness to go forward with a negotiated peace. Finally, the Irish Republic saw a change of government as Albert Reynolds' Fianna Fail Party came to power in coalition with the Labour Party, headed by Dick Spring.

The Social and Democratic Labour Party

Led by John Hume, the Social and Democratic Labour Party was a prime mover in bringing Sinn Fein and the IRA into the negotiating process by initiating the Hume–Adams talks in March 1993.

The SDLP is not officially a Catholic party, although its commitment to a united Ireland has tended to attract Catholic support. It wishes to see unification only with the approval of the majority in the north, and it denounces violence.

The first step was the **Downing Street declaration**, made in December 1993. Although the statement was vague and the two governments did not fully meet each others' demands – the Irish government agreed only to *review* its constitutional

Downing Street declaration

provision that it would seek a united Ireland, while the British government had hoped that this would be dropped completely – the two governments agreed to safeguard the interests of all parties in the conflict while encouraging the IRA to become a part of the negotiation process.

Initially, Sinn Fein called for clarification of the declaration from the British government, but John Major refused to be drawn into negotiations with the organization. In July 1994 Sinn Fein formally rejected the declaration, but on 31 August the IRA declared a 'complete cessation' of violence, i.e. a ceasefire.

Ceasefire

Unionist reactions to the ceasefire ranged from scepticism to condemnation. Nationalists were pleased and in September 1994 Albert Reynolds, John Hume and Gerry Adams met in Dublin to declare that they were 'all totally and absolutely committed to democratic and peaceful methods of resolving our political problems'. The British government professed itself disappointed by the wording of the IRA proclamation because of the absence of the word 'permanent'.

The British government was criticized by some for 'dragging its feet' over an acceptance of the ceasefire. John Major, however, walked a tightrope between those who desired rapid progress towards talks and the sceptics, particularly the unionists, who feared that the Protestant majority in the province would be 'sold out'. Another concern revolved around the IRA's refusal to give up its weapons, arguing that this should be part of the negotiating process not a prerequisite to talks. Some observers suggested that the IRA was asking for talks while reserving the right to return to armed conflict should the outcome not suit its purposes.

Nevertheless, since then the British government has accepted the ceasefire, and talks between the government and Sinn Fein began at the end of 1994.

Exercises

Short questions

1 a Outline *one* government initiative in relation to Northern Ireland since 1972.
   b Assess its effectiveness. (ULEAC, June 1994)
2 a What were the main features of the Anglo–Irish agreement of 1985?
   b What did the agreement achieve? (ULEAC, January 1992)

Essay questions

1 'Its best chance since 1974 of moving towards some sort of acceptable accommodation.' Discuss this conclusion of what the Anglo–Irish agreement has given to Northern Ireland. (ULEAC, January 1991)
2 Is the problem of Northern Ireland insoluble? (ULEAC, June 1991)
3 'The only contribution the British could make to solving the problems of Northern Ireland is to leave.' Discuss. (Oxford, June 1994)

Data response question

Read the following extract from John Major's statement to the House of Commons on the Downing Street declaration, 1993.

'Let me make it clear what is in this declaration and what is not. What is in the declaration is:

A renewed commitment by the British government to Northern Ireland's constitutional guarantee.

An acknowledgement by the Taoiseach that a united Ireland could only be brought about with the consent of the majority of the people in Northern Ireland.

A willingness by the Taoiseach to make changes to the Irish constitution if an overall settlement can be reached.

A confirmation that if Sinn Fein renounce violence they will be able to participate in future democratic discussions.

What is not in this declaration is:

Any suggestion that the British government should join the ranks of the persuaders of the "value" or "legitimacy" of a united Ireland; that is not there.

Nor is there any suggestion that the future status of Northern Ireland should be decided by a single act of self-determination by the people of Ireland as a whole; that is not there either.

Nor is there any timetable for constitutional change.

Or any arrangements for joint authority over Norther Ireland.

In sum, the declaration provides that it is – and must be – for the people of Northern Ireland to determine their own future.'

Source: David McKie, *The Guardian Political Almanac 1994/5*, Fourth Estate, 1994

1 How successful was the previous attempt at co-operation between the British and Irish governments: the Anglo-Irish agreement?
2 Why might unionist groups in Northern Ireland object to such co-operation?
3 Can the 'Irish problem' be solved by political means?

Sources

Andrew Adonis, *Parliament Today*, Manchester University Press, 1993

Samuel Beer, *Modern British Politics*, Faber, 1969

Tony Benn, *Arguments for Democracy*, Penguin, 1979

BBC Television, *Thatcher, The Downing Street Years*, Fine Art Productions, 1993

Richard Crossman, 'Introduction', in Walter Bagehot, *The English Constitution*, Collins, 1964

A H Birch, *The British System of Government*, Allen & Unwin, 1980

Hugh Collins, *Marxism and Law*, Oxford University Press, 1987

Julian Critchley, *Heseltine, The Unauthorised Biography*, Coronet, 1988

Richard Crossman, *The Crossman Diaries* (condensed version), ed. Anthony Howard, Methuen, 1979

Robert Dahl, 'The concept of power', *Behavioural Science*, 1957

A V Dicey, *Introduction to the Study of the Law of the Constitution*, 1885

Anthony Downs, *An Economic Theory of Democracy*, Harper & Row, 1957

Patrick Dunleavy and Chris Husbands, *British Democracy at the Crossroads*, Longman, 1985

Government policy paper, 'The civil service: continuity and change', HMSO, 1994

Government white paper, 'Efficiency and effectiveness in the civil service', HMSO, 1982

Wyn Grant, *Pressure Groups, Politics and Democracy in Britain*, Philip Allen, 1989

John Griffith, *The Politics of the Judiciary*, Fontana, 1977

Alan Griffiths and John Wall, *Applied Economics*, Prentice Hall, 1986

John A Hall, *Liberalism*, Paladin, 1987

H L A Hart, *The Concept of Law*, Clarendon Press, 1961

Anthony Heath, Roger Jowell and John Curtice, *How Britain Votes*, Pergamon, 1985

Peter Hennessy, 'The throne behind the power', *The Economist*, 24 December 1994

Peter Hennessy, *Whitehall*, Secker & Warburg, 1989

Ivor Jennings, *Cabinet Government*, Cambridge University Press, 1958

Bill Jones et al., *Politics UK*, Harvester Wheatsheaf, 1991

Dennis Kavanagh and Anthony Seldon (eds), *The Major Effect*, Macmillan, 1994

H C G Matthew, *Gladstone 1809–74*, Clarendon Press, 1986

Robert Michels, *Political Parties*, The Free Press; first published as *Zur Soziologie des Parteiwesens in der Modern Demokratie*, Leipzig, 1925

L Minkin, *The Labour Party Conference*, Manchester University Press, 1980

Philip Norton, *The Commons in Perspective*, Basil Blackwell, 1985

Philip Norton, 'The pattern of backbench dissent', *Parliament in the 1980s*, Basil Blackwell, 1985

David Pannick, *Judges*, Oxford University Press, 1987
Clive Ponting, *Whitehall: Tragedy and Farce*, Hamish Hamilton, 1986
James Prior, *A Balance of Power*, London, 1986
R A W Rhodes, 'Local government', in B Jones and L Robbins (eds), *Two Decades in British Politics*, Manchester University Press, 1992
Geoffrey Robertson, *Freedom, the Individual and the Law*, Penguin, 1993
Joshua Rozenberg, *The Search for Justice*, Hodder & Stoughton, 1994
George H Sabine, *A History of Political Theory*, Harrap, 1937
David Truman, *The Governmental Process*, Alfred A Knopf, 1951
Erik Ohlin Wright, *Class, Crisis and the State*, Verso, 1975
Hugo Young, *One of Us*, Macmillan, 1989
Hugo Young, *The Judges*, BBC Radio 4, 13 April 1988
Hugo Young and Anne Sloman, *No, Minister: an Inquiry into the Civil Service*, BBC, 1982

Index

unemployment, inflation, 177, 179
Uniform Business Rate (UBR), 150
unitary state, 5, 143
United Nations (UN), 4, 10
United States of America (USA)
    Bill of Rights, 8, 133, 138
    civil rights, 133
    civil service appointments, 106
    comparison, 6, 7–8, 36, 74
    election campaigns, 36
    federalism, 6
    funding for campaigns, 34
    House of Representatives, 74
    judicial politicization, 133
    political parties, 32

presidential government, 68, 82
separation of powers, 6, 70
Supreme Court, 11, 130, 132, 133

voting
    behaviour, 27–30, 35–7
    Liberal Democrat Party, 41
    voters, 17–18, 40
    wasted, 22

Waldegrave, William, 108
Wales
    devolution issue, 48
    political parties, 39–40
Walpole, Sir Robert, 116

Walters, Alan, 87, 180
wards, local government, 141
Weber, Max, 3, 104
Westland affair, 99
Wets, definition, 43, 84
whip system, 38, 64–5, 70–3
winner-takes-all system, 20–1
winter of discontent, 179
women
    judiciary imbalance, 129
    local councillors, 141
    parliamentary representation, 32, 67
working peers, 58
workload, MPs, 73
Wright, Peter, 136